THE ENCYCLOPEDIA OF

military
MODELLING

THE ENCYCLOPEDIA OF
military
MODELLING

General Editor:
VIC SMEED

Consultant Editor:
ALEC GEE

GREENHILL BOOKS, LONDON

STACKPOLE BOOKS, PENNSYLVANIA

First published 1981 by Octopus Books

This edition of *The Encyclopedia of Military Modelling* published 1998 by Greenhill Books, Lionel Leventhal Limited, Park House, 1 Russell Gardens, London NW11 9NN, England and Stackpole Books, 5067 Ritter Road, Mechanicsburg, PA 17055, USA

© Reed International Books Limited

Library of Congress Cataloging-in-Publication Data available

ISBN 1-85367-317-X

Printed in China

Pages 4 and 5 A Tamiya 1:35 scale StuG IV assault gun built by Don Skinner. Note the additional skirt armour – some of which has been lost or discarded – which served as an anti-bazooka shield.

Pages 6 and 7 Johnny Reb, a Confederate infantryman from the American Civil War. This conversion from the 1:12 Airfix French Grenadier was carried out by Charles Wembridge.

Contents

Foreword

by ALEC GEE Managing Editor, Military Modelling magazine

This *Encyclopedia of Military Modelling* is unique; it represents a bringing together of military model-making talent on a quite unprecedented scale and its pages offer the combined skills and experience of most of the significant present-day exponents of the art.

I choose the term 'art' advisedly for that, in my opinion, is exactly what this exciting pastime of ours, at its highest level, has become. The creation of an outstanding model – be it a single military figure, a set-piece involving several figures and equipment, or a diorama with masses of groundwork and activity – calls for a remarkable set of abilities on the part of the creator. He (or she) must be part sculptor, poet and painter. He must possess the ability to carry off successfully that most difficult of all visual tricks, namely the miniaturization

reduced form, then, I believe, the modeller ascends to artist and the model becomes art.

The Encyclopedia of Military Modelling not only illustrates graphically exactly what I mean but also provides all the practical knowledge – culled, as stated earlier, from the united expertise of a host of acknowledged modeller/artists – to inspire and enable others to do likewise. There are few of us who would aspire to military modelling greatness but we all, possibly unwittingly, strive to improve the quality of what we do – our art, if you like – model by model. This encyclopedia, filled as it is with sound advice and proven ideas, will undoubtedly help and encourage all those who read and enjoy it to get the most from their hobby – and it will certainly introduce many to this remarkably satisfying interest for the first time.

of an episode or moment from 'full-size' life, while preserving all of the emotion and atmosphere that would have attended the event in reality. And he even has to find a means to tame the elements and reduce sun, rain, and snow to manageable proportions!

But when the military modeller of today (armed as he is with a wealth of modern tools, accessories and aids) manages to work this special magic, his simple craft takes on a new sophistication. When something of the power and glory, the horror and the hell, the good times in warfare and the bad are successfully captured and convincingly reproduced in

It is published at a point when the state of the art has never attained such a high level – a fact which the following pages so clearly illustrate.

Alec Gee
Hemel Hempstead

Introduction

When cataloguing the colossal number of artifacts with which the noblemen of Ancient Egypt were interred, archaeologists found many dioramas made up of small carved wooden figures. One prince of the 11th dynasty was entombed with whole companies of miniature spearmen and archers mounted in formation on wooden boards, with their weapons and costume very accurately depicted.

These Egyptian figures are the earliest known model soldiers but from the Sumerian civilization at Ur, archaeologists have found little clay models of chariots, dating back to 2800 BC. Although these and many other little models found in pre-Christian graves are of a votive nature, it is reasonable to assume that similar models were made as decorative ornaments and as playthings. In fact, classical writings refer to a game where a model Trojan Horse containing miniature warriors was used to re-enact Odysseus' ruse, to get into the walled city of Troy.

When we get into the 3rd century AD, we find there were little toy figures of Roman soldiers, moulded in flat shapes from lead. These are the first known quantity-produced toy soldiers and are found throughout the lands of the Roman Empire.

Many wood, ivory and metal figures survive from medieval times. Some are naïve interpretations of a knight or soldier, but in almost every instance there is evidence of great care on the part of the creator, in trying to depict the essential details of dress and weapons. This seems to be the common aim of virtually everyone, past and present, who makes military models of any kind.

Because of this attention to detail, it is easy to date early figures, and we are able to discover curious innovation that may not exist in any other source of reference. For instance, there is in existence a delightful 13th century model of a galloping knight in full panoply that distinctly shows the curious square-shaped plates called *ailettes*, worn at that time to protect the neck. However, it also shows something most unusual, a similar device being worn to protect the horseman's shins. One of the most magnificent military models ever made is the 14th century silver statuette of St George now in the Metropolitan Museum of Art, New York. It epitomizes the popular idea of chivalry and romance, and at the same time has incredible detail and a poetry of motion which make it a work of art.

There must have been a vast quantity of military models down through the ages that were doomed from the time they got into the hands of children to be used as playthings. There might even be a lesson to be learned here, because it is largely those figures made in precious metals that have survived.

The great Italian silversmith Benvenuto Cellini was, in miniature work, the equal of Michelangelo, and he made many statuettes of Renaissance period soldiers. These figures wear Neo-Roman armour made of sculptured metal and moulded boiled leather and his work has never been surpassed. Most modellers could not do better than study his statuettes if they want to get some poetry into the stance of their figures.

It is interesting to note that up until the 18th century, very few artists or modellers ever attempted to depict the costumes or uniforms of a previous age. This is why the surviving figures are such a valuable source of accurate information. When an artist or modeller did step outside the sphere of his knowledge to portray a soldier of the past, he resorted to conjecture because he did not have the vast amount of information that is available to modellers in books and museums today.

King Louis XIII of France, when Dauphin, was given by his mother Marie de Medici a miniature army of silver figures and it is recorded that he cast his own soldiers, which were 70mm high and had a peg instead of a base, so that they could be mounted on a board and arranged in various formations. The royal child also had miniature cannon which could be primed and fired with real gunpowder. This model army was inherited by a succession of Dauphins and each generation reinforced it with more silver pieces until it became an extraordinarily elaborate affair, mounted on complicated mechanisms that would synchronize the movements of troops changing formation and even move their arms up and down. Alas, in this case it would have been better if the figures had been made of a base metal, because the vast collection disappeared, probably melted down to provide funds for a full-sized army to go to war.

In Eastern Europe there was a long tradition for skilful woodcarving, and wooden model soldiers were common in the Austrian and German States. The Prince Elector of Bavaria had a collection of such models in about 1670, but few have survived from this period.

Left This superb model of a Japanese Samurai designed by Ray Lamb shows the finish that can be achieved with experience. Samurai are probably the most colourful figures to be found in military modelling and require very careful painting.
Far left A selection of flats, beautifully painted by Jim Woodley.

However, it was from Germany during the time of Frederick the Great that a new form of model soldier emerged and has continued to thrive there ever since. These are the traditional German flats; cast figures which are two-dimensional with quite a lot of detail engraved on the surface. They were originally made in tin at Nürnberg by Johann Gottfried Hilpert in about 1775 and depicted various regiments from Frederick the Great's army. A little later, a whole industry of small manufacturers emerged throughout Germany to make these little flat figures and, although intended as children's toys, the skill of the engravers made them an art form in their own right. The moulds were all engraved by hand and some designers excelled themselves with artistry and detail. However, the final result depended on good painting, which could not be achieved during mass production in the toy industry. This started collectors, many of them artists, purchasing unpainted castings and delicately colouring them for their own pleasure.

The largest collection of these flat figures is housed in Bavaria, at the Deutsches Zinnfigurenmuseum at Plassenburg Castle, Kulmbach, where there are something in the region of a hundred thousand figures. From 1870 a few German makers such as Allgeyer and Heyde

changed to making solid metal figures, but their early products still had the characteristics of flats.

The bewildering complexities of military dress worn by the Grand Armée of Napoleon Bonaparte affords many enthusiasts a lifetime's study in itself. Models of figures from this epoch are among the most popular. An enigmatic Frenchman called Lucotte (who stamped LC and an Imperial Bee on his figures) made very fine metal pieces during and just after the First Empire, and a little later Mignot of Paris followed suit and founded one of the oldest established model soldier makers. Since then, a whole succession of manufacturers have offered collectors, both children and adults, most of the regiments of the Napoleonic armies and these models have culminated in the superb plastic construction kits by Historex.

The collecting of old toy soldiers, and the resultant appreciation in their value, has in recent years reached craze proportions. This spiral started in English-speaking countries soon after the British manufacturers, W. Britains Ltd, ceased production of their hollow-cast metal figures in the 1950s. On the surface, it would seem to have been a case of scarcity creating a demand; however, the reasons probably go deeper than that. William Britain of North London started making hollow metal figures in 1893, during the reign of Queen Victoria, upon whose Empire the sun was said never to set. They continued to turn out boxed sets of nicely cast, brightly painted soldiers throughout the intensely patriotic era when Edward VII and George V were on the throne of Britain. In fact their production period of lead soldiers spanned the reigns of six British monarchs and it recorded, in miniature, the changes of uniform not only of the British and Commonwealth army but also the troops of other countries.

What they did not tell the would-be purchaser was that they would be buying the antiques of tomorrow.

Just after World War 2 various plastic toy soldiers appeared on the market – Elastolin of Germany, Starlux and MDM of France and Herald of Britain offering some of the better quality pieces. W. Britains Ltd merged with Herald in 1955 and are today the world's largest manufacturer of toy soldiers. In the USA in the early 1950s Imrie Custom Miniatures and later, in 1956, Hellenic Miniatures were some of the first commercially produced models available and, like early Britains' pieces, they are much sought after collectors' items today. Designed and produced by William Imrie (to be joined in 1962 by Clyde Risley to form the famous Imrie/Risley partnership still prolific today), these were metal models, and plastic figures did not arrive on the American scene until later with the appearance of manufacturers like Revell, Squadron/Rubin and Monogram.

A renaissance of metal toy soldier collecting began two or three years ago when collectors, responding to the increasing scarcity and higher prices of antique metal soldiers, turned their interest towards modern-made toy soldiers. Sculpted and painted in the traditional style, these modern toy soldiers have gained enormous popularity and, in answer to a constantly growing demand, such firms as Blenheim, Dorset, Mark Time, Steadfast, British Bulldog, and others now offer a vast array of subjects. A number of these so closely approximate antique toy soldiers that differences are

Opposite *One of the 6,000-plus Chinese terracotta soldier figures dating from 210 BC discovered in 1974 near the tomb of the first Emperor of China, Shih Huang Ti, at Mount Li in the valley of the Yellow River. Originally painted, they are near life-size and it is thought that many more await discovery.*
Top left *A fine example of a flat in its unpainted state. Some such figures have plain backs; others, like this Belgian Lancer Officer of 1831, carry detail on both sides.*
Top right *Seaforth Highlanders with fixed bayonets, from Under Two Flags. Note the officer with the Colours. Palms and other trees are also available as painted flats from this company.*
Above *Panzer Grenadiers in a street battle diorama by Don Skinner, using 1:35 scale Tamiya figures. Many modellers prefer to put their figures in dioramas to make them more realistic. For details about dioramas, see page 176.*

almost indiscernible. An interesting recent development in toy soldier collecting has come from the American Society to Advance the Retarded, under the trade name Star. This Connecticut organization produces modern-made unpainted toy soldiers, available individually rather than in sets, and ready to be painted.

In recent years there has been a phenomenal increase in the hobby of wargaming, although the pastime has been with us a very long time (chess, for example, is a type of wargame). Wargaming today is essentially a method of recreating a battle or a campaign on a table top using miniature figures to represent actual troops. Using a set of rules and dice, it is possible to calculate troop movements and casualties as well as the conditions and stresses of real warfare including morale and fighting ability.

Wargaming covers virtually all the major periods including Ancient, Medieval, 'Pike and Shot', 'Horse and Musket', Napoleonic, American Civil War and World War 2. The size of the battles can range from a full-scale campaign to a minor skirmish depending on the size of the table and the scale of models used.

There are no common rules for wargaming, and societies and clubs throughout the world devise their own rules or use those supplied by such organizations as the Wargames Research Group in the UK. However, they all have tremendous fun researching campaigns and getting the historical detail right, whether it be terrain, uniforms or vehicles. In wargames, accuracy and attention to detail are just as important as with display figures, although, because the models have to be produced in far greater numbers and have to be handled regularly, painting need not be to showpiece standard. Not surprisingly, the scales of figures and vehicles used are rather small – 5mm, 15mm and 25mm, the latter being the most popular – and the terrain placed on the board is simplified so that the table is not too cluttered and the figures can be moved with ease.

In addition to traditional wargaming, there is the relatively new hobby of board games in which markers are used instead of figures and the base is in the form of a pre-printed map. Not only are board games far more economical than armies of model soldiers, they are much easier to store and carry around. This particular form of wargaming is now very popular in the United States.

Wargaming appeals to people of all ages and skills, and can be simple or complex depending on the rules used; tank wargaming, for example, can include rates of fire, armour penetration, performance data, firing ranges and such like. Although wargaming does not fall within the scope of this book, it is a fascinating subject in its own right, and there are now a number of excellent publications covering the subject at all levels.

For the collectors of the standard-sized 54mm figures, there are today enormous numbers of small manufacturers who offer stock figures to choose from. Most of the makers offer plain, solid metal castings ready for painting or painted figures that are rather expensive.

Scale measurements do cause some confusion and variation in sizes. 54mm (also called 1:32) is the most common, but some makers take the measurement from base to the top of the head; others from eye down, and some the total height of the figure including headgear.

This difference is not so obvious with a standing figure, but if a horse is made in proportion, you will notice a vast difference in scale when you compare mounted figures. Some of the first, and best, specialist 54mm figures were made by W. Y. Carman (who was one of the founders of the British Model Soldier Society), William Murray and Imrie/Risley in the USA, Charles Stadden (Tradition), Russell Gammage (Rose Miniatures) and Les Higgins. To them, and to the publishers of books and magazines on the subject, should go much of the credit for the healthy growth in military modelling in the last 15 years.

The plastic construction kits such as Historex, Airfix, Revell, Monogram, Tamiya and Helmet have also done a great deal to popularize the hobby, and they have given unlimited scope to modellers to develop their skills in converting standard kits into the most unlikely subjects. Some ingenious modellers combine bits and pieces from several figures or kits, both metal and plastic, even using proprietary-made toy figures.

Many people prefer small groups of model soldiers, similarly dressed to give a sense of uniformity. There is nothing nicer than a little cavalcade of Napoleonic Dragoons with glittering helmets, led by an officer in green coat and tall white plume, followed by several trumpeters on grey horses with jackets of the regimental facing colour.

There are on display some brilliant collections of soldiers, assembled in groups to represent a whole army of a particular period. The Musée de l'Armée in Paris has a marvellous display, and so does the US Military Academy at West Point, which displays Napoleonic figures particularly well. Blenheim Palace in England has several hundred of the rare Lucotte figures on public display. These are arranged in a gilt-framed case with mirrors at the back, which effectively doubles the number of figures that appear to be on display.

Moving on to larger scales, there are many suppliers offering castings that range from 75mm, 90mm, 100mm, 150mm and 175mm. Outstanding English master modellers in the larger scales are Ray Lamb and Charles Stadden, the latter having made the masters for some fine statuettes that are sold in natural pewter, while in America another Ray Lamb has created a handsome series of 90mm figures for Superior Models, a number of which are also available in pewter. Pat Bird of Series 77 has produced three masterful 154mm figures of exquisite detail: a German landsknecht, a pirate of the mid-1600s and a Napoleonic officer of carabiniers.

Running parallel with the making and collecting of model soldiers, there has been a massive interest in military vehicles, particularly tanks and armoured cars. In the past these were very difficult to make from wood because of the need for wheels, sprockets and flexible tracks. There were very few military vehicles offered by toy manufacturers before the 1939–45 war; Skybird and Dinky Toy come to mind with some excellent 1:72 diecast metal vehicles. The latter continued the range in postwar years with British army and even a few French military vehicles. Solido of France entered the market with some very well made cast models of a slightly larger scale.

However, it was the plastic construction kits that offered modellers most scope. Airfix and Aurora were two of the first to make military vehicle kits, but their sales did not prove to be as successful as the aircraft and warship models and it was left to firms like Revell and, in particular, Monogram to carry the US flag in the field of military plastic kits. However, it was the Japanese manufacturers such as Tamiya who really exploited the market. At first they offered kits for only the more famous types of battle tank, mostly 1:35 scale, and, as modellers strove to find ways of converting the standard kits into other versions of the basic tank, their interest became stimulated. This created a further demand for specialist books on the subject and the hobby started to breed on itself, until today we have an enormous selection of superb vehicle kits to choose from, in several different scales. Some are motorized kits with remote control and there are now large radio-controlled models available in kit form. The capital investment in plastic injection tools is very considerable, and it is amazing that kits of even obscure military vehicles sell in sufficient numbers to pay for the tooling.

It is interesting to speculate as to the reasons for the great interest in military models today. It might have something to do with the fact that the larger nations are passing through the longest period of their history without being involved in a major world-wide war, and they are looking at the past.

The hobby attracts people from all walks of life and every income group, and their common interest is a great equalizer. I remember enquiring into the professional occupations of enthusiasts a few years ago and found it weighed towards actors, government employees, the clergy and retired naval officers. The latter raised some amusement, and it was reckoned to have something to do with the fact that naval officers, when in service, all wore the same dark blue uniforms with collar and tie and black shoes, and secretly they longed for the wealth of distinctive colours worn by their military colleagues.

A group of players from the South London Warlords taking part in a typical wargame. One measures the distance to be advanced, while the other consults the booklet of rules. One throw of the dice can introduce several options, and choice can be crucial.

The hobby is by no means the domain of the male, there being many exponents among women, and their skill especially at exquisite painting has long been recognized. France in particular can boast Mme Metayer and Mlle Desfontaines, whose figures and dioramas are renowned in Europe and America.

There are collectors who lack the skill and inclination to use their own hands and they acquire models ready made; others purchase kits or castings and complete the models themselves. However, there are a few who scratch-build their own and, when they have mastered the techniques, this probably provides the ultimate satisfaction.

General Angenot of France made the most charming cavalry pieces by carving and sandpapering wooden horses and riders and attaching pieces of paper, fabric, and silken hair. The finished results have a delicate poetry of motion that is unique. Two other Frenchmen, Eugene Leliepvre and Lucien Rousselot, both Painters to the French Army, have made a number of incredible models, the swords and helmets beaten from metal and the sculpted figures dressed in cloth uniforms, a com-

plete mounted figure standing 41cm high. Yet another Frenchman, Pierre Conrad, working exclusively with Historex miniatures, creates beautifully oil painted unique figures. Some master craftsmen, like Peter Wilcox, who is famed for his splendid models of barbarian warriors, cast their own figures in metal, while others use such clay-like self-hardening materials as Barbola and DAS Pronto. Chicagoan Sheperd Paine sculpts his miniatures in an epoxy compound, while New Yorker Ron Tunison builds his lifelike large-scale figures of clay, then fires them in a kiln.

Hardwood is an excellent material but few have the skill to carve it well. An exception is C. Pilking-Jackson, whose beautiful carved wooden figures show all the uniforms worn by the Scottish regiments. These can be seen in the United Services Museum in Edinburgh Castle. Another master of wood carving was the late Cliff Arquette, best known as his television character, Charlie Weaver. In his small private museum at Gettysburg, Arquette displayed a number of wooden, painted figures he had carved, depicting soldiers of the American Civil War.

More and more people are getting bored with watching ball games and banal spoon-fed television entertainment and, with rising fuel costs making travelling a luxury, they will be inclined to adopt hobbies that can be pursued in their homes. We welcome you to the world of Military Modelling.

Major modelling periods

Military history covers such a vast field that few modellers could hope to find time to build a collection of miniatures representing every development in dress or weaponry. The tendency has therefore been for individuals to specialize in periods of particular personal interest, and over the years these periods have fallen into an established pattern. In this chapter experts discuss the attractions of their favourite periods and give an idea of the degree of commercial support, some suggestions for research and, occasionally, constructional hints.

An A7V German World War 1 tank model built by Dennis Green. It had an 18-man crew.

Ancient

Thanks largely to wargamers, the Ancient period has steadily extended from Egyptian, Greek and early Roman times to include any military activity of the pre-gunpowder era. With the extension of the time-span has come an increase in interest both amongst modellers and wargamers, making it now the fastest growing area and rivalling the popular Napoleonic period.

Such is the variety of troop types, arms and equipment in a period ranging from 3000 BC to AD 1000 or so that it will never be fully covered by commercial suppliers but, far from being a handicap, this is accepted as a challenge by devoted modellers who are continually finding new subjects to test their skills. Even those not talented at converting and scratch-building need not be downhearted, as manufacturers and publishers have paralleled the growth in interest with an expanding range, so that the Ancient enthusiast is now as well catered for as his counterpart in any other era.

The period has wargame rules used internationally and a comprehensive range of reference books. Backing these up are more specialized books by historians and archaeologists, some readily available, others only through the services of central lending libraries. References to many of these are given in the 'Armies and Enemies' series from Wargames Research Group and are invaluable to the modeller who wants to research less common or uncommercialized subjects in depth.

This period also has the distinction of having its own organization, the Society of Ancients. This is a British-based international group devoted to ancient military history and wargaming. Membership now approaches 2,000 and members are kept in touch through the Society journal, *Slingshot*, published six times a year and containing well-researched articles on military history, as well as wargaming and modelling.

Modelling falls into three main categories. First, there are the wargamers and figure collectors. Both are interested primarily in finishing and painting ready-made figures, the wargamer in massed formations for his armies, the collector with single figures or dioramas showing scenes from history, or individual heroes or great captains. Foot figures range from 12 to 30mm high for wargaming, through 54mm up to 90mm and bigger for individual personality figures. Painting techniques are a fascinating study alone and one aspect of modelling which is attracting growing attention is the art of the weapon-maker. This involves substituting the cast metal or plastic weapons with properly made-up arms to scale, using high quality hardwood and suitable metals. Immensely satisfying, this touch adds just that extra something to a well-painted figure.

The next step is converting. Again both wargamers and collectors are involved, bringing types into an army, or creating particular figures which are not available commercially. Most of these conversions are of plastic figures, alterations to metal figures tending to be left to the expert few, but whether it is swopping heads and limbs on Airfix wargames figures or fine sculpting and alteration on larger figures the effort is always worthwhile. Some of these alterations show imagination and ingenuity at their peak. Many a 54mm scale plastic Hussar kit has become a Hun or an Arab!

Two subjects almost exclusive to the Ancient world are elephants and chariots. Both make impressive subjects for the painter or converter, and chariots, ranging from the ultra-light Egyptian to the heavy Indian four-horse type, are also very popular for scratch-building. All were highly decorated with elaborate trappings, horse plumes and sometimes armour for elephants.

Finally comes the modelling of siege engines and warships. A great variety of engines was in use, ranging from light catapults to immense siege towers several storeys high, mounting dart- and stone-throwing engines. Warships could be anything from a light Saxon galley used to raid the English coast to the monsters created by Alexander's successors. Here is the chance for modellers to build pieces of Ancient history, and all the better if plastic is put aside and the models are made of wood, as were the originals.

If there is a snag to this era it is the tremendous choice. Many a modeller has foundered under the weight of unpainted wargames armies or models as, magpie-like, he collects at random. Reconnaissance is seldom wasted, so do read up first before deciding on a subject. But with Assyrians gleaming in scarlet and gold, Byzantine cavalry armed to the teeth, an Indian king on his elephant, a Viking ship or a Chinese crossbowman, who can blame the modelling magpie when faced with the possibilities of this fascinating period?

Below *A 75mm Sutton Hoo warrior by Peter Wilcox.* **Opposite** *Macedonian archers on an elephant, also by Peter Wilcox. The elephant is from Britains' Zoo series, the figures from Sovereign Miniatures.*

Medieval

Medieval means 'of the Middle Ages' and in its widest sense this covers a period of history stretching from the fall of the Roman Empire in AD 476 until the late 15th century. Thus in the medieval period we have a truly vast span of history, and the modeller is confronted by a bewildering array of potential subjects ranging from the Byzantines and their various 'barbarian' allies or mercenaries, to the start of the Renaissance: Visigoths, Lombards, Vikings and Saxons, Arabs and Moors, Mamluks and Seljuks, Mongols, Normans, Crusaders and the Military Orders, with further east the Sassanids, Slavs, Bulgars, Magyars, Poles and Russians – all names to conjure up pictures of a violent past. There are also the armies of France, England, Spain, the Italian states and the German princes of the Holy Roman Empire, confronting each other in prolonged wars enriched by the splendour of medieval heraldry.

The choice of modelling subjects in such an era is obviously endless, and presents the modeller with a great deal of research because of the diversity of arms and armour employed. However, modelling in this period may be said to be characterized by the emphasis on single figures, or pairs locked in personal combat, to a degree not found in other periods of history. Generally speaking, once battle was joined, each warrior fought as an individual, no matter what the organization or training of the army to which he belonged. And the choice of individual figures is wonderful – the simply dressed but deadly English longbowman, the magnificently attired Italian *condottieri*, the tough mercenaries of the multi-nation Free Companies which roamed Europe, the more orderly dress of the English liveried retainers in the Wars of the Roses, Swiss pikemen and halberdiers insolently standing against and conquering the lordly knights of the Holy Roman Empire, as did the Bohemian peasants in their war waggons during the Hussite Wars, the Spanish and Italian city militias, the colourful Landsknechts towards the end of the period, and the equally colourful and arrogant knights of the great Military Orders – the Templars, Hospitallers, and Teutonic Knights, who neither gave nor received quarter in their fight against Islam.

Broadly speaking, all these troops may be divided into four major categories: unarmoured, or armoured in lamellar, chain mail or plate armour. The first two usually present few problems to the modeller, but the painting of mail or plate is, next to heraldry, the major difficulty confronting any modeller when first tackling this period. There are a number of ways to paint mail and plate armour, few of which are totally successful: it is mostly a case of personal preference in the end. Some modellers undercoat their figures with black, then apply silver paint over. Others mix a little black or blue into the silver paint, then use pure silver for highlighting. Still others mix gunmetal and silver, or silver and black paints, or merely apply a silver or silver and black wash on the bare metal. If you are starting with a metal figure, the best way to represent metal is obviously to use the metal of the figure itself: simply apply a black wash to create shadows, or paint black overall then wipe the paint off to leave small amounts outlining joints, rivets, engraving, etc. If using a wash or the 'paint and wipe' method, a *fine* coat of gloss varnish should be applied afterwards.

Metal figures are manufactured by all the major companies in a wide range from 54 to 90mm scale, but there is a less plentiful choice in plastic, three main sources of which are Elastolin, Figurines Historiques, and Airfix. Information on arms, armour and equipment may be found in *The Age of Chivalry* (L. and F. Funcken), *European Armour* (C. Blair) and a series of small books by R. E. Oakshott. There are many other sources, including general fashion and costume books and the small booklets and postcards available from various museums such as the Musée de l'Armée in Paris, the Metropolitan Museum of Art in New York, and the Tower of London.

The problem of heraldry bedevils many modellers in this period. There is little one can say, except heraldry *must* be correct; if it is it will look magnificent, if it is wrong it will look dreadful. The basics of heraldry can be learnt from the *Observer's Book of Heraldry*, and some individual medieval examples may be found in the Funcken books and in Blandford's *Heraldry of the World* by von Volborth. The Wargames Research Group books on the Dark Ages and Feudal Europe also provide examples of flag and shield designs. Certainly among the most magnificent volumes published on heraldry was Ottfried Neubecker's *Heraldry: Sources, Symbols and Meaning*, published by McGraw-Hill Book Company.

Opposite left *A John Tassel metal figure of a 14th century crossbowman with a type of headgear known as a 'pot de fer' and a mixture of chain and plate armour.*
Opposite right *The Billman, 1485. A clever conversion from the big (1:6) scale Revell 'Spartacus' kit, by W. M. Ganley. The single figure, sitting on a well coping and bandaging his hand, engages the imagination as well as recording the arms and armour of the time.*
Above right *A 15th century Belgian knight, one of a large range of 75mm metal models of this period by Sovereign Miniatures.*
Right *A mounted Landsknecht by Barton Miniatures. Horse armour is a fascinating subject in itself, but this whole era is colourful and full of interest.*

English Civil War

'The first dry rattle of new drawn steel changes the world today.'

Thus did Rudyard Kipling in his poem 'Edgehill Fight' describe the impact of the first major engagement of a war which established the progress of the 'mother of parliaments' and ended the concept of absolute monarchy.

The field army of the period comprised four main elements: infantry, dragoons, horse and artillery. Infantry regiments – usually around 800 strong – consisted of pikemen and musketeers. The latter carried matchlock muskets and a bandolier of charges. Pikemen were selected from the tallest and strongest recruits. They needed to be: wielding a 14-foot pike of ashwood took muscles and nerves of steel!

Dragoons were simply mounted musketeers, although they carried flintlocks rather than matchlocks. Their function was skirmishing and outpost duty, and in the battle line they performed as light infantry. The horse were all, in effect, heavy cavalry. Armed with long straight swords, pistols and sometimes carbines, these were the troops that formed the regiments of dour 'ironsides' and spirited 'cavaliers'. Cavalry standards were highly decorative, often carrying political or religious cartoons and slogans.

Artillery was sometimes a problem: gun carriages tended to be too heavy for easy manoeuvring in the field and only the lighter guns were of great tactical use. However, both sides were generally well served by their artillery, and in several battles the big guns played a decisive role.

The development of uniform was in its infancy. Though most units were clothed in coats and hats, and occasionally breeches and stockings, of a uniform colour, there was no consistent pattern and often the only way to differentiate between royalist and roundhead was by the wearing of sashes – crimson or blue for the king; orange/tawny, white or scarlet for parliament.

Of the infantry only pikemen wore protective armour – a helmet known as a 'pot', a breastplate, and sometimes 'tassets' – thigh guards – but the latter were seldom worn in action. Often a thick buff leather coat replaced the breastplate. Cavalrymen also wore breastplates and tassets and were equipped, whenever possible, with the famous and curiously menacing 'lobster-pot' helmet. It is a myth that this headgear was peculiar to the Roundheads. Simple lack of equipment forced some Royalists to rely on felt hats, but a helmet was usually preferred. Armour was frequently painted black, or black leaded, to protect it from rust.

Modellers should bear in mind that the mid-17th century was a very cold period; clothes were bulky and many-layered, and in most cases the use of vegetable dyes produced muted colours. Also, this was an extremely 'dirty' age – even peacetime standards of hygiene were at a particularly low ebb – so forget about shirts with whiter-than-white collars! Most soldiers – including parliamentarians – wore long hair, and small beards and moustaches were popular.

Figure models for the period abound and both Parliamentarian and Royalist troops are covered in all of the major scales from 15mm upwards. In plastic, Airfix offer a 54mm scale pikeman and musketeer while, from the metal figure producers, come Ironside troopers, ensigns and standard bearers (Series 77 of California offer a particularly good selection in 77mm scale) and there are even personality figures like Phoenix Model Developments' Oliver Cromwell and Jupiter Models' Charles I, to say nothing of literally hordes of wargames figures in diminutive 15 and 25mm scales (for example, Rose Miniatures' range).

Recommended reading on the subject includes *The English Civil War* published by Arms and Armour Press, and the *English Civil War Armies* from Osprey Publishing in their 'Men-at-Arms' series. The museums of many English towns and cities – in Warwickshire, Northamptonshire and Oxfordshire in particular – contain much in the way of artifacts relating to the period and, of course, it is still possible to visit many of the battle sites (like Edgehill and Marston Moor) to gain modelling 'atmosphere'.

Opposite *Part of a large diorama by K. M. Yuill depicting Royalist forces defending a rather open position with pikes and muskets. The shortage of helmets and other equipment is brought out in this scene.*

Below *A part of the other half of the same diorama, with the comparatively well-equipped Roundhead heavy cavalry charging the defences. Little protection was provided for the horses in this period. A diorama of this complexity will involve hours of patient work. Before modelling can commence, a great deal of time must be spent on research and this means consulting the recommended histories of the period and studying carefully the illustrations of weapons and uniforms. Visits to museums and libraries may also be necessary. It is helpful – if not essential – to make a rough sketch showing the intended disposition of the figures before construction is actually begun.*

Napoleonic

Without doubt this is the most popular period for collectors and modellers of all ages; possible reasons can be summarized under five headings:

(a) The reverence rightly or wrongly attached to the military prowess of Napoleon Bonaparte and his conduct of the art of warfare.

(b) The similar attraction of the character and expertise of the Duke of Wellington.

(c) The extraordinary number of nations, states, principalities, dukedoms, and electorates engaged in the Napoleonic Wars and the exotic nature of their infinite variety of uniforms.

(d) The fascination of military historians, researchers and serious wargame students in the classic military confrontations of the period and the strategies adopted by the major protagonists.

(e) The enormous fund of information available on the uniforms, equipment and weapons of the period.

Between 1795 and 1815, Bonaparte fought a series of always dramatic campaigns, opening with the war in Italy between 1795 and 1798, and ending with the Battle of Waterloo. His army fought Austrians, Mamelukes, British, Russians, Prussians, Spanish, and Portuguese armies and finally engaged the combined might of Europe in a series of now legendary battles culminating in the incredibly dramatic Waterloo, when Napoleon and Wellington finally came face to face to fight the classic battle, utilizing their particular strategies in one horrendous engagement.

It can be said that Napoleon used an almost stereotyped strategy, attacking the enemy with massed artillery bombardments, followed by attempts to turn his foe's flank with either a mixture of line and column but more usually with massed solid columns of infantry, punctuated by support from enormous cavalry charges.

Against lesser opponents the system usually proved successful but it was effectively countered by Wellington's refusal to be panicked and his infantry's coolness under extreme pressure. Facing enormous columns in line, the British waited until they were within musket range and then fired by battalion volleys, smashing the heads of the columns and then attacking with cold steel before the shattered French could redeploy. At Waterloo, Napoleon had been warned that these would be Wellington's tactics, but he ignored the advice and was beaten. The scenario is perfect for wargamers and has provided unbeatable excitement for modellers.

The Napoleonic period fostered an enormous literature and great interest in the military costume of the day. As a result, contemporary print makers edited prodigious series of plates illustrating the uniforms of the various nations. Even Napoleon believed in the adage 'uniform maketh the man' and encouraged the

Below *Modified 54mm Historex figures were used in this diorama of a French artilleryman defending himself against a British cavalryman.*
Opposite *A Chasseur à Cheval of Napoleon's Imperial Guard, from the Barton Miniatures range.*

quartermasters to clothe his Grand Army in a kaleidoscopic variety of colours. Amateur artists, such as the mayor of Hamburg and his brother, patiently recorded the style and colour of the dress of the troops who passed through the city in 1806, while in France, Britain and other countries, artists were sponsored by royalty and the rich to produce volumes of military-inspired drawings.

The basic male costume of the period, the short-waisted, long-tailed coatee and the shorter-skirted but equally high-waisted Spencer, together with the skin-tight breeches and lacquered boots of the time, lent themselves to the design of richly diverse uniforms exaggerating the male figure. Soldiers were given crested helmets, tall shakos, towering plumes, huge epaulettes, tight breeches, and masses of glittering lace and embroidery, with the object of instilling a feeling of inferiority in their foes. The French had failed to learn the lesson of the American Revolution and dressed their skirmishers in bright yellow facings and multi-coloured plumes, in contrast to the sober, workmanlike costume of the Allied riflemen. In Russia, France, Prussia, Austria and Great Britain, the dress of hussars became excessively fantastic. They were dressed in pink, white, lemon yellow, sky blue, green, red, and brown, with tight jackets and fur trimmed slung pelisses, resplendent with braid and buttons.

In America, the period encompasses a wealth of uniform colour; the war with Britain of 1812 saw American Marines, for example, smart in their dark green faced-red, long-tailed coats (later blue) and buff breeches who, having seen the Redcoats burn the White House and the Capitol in 1814, gave such a good account of themselves at the Battle of New Orleans a year later.

After Waterloo, a vast collection of hand-painted paper cut-out figures of soldiers of the time was made in Strasbourg (the Wurtz Collection of several thousand is now in the Army Museum in Paris) and during the Victorian era a number of major works were published which provide an almost infinite fount of knowledge. In Germany, for example, Richard – and later Herbert – Knötel produced volume after volume of *Uniformenkunde*, comprising thousands of plates of uniforms of all armies, with emphasis on the Napoleonic period. In 1904, H. Malibran prepared a record of uniform regulations of the French army of 1791–1848. It has 941 closely printed pages detailing every minutiae of uniform and a complementary album of 248 beautifully drawn plates.

In Austria, Teuber's huge two-volume work and, in Russia, the 16-volume colossal study by W. Viskavatov record the uniforms of those countries. In Britain, the Royal Collection, regimental inspection reports, and portraits of the period provide a wealth of information. French sources include Commandant Bucquoy's 3,000-plus coloured postcards of the uniforms of the First Empire, and his *Le Passepoil*, a magnificent magazine which ran for nearly 30 years and was devoted to uni-

DRUMMER-DRAGOONS À PIED
27th Regt-1806

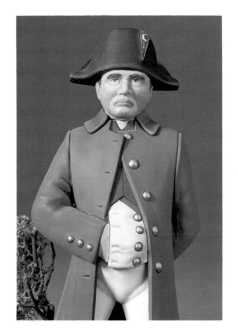

EMPRESS DRAGOON (1809)
Imperial Guard

Opposite left *A conversion of a plastic 1:12 Airfix Foot Dragoon drummer by B. Harris; note that there is just enough on the base to indicate the terrain without proving a distraction.*
Opposite right *A John Reagan Milliput figure, this is an officer of the 79th Foot (Cameron Highlanders), c. 1815. Milliput is an epoxy putty which remains workable for up to three hours and is water soluble in the early stages.*
Above left *A 1:12 Airfix conversion by B. Harris, an Empress Dragoon of the Imperial Guard. Uniform colour and variety reached their peak during the Napoleonic period, so there is enormous scope for modellers.*
Above centre *A beautiful little Marlburian drummer by John Reagan. Elements of the dress of this earlier period carried over to Napoleonic times.*
Above right *Napoleon Bonaparte himself – a converted 1:12 Airfix kit, yet another by B. Harris. Easily recognizable military figures attract quite a number of people, but naturally this area of modelling requires extra time and effort in the painting and finishing, especially with facial features.*

forms of the French army, particularly the Napoleonic period. Generals Vanson and Jolly produced collections of notes and drawings and in later years, Lucien Rousselot produced, in a unique two-page plate style, a history of the uniforms of the French army, its arms, and its equipment.

Happily for military historians and modellers, much of the material produced around the turn of the century, which has only existed in libraries and museums, is now being republished. Bucquoy's monumental card series is now being reprinted in a series of volumes headed *Les Uniformes du Premier Empire*. Knötel's *Uniformenkunde*, or at least a large portion of it, was re-issued as a series of colour plates, and Malibran's documentation of the French army is again available, republished in two volumes. The series on the French army by Lucien Rousselot, begun during World War 2 in German-occupied Paris, is now being reprinted, with text in French and in English.

Contemporary works have resulted in a glut of

books and plates on today's market, some of it excellent and flawless, much of it, sadly, misleading and with numerous errors. Among the finest modern sources on the Napoleonic French army are the series of full-colour, impeccably accurate 'Le Plumet' plates, produced near Paris by the French artist, Rigo. Andrea Viotti has recently begun documenting the dress of the cavalry of Murat, one of Napoleon's most colourful cavalry commanders. Each volume contains numerous black and white and colour drawings, with a text in Italian and in English. Emir Bukhari has produced a fine series of volumes on the French Napoleonic army for Osprey Publishing Ltd, while a French publisher, Forthoffer, has produced an excellent continuing series of colour plates on the Napoleonic French army and its allies.

In addition, magazines such as *Military Modelling*, *Campaigns* and *Uniformes* devote considerable attention to the armies of the Napoleonic era.

This brief list only taps the surface of authoritative information; there are other prime sources in the Netherlands, Italy, and in numerous libraries in the United States, Europe, and Great Britain which collectively provide modellers with an almost complete record of the stupendous variety of uniforms of the period.

For collectors interested in the antique market, there are the figures of Lucotte, Mignot, Algeyer, Haffner and Metayer. For the collector or painter of Continental flat tin figures there is the work of Almont and Mignot in France, as well as the thousands of figures produced by Ochel, Neckel, Scholtz, and many other manufacturers in Germany and Austria.

For modellers and collectors of the 'ronde-bosse' (the sculptor's term for the fully three-dimensional rather than the flat or bas-relief figure) models, the choice is enormous and still growing. Space precludes listing all the modern manufacturers.

The combination of such a rich research reservoir and the art of so many expert model producers makes the Napoleonic period a never-ending source of interest to experienced modellers and newcomers alike.

American Civil War

The years 1861–65 witnessed a terrible struggle between the forces of those of the United States of America which supported the Union, broadly termed 'the North', and those of the seceding states, grouped together as the Confederacy and known as 'the South'. Causes of the conflict were many and varied, but included the vexed question of slavery together with much bitterness in the South over damage to its interests from growing economic and political power in the Northern states. Like most such struggles, the Civil War was pursued with great intensity of feeling on both sides and it has been estimated that during its four-year course more than half a million of the men involved died in action or from disease, with several times that number surviving wounds and sickness.

Often described as 'the first of the modern wars', it occurred at a time when enormous leaps forward were being made in the efficiency of weapons, communications and industrial production, although military thought and tactics adapted but slowly to the opportunities made possible by these developments. Nevertheless, the period saw the introduction of practical machine-guns, repeating rifles, submarines, armoured warships and breech-loading artillery, setting a pattern for warfare that began to steer it inexorably away from the concept of gaily caparisoned troops advancing in massed formations to hand-to-hand combat.

For modellers, the Civil War provides ample scope for the depiction of uniforms, unusual and interesting artillery pieces such as the 13-inch mortar 'Dictator', siege works, engineer equipments, vehicles of all kinds and innovations in the design of naval vessels. Situations involving the confrontation of mounted and dismounted men were still a feature of campaigning, while the terrain manoeuvred and fought over encompassed mountains, forests, swamps, plains and farmlands, with fortified townships and elaborate trench systems included for good measure. There is certainly no lack of varied subject material both of a combat and 'out-of-action' nature to stimulate imaginations and provide scope for the full employment of skills and techniques.

Manufacturers on both sides of the Atlantic list ranges of Civil War types in their production of wargames, toy and connoisseur figures, artillery equipment and accessories. Imrie/Risley Miniatures offer a vast assortment of infantry, cavalry and general officers in 54mm; Rose Miniatures produce a nice selection of British-made figures in this scale, as does Tradition. Larger-scale Civil War figures are not so plentiful, though several are available: Series 77, for instance, offer an excellent Civil War zouave in 77mm. With a modicum of conversion or scratch-building

19th century

work virtually every aspect of personnel and impedimenta can be represented faithfully in review, campaign or informal order. There is plenty of reliable information available giving details of dress, organization, armament and so on, as well as accounts of actual operations. Perhaps the most fruitful sources of useful information are the superb plates prepared by Matthew Brady, one of the first war photographers (350 of his illustrations appear in *Mr Lincoln's Cameraman* by Roy Meredith published by Dover Publications). Brady's pictures give a marvellous impression of the times and, with the many prints of artists and illustrators contemporary with him, afford innumerable excellent modelling subjects. Be cautious with wood engravings or lithographs produced during and just after the war, as many are fanciful rather than factual.

With such a wealth of inspirational events, copiously reported and pictured at the time, and subsequently covered in all aspects by a continuing stream of written and illustrative material, the American Civil War is ideal for representation in miniatures.

Opposite left *A General Custer figure conversion by David Hunter.*
Opposite right and below *Mid-19th century American Army figures by Norman Abbey and David Hunter.*

After Waterloo the cessation of the wars against Napoleon ushered in an era of 'peace' for Europe, at least as far as international conflict was concerned. There were, it is true, struggles for self-determination, revolutions and much civil disorder, but it was left to the Americas to add wars between the United States and Mexico, with several outbreaks in the Southern continent, to these 'minor' conflagrations. Just past mid-century the precarious calm was shattered by the Crimean War, followed by the American Civil War, the outbreak of hostilities between Austria and Prussia, and a few years later between Prussia and France, resulting in the establishment of yet another republic in the latter country after the collapse of its monarchy.

Yet this was an age of expansion, exploration and colonization: industry in Europe was producing great quantities of goods, with a consequent demand for raw materials and an ever-increasing need for markets. Explorers, pioneers, traders, colonists and administrators often needed protective action for one reason or another, and the passage of the 19th century was troubled throughout by a succession of colonial outbreaks and small wars. British troops fought campaigns all over the world, so to a lesser degree did the French and Germans; the Americans and Russians saw action in their own territories, and there was much fighting in South America. The century came to a close with wars between Britain and the Boer republics in South Africa, the US and Spain and, in the Far East, China and the fast-growing Japanese empire.

This too was an age of discovery, invention and development in all kinds of technical fields, including that of weaponry, in which firearms particularly underwent spectacular change and improvement. Replacing the cumbersome flintlock, the simpler, more reliable percussion system had its day, only to yield to breech-loading weapons using metallic cartridges incorporating their own primers. Rifling of barrels increased range and accuracy, and the introduction of smokeless powder, by enabling marksmen to remain concealed when shooting, revolutionized tactics.

Artillery benefited equally from breech loading and rifling of the bore, with the result that fire could be brought to bear on targets with rapidity at distances undreamed of with smooth bore, muzzle-loading cannon. Multi-shot weapons, in the form of pistols with revolving chambers, repeating rifles and machine-guns, mechanically operated by crank or, latterly, working by means of the blow-back from each successive round's explosion, also played their part in changing the face of warfare. At sea, the advent of steam propulsion and armoured protection for warships, the invention of practical submarines and the increased performance of ordnance, both in range and quick-firing capacity, had a similarly deep effect on naval design and strategy.

Because of the improvements in the armaments used by and against them, as well as the requirements and limitations imposed by campaigning in all sorts of climates and countries, soldiers found that their uniforms underwent gradual but, eventually, comprehensive changes. In the days of massed formations employing relatively short-range weapons which produced dense clouds of smoke when discharged, the brightly coloured, elaborately decorated dress of the parade

ground had relevance in the field, providing instant recognition of friend and foe. The arrival of arms that delivered their missiles accurately to great distances without obscuring the battle field made it necessary to use ground as cover, and turned conspicuous clothing into a definite liability.

Extremes of climate and unfriendly terrain, frequently met with on colonial expeditions, also indicated that uniforms should be more suitable for conditions if men were to operate efficiently. As a result, neutral tinted foreign service dress, which offered protection from the enemy's observation and from the vagaries of weather and environment, began to be issued, although in most armies ceremonial and home service uniforms continued in traditional colours to the end of the period.

As a source of modelling subjects the 19th century is unrivalled, spanning as it does the gap between horse and musket campaigning and the increasingly mechanized warfare with sophisticated weaponry that characterizes the present epoch. Opportunities abound for the depiction of those gorgeous uniforms worn in the earlier times of European peace, whose magnificence has never since been seriously challenged, not to mention the intensely interesting stages in the development of combat clothing. Similarly, the enormous range of types involved, from Bashi Bazouks to Zulus, unusual, exotic, even bizarre, as well as the soldiers of more conventional armies, is full of possible modelling ideas and themes. It is also noteworthy that the whole military scene relied to a very great extent on animal transport in the field, despite the availability later on of steam ships and trains for long-distance movement of men and supplies. Modellers using this period for their inspiration really do have a tremendous choice.

Top *Metal Zulu War figures by Hinchliffe Models, painted by Norman Abbey. The Zulu shield on the base immediately sets the scene.*
Above *The 'other side' of the Zulu wars is typified by this proud Zulu warrior figure by W.M.H. Models.*

World War 1

The 1914–18 war was a war of attrition, with *materiel* replacing humans as the leading participants; guns, guns and more guns striving to breach the never ending lines of fortifications, and the infantry just cannon fodder, to be counted at the end of the day to see who had lost the most, for success was measured in casualties and shell production, not ground gained. In this horrific trench warfare of the Western Front more men died than had ever perished in a war before – or since. The French Army and, to a minute degree, the British Army mutinied. The Russians had a revolution and simply climbed out of their trenches and walked away. The world has literally never been the same since.

What possible fun can there be in modelling such scenes of suffering? How can anyone model World War 1 scenes or figures without insulting the memory of the participants, or upsetting those who lived through it? Firstly, it is important that those born since World War 1 be reminded of this most horrible of conflicts, in the hope that there will never be another like it. Secondly, there is the great range of *materiel* which can be modelled without offending anyone. Thirdly, and most importantly, it is essential that we record – whether it be in words, pictures, songs or models – the fact that the front line soldier's spirit rose above the horrors of the war. Think of the wry humour of the Old Bill cartoons by Bruce Bairnsfather, re-published continuously over the years. At the time these cartoons were accepted with acclaim, and Bairns-

Some of the finest military artists were producing their work during the 19th century, war correspondents made their fascinating on-the-spot sketches, and photography was fast coming into its own. All these factors contributed to the fund of information on the period that is available today. However, it is as well to sound a note of caution, since not all these sources are completely reliable. Many changes of uniform and equipment, for instance, lasted for such a short time that they did not receive adequate description or representation in printed word or illustration. It is therefore essential that reference data be carefully checked with all likely sources, comparing one with another and even using inspired guesses in some cases. Obviously the more background information that is acquired the easier it is to make logical assumptions, and fortunately there are many reference libraries and galleries where such data can be gathered.

Connoisseur figure manufacturers have not been as thorough in their coverage of the 19th century as they have with other periods, though there are masses of toy soldiers, both contemporarily produced and of modern origin. The British and Zulus in the Boer War have been fairly well covered in miniature by Minimen in the United States and Tradition in Great Britain, with other manufacturers, such as Realmodels, producing smaller samplings of the subject. The Indian Army has been well represented by both Rose Miniatures and Tradition, as well as by Dek Model Soldiers.

As with miniatures, reference material is scattered and difficult to come by. However, this situation does appear to be changing now, slowly but surely, with Philip Haythornthwaite's *World Uniforms and Battles 1815–1850* and Series 77's US infantrymen of the Spanish–American War beginning to show the way.

But by and large, to depict many subjects enthusiasts must have recourse to conversion and scratch-building. This, however, has an advantage in that it leads to creations unique to the individual and such extra trouble is well worthwhile to depict types and incidents from this most fascinating era.

Top *90mm Bengal Lancer figure from Chota Sahib.*
Above *54mm Historex/Airfix mixture for a General Foch figure by David Hunter.*

father became the voice of the common soldier, a means of expressing his scepticism and even disgust at the way the generals and politicians were handling the war. Think of the scathing sarcasm and self-mocking melancholy of the soldiers' songs so well preserved in the musical *Oh! What a Lovely War*. This is what it is important to remember about World War 1; that the ordinary soldier not only survived but rose above the appalling conditions and battles into which his alleged superiors threw him.

If you take excerpts from the songs, or cartoons from Bairnsfather's books, and use them to create model dioramas, you have the *spirit* of the World War 1 soldier encapsulated. Both sources are rich in ideas for such models: brewing tea in a water-filled shell-hole, hanging equipment on a dead man's arm sticking out of the trench parapet, sardonic notices over dug-out homes, scenes of outdoor life where uniform disappeared as men tried to keep warm and dry, sometimes up to their waists or even shoulders in water, alone on sentry duty at night when spit froze before it could reach the ground, and always the mud, the barbed wire, and the raids into No-Man's-Land for prisoners, information and to keep the enemy on his toes.

But it should not be thought that World War 1 was fought entirely at the Western Front, or entirely in trenches. Far from it. It was a *world* war, and numerous nations were involved on many fronts. There were the Alpini and Bersaglieri in the snow and ice of the Alps, the more mobile Eastern Front with its terrible Russian winters, the Indian Army with the askaris in East Africa as well as at the Western Front, armoured cars and Australian cavalry in the Western Desert and Mesopotamia, the sea-borne landings against the Turks at Gallipoli and Suvla Bay – the variety is endless.

Nor was the war fought only by the armies. There were launches and small gunboats fighting on African lakes, midget submarines in the Sea of Marmara, naval brigades fighting on land, and the fragile aircraft of those days which can provide many original diorama ideas, either crashed in No-Man's-Land or portrayed in the rear areas.

World War 1 offers the modeller for his choice of subject all the armies of the world, in all terrains from desert to Arctic, and ranging from individual soldiers to large-scale raids in 25mm scale. There is also a wide range of equipment, from the new tanks, monster guns and extensive use of small railways behind the front, to the first major use of tractors and lorries in war. Yet horses remained a major part of the transport scene, so there is really something for everyone – even cavalry, either muddy and heavily laden at the front, or immaculate with pennanted lances on escort duty in the rear.

World War 1 is not a popular modelling period at present, and the miniatures available are few. However, this in itself is a challenge – to create a model in an area where others are reluctant to venture. A number of the major figure manufacturers do provide a starting point: German infantry in 54mm by Greenwood & Ball, Cavalier Miniatures, and Tradition; 75mm Scottish officers and men by Scottish Soldiers Collection; British and German infantry in 54mm by Old Guard and Squadron/Rubin, who also make RFC and East African figures; and 75mm Italians and 54mm British artillery by Hinchliffe. Perhaps the widest range of 54mm figures is by Rose Miniatures, producers of a complete variety of German, French and British soldiers. American doughboys are virtually non-existent in miniature, but British

Dennis Green's revealing diorama of a section of World War 1 trench, a subject full of possibilities for showing the humour as well as the horror of war.

World War 2

World War 2 lasted from 3 September 1939 until 2 September 1945. Initially it was limited to north-west Europe with Germany and Russia invading Poland, and then the former over-running Norway and Denmark, the Low Countries, and finally France (which was supported by the British Expeditionary Force) in early 1940. When Italy came in on the German side in June 1940 the conflict spread to the British and Italian colonies and areas of influence in north and east Africa, and in early 1941 to Greece and the Balkans. In the meantime naval warfare on the Atlantic trade routes and air warfare over England and the Continent were increasing in intensity. In June 1941 the first major escalation occurred with the German invasion of Russia, and in December the conflict became effectively world wide following the Japanese attack on Pearl Harbor which brought in the Americans and Chinese, and extended the area of operations to the Pacific and south-east Asia as far west as the borders of India.

Until mid-1942 the war went generally in favour of the German–Italian–Japanese Axis, with the Germans advancing deep into Russia, the Japanese capturing the American Pacific islands, Malaya, Indonesia and Burma, and Britain suffering heavy losses in the Battle of the Atlantic. Thereafter, however, as America played an increasing part, both directly and by supplying material to her allies, the tide turned. The German-Italian army was driven from North Africa in early 1943, and there followed the Allied invasions of Sicily and Italy which led to the Italian surrender, although not to the end of fighting on the Italian mainland. Following Stalingrad in February 1943 the Germans were gradually pushed back out of Russia, and in June 1944 the Anglo-American invasion took place in Normandy. By May 1945 the Russians and the Allied armies had met in Germany and the war in the west was over.

In the Far East, 1945 saw the reconquest of Burma by British and Imperial troops while the Americans, having inflicted crippling defeats on the Japanese fleet, were able to start 'island-hopping' invasions towards Japan itself. In the event, however, the dropping of the atomic bombs on Hiroshima and Nagasaki in August forced the Japanese to surrender.

With such a total combat the scope for the military modeller is clearly enormous. Soldiers from Brazil to Poland, or Yugoslavia to China, can be portrayed in settings ranging from primary jungle to snow-covered steppe, or from empty desert to ruined cities, while numerous auxiliaries ranging from partisans to NAAFI canteen staff are also legitimate subject matter! From the modeller's point of view World War 2 has a number of special characteristics apart from its sheer size. The most obvious difference from previous campaigns was the replacement of the horse by the machine, and the vast increase in the scale of mechanical equipment and sophisticated weapons generally. Although some armies, such as the Germans and Russians, continued to rely heavily on horses right through the war, the variety and frequency with which not only tanks and other fighting vehicles, but also the soft-skinned support vehicles, were replaced as they became obsolete, and the introduction of new and specialized anti-tank and anti-aircraft artillery, means that World War 2 is at least as much the field of the hardware modeller as the

Cavalry was used in World War 1 but no kits exist as such. This model by Harry Heaviside is a conversion from a 1:12 Airfix kit with a particularly fine horse's head. Convincing horse modelling is an art in itself.

soldiers in helmets may be modified to represent them.

The dress uniforms of the period have received more attention from manufacturers. Tradition has produced a wide selection of German and Austrian troops; Monarch Miniatures' 54mm German infantrymen and bandsmen are especially handsome; Superior Models has made 90mm figures of the Kaiser, von Mackensen, a kürassier and a Uhlan. Series 77 offers an excellent selection of Germans in 77mm, including a striking *Garde du Korps* standard bearer. The dress uniforms of this period are especially colourful, particularly those of the German armed forces, which may explain why they have received so much attention.

For dioramas, a number of early cars produced in kit form may be used as staff vehicles, and there is the famous Old Bill 'Bus of 1914 by Airfix. After that it is balsa, plastic card, modelling clays and plasters, and *your* skill – and that is the most rewarding part of modelling World War 1 subjects.

Apart from the Bairnsfather books there are one or two other handy reference sources for ideas and uniform and equipment detail: Volumes I and II of the Funckens' *L'Uniforme et les Armes des Soldats de la Guerre 1914–18*, and Blandford's colour books on *Army Uniforms of WW1* by A. Mollo, *Tanks & other AFVs 1900–1918* by B. T. White, and *Railways and War before 1918* by D. Bishop and K. Davis. Purnells' part-work *History of the First World War* not only contains illustrations of the men and machines, but is also a treasure house of ideas for settings.

figure enthusiast. Although ships and aircraft are separate modelling subjects in their own right, even they can become involved in military scenes such as beach assaults or airfield defence dioramas.

As with World War 1, and to some extent the inter-war period (which should not be forgotten as an interesting topic for modelling), drab uniforms and camouflage schemes for equipment do not give as much scope to the painter as some earlier periods, but detailed camouflage patterns and the intricate systems of markings and badges used both on vehicles and personal uniforms often need much research and considerable skill to reproduce on a small scale.

With the end of the war less than 40 years ago it is natural that there is more information available to the modeller than earlier conflicts. This is not only because there are still people around who can remember the actual events, but many vehicles, uniforms, weapons and fortifications still remain both in museums (for example, the Royal Armoured Corps Tank Museum, Bovington Camp, Dorset; the Imperial War Museum, S. Lambeth, London; US Army Ordnance Museum, Aberdeen Proving Ground, Maryland, USA; and the Patton Museum, Fort Knox, Kentucky, USA) and in private hands. Probably the most useful source is the very large number of photographs taken as a result of the rapid developments in photographic equipment between the wars. Nowadays many books and periodicals reproduce these in forms useful to the student or modeller. Particularly helpful are those titles published in the Squadron Signal series, numerous of the Almark and Osprey 'Men-at-Arms' publications and the excellent 'Tank Data' range by Sycamore Island Books (US). As the World War 2 period attracts a large number of military enthusiasts and modellers, new books appear regularly on the bookstalls. Unfortunately, few include many contemporary colour photographs – mainly because the film was very hard to come by at the time – and most rely strongly on colour drawings which can vary in quality.

For the making of World War 2 models, there are sizeable numbers of plastic and metal kits on the market for both figures and hardware. Imrie/Risley have available to modellers a large variety of 54mm metal German and British troops, with a sprinkling of Americans. The New York firm of Cavalier Miniatures offers a number of excellent 54mm German World War 2 subjects, including a superb motorcycle and driver. Though their figures are not as precisely detailed as some modellers may want, Heller is producing a number of French subjects in plastic. The Japanese manufacturer of armoured vehicle kits, Tamiya, quite naturally added a full range of plastic figures to their line; though emphasis is on German troops, Tamiya also produces Russian, American and British soldiers in scale to their tanks, as well as equipment to go with them. Manufacturers in England offer various scales from Matchbox, Hinchliffe, Greenwood & Ball, Airfix, and many others.

Such is the range of subjects for the World War 2 modeller that all the kits produced cover only a fraction of possible subjects, and so perhaps more than any other it is a period for the converter and scratch-builder (unless one is content to make up standard kits, which tend to be infantrymen of the principal combatant nations and tanks, predominantly the German types). World War 2 therefore not only provides great scope for the modeller prepared to try his hand at converting and scratch-building, but also a wealth of information to give him ideas and help him do so.

Opposite *Clever posing of 1:35 Tamiya figures gives this American World War 2 communications post a remarkable degree of atmosphere. The arrangement of only a very few simple pieces completes a little masterpiece by Don Skinner.*
Below left *World War 2 German infantryman, another 1:12 Airfix conversion, this one by Mac Kennaugh.*
Below right *Large models need be no less convincing than small ones. This 1:10 scale Hellcat tank is actually a radio-controlled model built by Keith Lister and skilfully photographed by John Wylie.*

1946-81

Following six years of global war, the period since 1945 has been described as one of 'limited war'. There have been a host of insurgencies, a dozen minor wars and four major ones, counting the Arab-Israeli conflicts as campaigns in one prolonged war. Battles have been documented, photographed and reported instantly from the scene of the fighting as never before, often from both sides of the action. Scale drawings, colour photographs and reference shots are readily available. The variety of terrain, location and style of war is as great as in 1939–45 and the range of weapons and equipments used covers all those of the later years of World War 2 up to the latest modern products.

The Vietnam war falls into two distinct phases. The first, from 1946–54, was the French campaign against the Viet Minh, ending with their defeat at Dien Bien Phu. After this there was a pause during which the states of Laos, Cambodia and North and South Vietnam were established.

Fighting flared up in 1958 and the Americans, starting as advisers to the South Vietnamese, gradually became totally involved. When their troops joined in the ground fighting in 1965 it became a war of material against guerrillas. The Americans used almost every piece of equipment in their inventory in large numbers and huge quantities of ammunition. Their use of AFVs for every kind of mission and their strategy of 'Fire Support Bases' give great scope to the modeller. The M551 Sheridan saw its only active service in Vietnam, though without using the Shillelagh ATGW. Probably the most typical vehicle of the whole war was the M113 APC in most of its roles, and modified locally with extra armaments and protection in bewildering array, a gift to the model converter. More than 7,000 Australians and New Zealanders served in Vietnam, mostly infantry but with their own artillery and armoured elements, including Centurion MBTs and ARVs.

Probably no other 'limited war' in history has been as widely documented as the Arab-Israeli struggle for Palestine. It erupted in 1948 and has since been through four major campaigns. Most of the fighting has been in classic desert surroundings, but in 1967 the Israelis took the war up on the Golan Heights and in 1973 there were two assault crossings of the Suez Canal.

The growth of the Israeli forces is a fascinating study in improvization; in particular the Armoured Force, which started with a Daimler armoured car and two Cromwells stolen from the British, augmented by a Sherman and some old Renault and Hotchkiss light tanks. Since then they have used American, British, French and Soviet tanks of many types, culminating with their own locally designed and built Merkava MBT. Kits are available covering many of the equipments used by all arms, but a major problem is the dearth of kits of modern Soviet AFVs, artillery and soft-skinned vehicles. So for the Arab armies (except Jordan) it is largely a matter of scratch-building. Luckily there is a huge reservoir of information on all phases of this war and, for small scale enthusiasts, some resin mouldings in 4mm (1:76) scale are available.

The war in Korea was totally different. It was the first United Nations war, involving troops from the Republic of Korea and from 21 other countries. The terrain was mostly mountainous and the war, from 25 June 1950 to 27 July 1953, moved from the 38th Parallel south to the Pusan perimeter (beach landings of equipment, for the diorama builder) and north to the Yalu River, before the huge Chinese army joined in to support the North Koreans and the fighting swung south again to stabilize on the 38th Parallel. There were many heroic actions in Korea, one of the most famous being the battle of the Imjin River, where the Gloucesters became 'Glorious'.

The variations in climate meant that troops wore clothing from Arctic to tropical, a bonus for the modeller, and kits are readily available, since both sides used World War 2 vehicles and weapons. One notable exception is the Centurion tank, which won its spurs in Korea and gained a tremendous reputation for its protection, its accuracy and its ability to climb seemingly impossible hills to positions from which it was used for 'heavy sniping'. Kits in a variety of scales exist for models of this famous tank; Tamiya produce a Mk III in two sizes (1:35 and 1:25 scales) and Airfix offer a later variant – the Mk X – in smaller 1:76.

Another area in which the Centurion showed its mettle was in the Indo-Pakistan wars of 1965 and 1971, where the Indians used it most successfully against the Pakistani M48s and T55s and T59s. Both campaigns were largely conventional battles fought in the arid west of India, but the 1971 campaign was remarkable for the brilliant 'Lightning Campaign' by which India defeated the large army in West Pakistan. The Indians fielded a large number of T54/55s and made good use of the amphibious PT76.

There has not been a year without a war or 'emergency' in progress. Other affairs in which the modeller may find interest and much information on which to work include: Malaya, Brunei, Suez, Cyprus, Kuwait, Yemen, Oman, Rhodesia, Congo, Angola, Nigeria and so on, with more lately Ethiopia, Somalia and Uganda.

These wars have been valuable testing grounds for the armourer nations of the world and most campaigns have had weaponry from both east and west, with successes to both camps. Over all this broods the threat of Soviet attack in Europe, providing an interesting challenge to the wargamers, amateur and professional.

Miniature soldiers of the 1946–81 period are not as readily available as models of armoured vehicles for the same years. While the tanks of the time capture the imagination of modellers, for some reason the regular troops do not. A few American infantrymen are produced by Valiant Miniatures, plus a Viet Cong soldier, and there are the plastic figures produced by Tamiya as adjuncts to their armoured vehicle kits. Modellers will, in general, have to modify and/or convert whatever modern-day figures they can find – not too difficult a task, aside from the mechanical aspects, considering the wealth of photographic material available for reference use.

Opposite *A British Army patrol in a Northern Ireland street scene by John Wylie. The troops wear the disruptive patterned combat clothing which is so popular with armies in most countries today. An enthusiast interested in present-day conflicts should have little difficulty in building up a scrap-book of useful references from newspapers and magazines.*

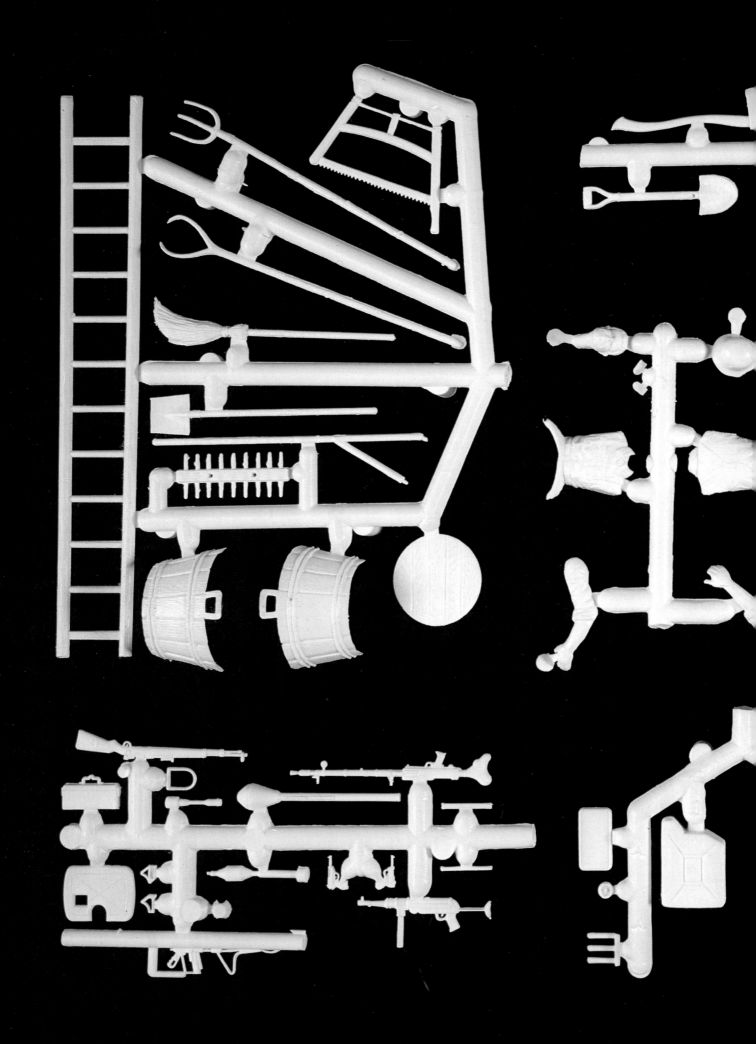

How to start

Not very long ago, making a model meant producing drawings, acquiring tools and buying raw materials to start a long process for a hard-won and frequently unsatisfactory result. Nowadays it is possible to buy a set of parts and simply assemble them to achieve a result far better than a beginner could previously have hoped for; the danger is that such simplicity can soon bring a loss of interest. A modeller needs a challenge to his skill and ingenuity, and in military modelling he finds this in the search for perfection in detail and painting, realism with authenticity, and the imposition of his own ideas by conversion of commercial kits or even, with experience, scratch-building.

Attachment of parts to sprues is common to kits from all manufacturers. Save the sprue because, as described, it will have many uses.

Visitors to exhibitions of models often say 'I could never do anything like that', to which the standard rejoinder is that everyone has to start somewhere and, taken step by step, there is nothing in modelling beyond the capabilities of average people. Most likely a plastic kit is the commonest starting point.

The first step is to buy a simple kit; keep to a very modest price and if the model shop owner offers advice, accept it willingly. Unfortunately many expensive and complex models never get beyond the just-started stage because they may be too difficult for the beginner. Better make a good try at a low cost kit first and be resigned to the fact that this effort will almost certainly not be a competition winner, and may not even reach your own potential standards.

Basic tools

A basic tool kit for a minimum start will include some small sharp scissors, a modelling knife, tweezers and a paint brush, with possibly a small Swiss file and some fine wet or dry rubbing paper. Some items can probably be borrowed from the household but, if you are going to be a modeller, get your own and always, *always*, buy the very best you can afford. If you intend to take matters seriously it is better to buy a cheap starter and save up for the good tool later. Such tools are most often available from hobby shops, and a copy of a modelling magazine will tell you which makes are those specially designed for modellers.

The knife should have replaceable blades and it is useful to have two or three different shapes. A sharp point straight knife is of most use, followed by a curved edge blade with a point. The tweezers should have a fairly narrow flat end, and for the file a half round Swiss or needle type is a good starter. The paint brush is most important. You will never paint successfully with a poor brush and, though some hobby shops stock quite good quality brushes, it is best to visit an artists' supply shop. Look for a high-quality water colour type sable brush which has a long bristle and comes to a fine point. Ask the owner of the shop to wet the point and shake it out to see that it is perfect, and reject those which are not. These brushes are expensive, so buy only the ones that are just right. The brush *must* be stored upright and the protective plastic tube kept on after use. Always clean the brush completely, for if looked after it should last for years.

This very basic outfit of tools can be considered stage one and will provide enough to build your first models, with the addition of a few extra items such as rubber bands, adhesive tape, bulldog clips and a modelling board. If you are very much a 'table top' modeller, use a cheap wooden tray with a beaded edge, as it will help keep small parts off the carpet.

Stage two comes as interest grows and brings the ambition to build something different by simple modifications or tackling more complex kits. Additions to the tool kit could be a small razor saw, extra files: oval, round and flat are probably all that are really necessary, as good ones are also rather expensive. Most other needs will be covered by a small pair of long-nosed pliers, some very small drills, starting at about $\frac{1}{16}$ inch and going down as small as you feel you can handle, with one or two pin chucks to hold them, a small steel rule, a protractor and right-angle square, and a compass and dividers.

Opposite *Typical inexpensive plastic figures available in model and toy shops and many chain stores. In this example of the Airfix range, parts and equipment for six figures are supplied; a beginner might do worse than assemble and paint two as supplied, try his hand at simple modification of two more and use the remainder as a nucleus for a 'spares box'.*

Below *A fairly comprehensive selection of basic hand tools and examples of that most important requirement, research material. The text lists minimum requirements for tools which are surprisingly modest and research material exists in plenty in libraries and museums. A safe procedure is to base a model on illustrations and the like already held.*

Spray guns and airbrushes

The third stage of tool-kit building brings in some of the more exotic and expensive equipment and is really only for the serious enthusiast. Unless you build, say, at least a dozen models each year, or intend entering competitions extensively, or specialize in, perhaps, large expensive vehicle models, it is probably not worth buying an airbrush. A really good finish can be obtained by hand brushing and some of the top modellers prefer to use a quality brush and consider that an airbrush is not really a substitute.

However, if you are convinced that your tool kit is incomplete without an airbrush, consider a few points. First, it takes a considerable amount of practice to achieve even quite modest results, and those who produce what can only be described as works of art are painstaking and patient.

Airbrushes as modelling tools fall into three categories, (1) simple venturi suction types, (2) single action and (3) double action. The simple type is not really an airbrush but a small-scale spray, and many years ago modellers used a device of a pair of tapered tubes, one end in a pot of paint, and the other either blown by mouth or a squeeze bulb. It actually worked, and now, brought up to date with a more accurate venturi and a sealed paint jar and powered air supply, an effective tool has been produced. This type is most suitable for putting an even layer of paint over a broad surface, and with careful masking off quite complicated work can be carried out, but because of the limitations some finishes can only really be achieved by a more controllable instrument.

Type (2) is a precision instrument where the paint and air are both adjustable. Usually the paint is regulated by a screw valve which operates by moving the finely tapered needle back and forth in the spray tip to allow more or less paint to pass. The air is turned on by means of a finger tip control operating on/off and, by varying finger pressure, also adjusting the volume of air. This gives more precise control and enables very fine work to be achieved. Finally, type (3), the double action, has a single control operating both air and paint simultaneously. This is possibly the most difficult to master but can cover a wide range of effects.

The first type is obviously the least expensive and is really all many modellers need, but for those looking for precision the most expensive type is necessary and will cost perhaps ten times as much. Choose carefully, as some expensive airbrushes are totally unsuitable for modelling; some types are made for graphics and will operate only with inks, so if you intend buying one it is useful to discuss types with someone who has experience and can advise exactly the right one for you.

A spray gun (above) has comparatively little application in average military modelling but can be useful for large models of tanks, bigger diorama details and wargame topography as well as for undercoating metal figures. For figure and small diorama work an airbrush (below) is more versatile, providing much more precise control and capable of spraying very small areas. Both illustrated instruments use a single control operating both paint and air flows.

Airbrushes need an air supply. Cans of pressurized gas are useful and readily available and it is more economical to buy the larger sizes. Don't leave the valve screwed on as the gas can leak, and *always* clean the airbrush most thoroughly after use. You will probably use more air cleaning the airbrush than painting. With economical use a large air can will paint at least half a dozen 1:35 scale AFV models. As cans cost quite a lot these days, it may be an investment to buy a compressor, which is about equal in cost to one of the higher priced airbrushes. Nothing is more irritating than to run out of air on a Saturday night with a half-finished model and a paint-filled airbrush.

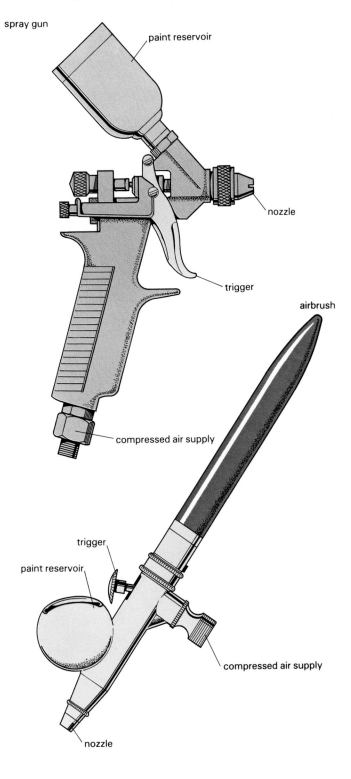

spray gun

paint reservoir

nozzle

trigger

airbrush

compressed air supply

trigger

paint reservoir

compressed air supply

nozzle

40

The Pyrogravure

Next on the list, or possibly first according to your needs, is a 'pyro'. The Pyrogravure is simply a heated tool with a variety of 'points' for working with a hot tip, and if not available at your model shop one could probably be purchased at an art and handicrafts store, as they are used for 'pokerwork' on wood or leather. For figure modelling in plastic it is invaluable, as the heat, confined to a variety of tips from small points to spoon shapes, can be used in a number of ways to work plastic.

Our luxury tool kit is almost complete and probably the final item would be a miniature power drill and

Bearskins and other hair or fur items provide a natural subject for pyrogravure work, though with time and patience similar results can be obtained with a simple heated needle. This is a 1:12 scale mounted Imperial Guard figure based on Airfix parts, by Bernie Harris.

tools. Some of these small units are very good, with excellent bearings and accurate chucks, and will drill or turn precisely, very important for small work. Others have rather crude and wobbly tool mountings and at least one of these has ended up, rather ignominiously, as a mechanical paint stirrer.

During your modelling years you will undoubtedly find many other useful tools for all sorts of purposes and it is important to get into the habit of looking at anything from the angle of 'how could I use that?'.

Kits and scales

Today model manufacturing is an international business and most countries will have kits from the USA, UK, Japan, Italy and France. Even kits from Eastern Europe find their way into the West, and the enthusiast with a well-stocked model shop nearby is spoiled by the wide choice. However, thousands rely on mail order, where it is difficult to choose because you have to hope the kit is just what you expect, and unfortunately sometimes the result is disappointing. It would be impossible to list all makers and kits, as the only lists ever produced filled a small book and were out of date even before printing was finished. However, it is possible to provide some food for thought for the beginner and perhaps alert him to possible pitfalls.

Scale is obviously a matter of taste and, to some extent, the modeller's facilities for storage. A modeller with fifty tanks in 1:76 scale has no problem, but where would he keep fifty in 1:25 scale? To generalize somewhat, manufacturers have, with a few exceptions, opted for small scales, covered by HO/OO, 1:76, 1:72; medium scales, covered by 1:32 and 1:35; and large, 1:25, 1:24 and giant 1:9. Figure manufacturers in the main have opted for 25mm, 54mm, 77mm and 90mm, or variations of these sizes.

Unfortunately, it is sometimes hard to be sure just what is what, though in some countries it is an offence to describe an item for sale with an inaccurate description. It is inevitable that errors and inaccuracies will creep in, and that some makers are stricter than others. Generally, as vehicles and aircraft can readily be checked dimensionally, these models are more or less accurate to scale, but figures are another matter, and as military modelling covers all the spheres of land warfare it is worth discussing exactly what scale is.

Taking the more popular scales and producing the most-used common denominator of one foot we get a table like this:

Scale description	1ft equals	Height of 5ft 8in man
HO (1:87)	3·5mm	19·88mm
1:76	4·01mm	22·76mm
OO (1:75)	4·06mm	23·06mm
1:72	4·24mm	24·03mm
1:35	8·71mm	49·42mm
1:32	9·63mm	54·06mm
54 (1:31)	9·82mm	55·80mm

Scaling dimensions sometimes seems to bother modellers. Modern technology helps if you have a calculator. Just take the full-size dimension in millimetres and divide by the scale fraction, which then gives the model dimension in the scale you require. The table above shows about 4mm difference in height for an 'average' man, in theory, in any of the small scale range, and about 6mm in the large scale. This represents a short man (i.e. less than 5ft 5in) against a man about a head taller, and rather less so with the larger scale. This would make the two scale ranges entirely compatible if some constant reference was used, and also if models were made with similar bulk. As it is, most

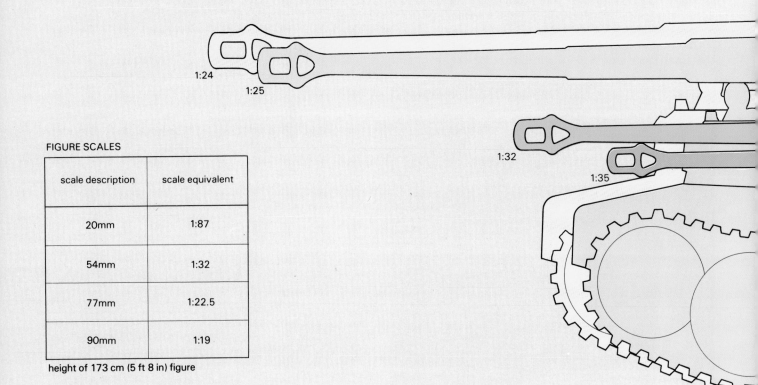

1:24

1:25

1:32

1:35

FIGURE SCALES

scale description	scale equivalent
20mm	1:87
54mm	1:32
77mm	1:22.5
90mm	1:19

height of 173 cm (5 ft 8 in) figure

Representative figures reproduced full size in each scale

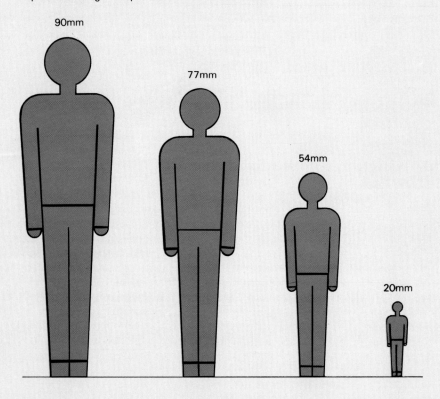

90mm

77mm

54mm

20mm

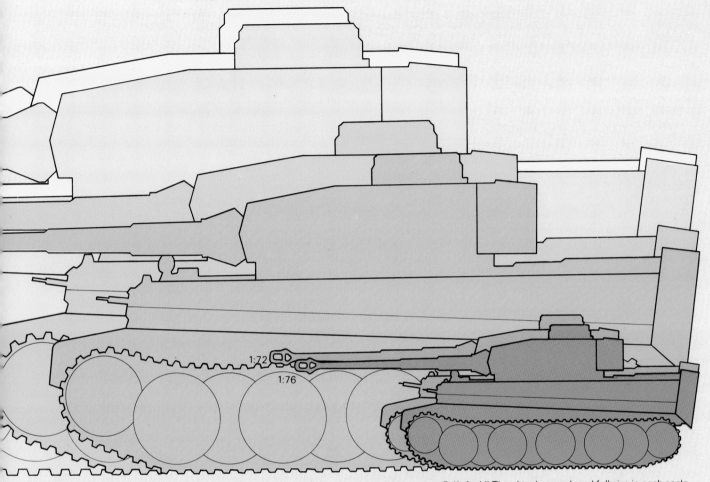

1:72

1:76

PzKpfw VI Tiger I tank reproduced full size in each scale

Differences in scales can be dramatic, as illustrated here. Most modellers experiment a little, then choose a scale which best suits their particular interests. Single figure modellers might be thought to be more fortunate as far as space requirements are concerned, but a move to dioramas can create storage and display problems; one major exhibition was forced to limit uncased dioramas to 300mm (12in) square. Tanks, too, can offer problems in the larger scales. Manufacturers respond to demand, so that a check on kits available will indicate the more popular scales and may well influence a new enthusiast's choice.

VEHICLE SCALES

scale description	scale equivalent		height of 173 cm (5 ft 8 in) figure
	1m	1ft	
1:76	13.16mm	4.01mm	22.76mm
1:72	13.89mm	4.24mm	24.03mm
1:35	28.57mm	8.71mm	49.42mm
1:32	31.25mm	9.53mm	54.06mm
1:25	40.00mm	12.20mm	69.20mm
1:24	41.67mm	12.70mm	72.08mm

models sold as HO scale look tiny besides 1:72 figures and a measured comparison of some examples from the larger scales shows some interesting results.

Make	Model dimension	Height scaled
Tamiya (1:35)	47mm	5ft 5in
Revell/Ital (1:35)	50mm	5ft 8in plus
Airfix/Max (1:35)	45mm	5ft 2in
ESCI (1:35)	48mm	5ft 6in
Heller (1:35)	47mm	5ft 5in
Nominal 54mm (metal, female UK)	58mm	5ft 11in
Nominal 54mm (metal US)	51mm	5ft 2in
Nominal 54mm (metal UK)	61mm	6ft 3in
Airfix (1:32)	53·5mm	5ft 7in

Lined up, all the figures are compatible except the Airfix/Max and the two large metal UK-made figures. Fortunately the Airfix/Max figures are in a vehicle and the small size does not show up against others when used in a diorama.

Vehicle kits
Kits of vehicle models are completely straightforward, and there is little technical difference among the products of the major manufacturers. In general, parts fit well, detail is good – in some cases excellent – and instructions, which most frequently use the exploded diagram method of showing assembly, are clear. It is usually most important to follow the assembly sequence shown in the instructions, as it is all too easy to find parts, or even sub-assemblies, not fitted in correct order, left over and unusable.

The largest range in any scale is probably that produced by Tamiya in 1:35. Scale accuracy is very good, though there is sometimes a tendency for their figures to be small in relation to the vehicles. Detail is excellent. Monogram has a range of 1:32 scale kits, some of which are very good, and also a few odd-scale models of interest mainly to general modellers.

Airfix produces military models in four scales, vehicles and figures in 1:32, 1:35 and HO/OO, plus figures in 1:32 and HO/OO as well as the 54mm Collectors' Series. Matchbox make figures and armour in 1:76 which tend to be rather simple in detail, and both Fujimi and Hasegawa offer excellent small-scale armour with some of the best detail, frequently only equalled by the 1:76 ESCI kits.

Revel/Italaerei kits are 1:35 and ESCI also model in

this scale. Heller, marketing through Humbrol in UK (though not yet including armour in the Humbrol range), do some excellent 1:35 kits mainly of vehicles and figures with French connotations. In addition, there are others in the field but rather less well known, so many makers have not been mentioned, not through lack of good products, but because of the sheer length of a full list. If metal figures in all the various scales were added the inventory would be almost endless. Experience will show which manufacturers can nearly always be relied upon but, to begin with, pick the big names.

First models

Where, then, to start? If you are commencing with armour, choose relatively simple models without complicated chassis or detail. Two or three like this can teach a lot, and to get your enthusiasm going a well-finished simple model is better than an unfinished complicated one. Experiment with simple modifications to the kit. Opened hatches, extra stowage gear, or a couple of figures, all add to the interest and the way to do it will be discussed later.

Figures are rather more of a problem. A good way to start is with the well-produced but low-cost kits, and possibly the best are by Airfix, either the 'Multipose' type for World War 2 enthusiasts or the Collectors' Series for the historical buff. With the latter, again pick an easy one, say the Rifleman rather than the Highlander. Study the assembly instructions and painting details as a preparation. Basically what follows applies to all kit models.

The parts are attached to a 'sprue' which is the moulding of the channel which carries the plastic through the mould. Identify the parts for the first assembly and carefully separate them from the sprue, using small sharp scissors, wire snips, or a modelling knife with a strong blade, pressing down on a cutting board. Separate near the sprue so that a sliver of plastic is left on the moulding and remove this by careful use of a thinner sharp blade.

Examine the mouldings and you will probably see a fine raised line on the surface. This is the line of separation of the mould halves (an old worn mould makes a pronounced line) and this should be carefully removed by gentle scraping with the blade edge, holding the blade at right angles to the moulding.

In some cases there will be 'flash', which is where the moulding has not closed tightly at the edge of the part and plastic has 'flashed out' under the flats of the mould halves. This must also be carefully removed.

Opposite *A tank kit is likely to include scores of tiny parts, each one of which must be detached from the sprue with equal care. Many modellers paint the parts while still on the sprue, touching up the cut surfaces when the parts are finally separated. An alternative is to cut and trim the various items, then place them on an adhesive foam pad, which avoids losing tiny parts and holds them firmly enough for delicate painting. The tank pictured is a Crusader in the Airfix 1:32 range.*
Right *Cutting parts from sprue requires a sharp blade and a clean cut. Always cut on a board with downward pressure – the cut tends to occur suddenly. A smaller, tapered blade can be used to pare away surplus sprue from the cut part, holding the part firmly on the cutting board rather than in the fingers.*

A typical tank kit

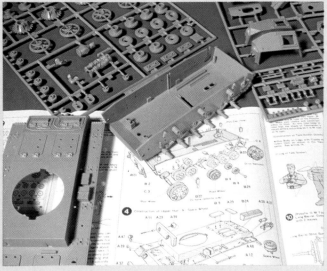

1 *Always unpack a plastic kit on a clear, clean surface and be careful not to drop any small part which may have become detached. Read the instructions, identifying the parts and checking that they are all present. Keeping related parts in separate boxes is helpful.*

2 *Do not separate parts from their sprues until they are needed, then cut, not break, them off and trim away any surplus. Some modellers prefer to paint small parts before removal from the sprue, especially where finished colours vary.*

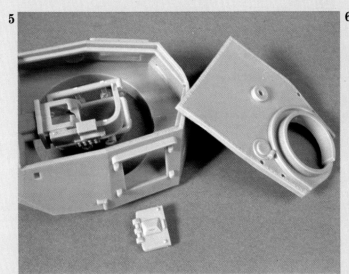

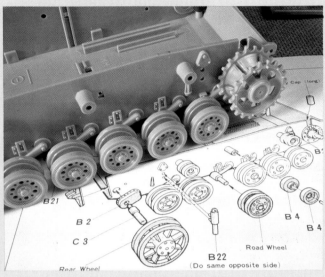

3 *Flash and moulding flaws should be removed by cutting or scraping with a very sharp blade. Scraping will not score the surface, as may happen with abrasive papers or files. Each part should be as perfect as possible before gluing.*

5 *Be careful to keep cement clear of any moving part, such as the elevating and traversing gear of a gun. Serious modellers normally lock parts in place permanently to suit particular needs, but only after mechanisms are completed.*

4 *Always assemble in the order given in the kit instructions, or it may be found that parts which should have been positioned earlier cannot be fitted. If in any doubt, try a dry run, i.e. fit the parts together without adhesive.*

6 *Small details should be attached only after major handling of main components is completed. If they have been pre-painted, it is essential to scrape away any paint from surfaces to be glued; plastic cements will not stick to paint.*

7 *Although this model is shown largely assembled, much of it is in dry-run stage and will be disassembled for painting, fitting of tracks and other work. The model is a Tamiya Panzerkampfwagen III and a completed example in Afrika Korps markings is shown below.*

Cementing

When parts have been cleaned up, glue where required, using tube cement applied by a wooden toothpick, or liquid cement by a small pointed brush. Liquid cement should be applied by holding the parts together, then touching the brush, loaded with the thin cement, (wet but not dripping) to the join line of the parts, when capillary action will cause the liquid to flow into the join. Allow sub-assemblies to dry properly before assembling together. Continue until you reach the stage where the next move will cover up a part and make it hard to paint. At this stage, paint the parts to be covered. In some cases it is better to paint detail before assembly and parts can be touched up later. Remember that cement will not stick to paint, so it may be necessary to scrape the paint off small contact areas to stick detail. Usually about 1·5mm ($\frac{1}{16}$ in) square is the smallest area that glue will hold; if the point of contact is very tiny, use one of the 'super glues' with a cyanoacrylate base. When you have reached the stage when you are ready to give the bulk of the model the final paint finish, it is useful to paint or spray overall with a thin matt white undercoat to ensure even paint coverage.

If you have any small gaps use model filler such as Squadron Green Putty or Humbrol Britfix Customizing Body Putty, and it is a useful tip that, if you use solvent liquids as glue, (e.g. methyl-ethyl-ketone or Butan 2-one) these will thin Squadron putty and it can then be applied to tiny gaps with an old paint brush. Some of the commercial model liquid cements will also do this, but not all.

Tube glue works perfectly well, though is a little longer hardening, and very small amounts of impact adhesive can be used instead of cyano.

Modification and conversion

Some customizing of a kit makes a personal model instead of one just out of the box. In addition, figures and vehicles are ideal subjects for miniature displays. Positioned on an attractive base a tank is more interesting than on its own, and a figure just asks to be 'doing something'.

A display of more than one item in the form of a vignette or a diorama is even better, but don't make the mistake of making every one an epic. Sheer lack of space will stop you making models of Custer's last stand or D-Day every time . . .

Look at the illustration on the box top and imagine just what you would like the subject to be doing. The Rifleman is firing his gun, but if his right arm was bent a little more and his left arm bent and brought across his body with legs together and crossed slightly, he could be leaning on a fence rail smoking a pipe. That tank crewman sitting on the turret edge could be smoking a cigarette and holding his water bottle. Such individual touches are not difficult to incorporate.

The very basic materials of conversion are a few sheets of plastic card of varying thickness, and some body putty. Examine the pose of the figure as kitted, then decide what needs to be altered to produce the pose required. To alter the bend of a limb, cut at the angle of the joint. To make a more pronounced bend, cut through and file the surfaces carefully until they fit at the correct angle, or cut a V-shaped notch, press

together and glue. To straighten a bend, cut about two-thirds through the joint, straighten, and pack the opening in the bend with scrap plastic, then glue.

In both cases clean up when dry with a fine file and fill as necessary with body putty. Hands can be cut off and replaced in their required positions, or when you have built up a 'spare parts' box, substituted for another hand in correct pose.

Heads can be cut off and changed or repositioned, and as the neck will be shorter after cutting, a thin disc of plastic card can be added to raise the head. Heads can be angled up or down by a small wedge of plastic at front or back.

If legs are spread apart they can be closed by cutting and filing the join to give the correct angle and possibly packing with thin plastic card if the hips become too narrow for the trunk to seat properly. Similarly if one leg is back and the other forward, they can be fixed as required, then filed, packed and filled to fit the trunk. Limbs can be lengthened by carefully adding a disc or

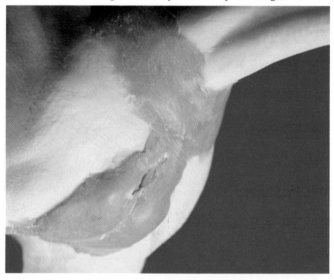

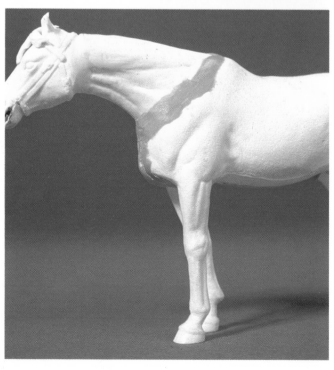

discs of thin plastic card to the correct dimension.

The best material for belts and straps is thin lead sheet, which can be obtained from some model soldier shops, or from the tops of wine bottles and toothpaste tubes. Cut into strips of the correct width with a steel edge and sharp blade and glue in place with cyano or impact glue. This material conforms to shapes better than any other, but other suitable materials are cigarette paper or several thicknesses of tissue soaked with polystyrene glue thinned with liquid cement. This latter is also useful for simulating tarpaulin covers and rolled blankets, etc.

Arranging opening hatches on vehicles is simple. Drill tiny holes at each corner with a drill about ·8mm ($\frac{1}{32}$in); if the corner is rounded, drill all round the bend. Then cut across the straight edges with a sharp blade and carefully open up. Trim the edges and if the hatch edge is a bit messy glue a thin strip of plastic all round. File the underside of the cover so that it is thinned and, if it is an armoured hatch, cut a plastic cover from thin card just undersize to the one you have. Glue in place on the underside leaving an equal edge all round.

Most armour hatches have lever locks and handles, so try to find pictures of what these look like and simulate them with scraps of plastic. The hinge can be made from plastic sheet and stretched sprue and the unit glued in the open position.

Opposite *These photos show the alteration of a horse's neck, with the cuts filled and smoothed over with body putty, to be rubbed down later.*
Below left *Modifications to figures can be reasonably straightforward using body putty or one of the epoxy equivalents. In this model the shorts have been lengthened to the World War 2 British Army standard issue length, a field dressing pocket has been added, and a new chin has been formed.*
Below *An extensive conversion using Milliput to build the tunic, kilt and gaiters. All these models in work by John Reagan.*

Stretched sprue

You never go far in conversion before the term 'stretched sprue' is mentioned. What is stretched sprue? Simply the sprue or runners heated and stretched as thin as required. Use a candle flame (the candle needs securing firmly in a holder) and do the stretching somewhere free of draughts. Cut about 100mm (4in) of straight sprue and holding across the flame and about 12mm (½in) above the flame tip, rotate gently between finger and thumb. When the plastic softens enough to sag, move from the flame and wait a few seconds. As it hardens, gently but firmly pull apart and the sprue will stretch to a thin section. If too hot it will go to a very fine string; if cold or pulled too quickly, it will break.

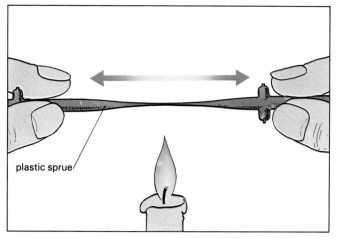

plastic sprue

With practice it is possible to draw any desired thickness, but it is worth noting that some sprue (i.e. in different makes of kit) draws better than others. When it has been drawn as desired, hold taut for a few seconds until cool and set.

If a dead straight piece is necessary, put in a couple of twists between finger and thumb as you draw and this removes any stresses left after stretching and helps the stretched piece to stay straight.

A development of this is to stretch and wind small rings or rectangles useful for handles and buckles. Odd pieces of wood or metal of suitable shape, i.e. half-round for D rings, rectangular for buckles or handles, etc., can be used for the formers. Hold the end of the former in the left hand and heat the sprue in the right hand. When ready put one end of the sprue in the left hand against the former and wind and stretch round the former. It takes a bit of practice, but you can soon learn to vary the thickness as you wish. Use a sharp blade and cut down the formed rings one side and they come off the former easily.

Another tip, particularly if you have a pyro, or even a small soldering iron which gets very hot, is to make buttons or rivets. Select some stretched sprue of the desired diameter and hold one end about 6mm (¼in) from the heat source (just glowing red is best) and the tip will curl back forming a small dome. The further you feed to the heat the larger the dome, up to a limit according to the sprue thickness.

Practise a bit and, when you want uniform buttons, drill a small hole in each button position and insert a length of sprue, leaving a protruding stalk long enough to make a pre-tested button size. Carefully bring in the

heat and the buttons form. On smaller models be careful that the heat source does not melt the model. A touch of liquid glue locks the sprue in place. This technique can also be used for rivet heads.

The conversion addict develops an eye for useful materials which are more often than not totally unrelated to modelling. Wire gauze or screening of the type used in laboratories and available in differing small sizes has many uses. Ladies' mesh stockings make an excellent source of small mesh net, old net curtains for larger, and some of the plastic nets used for supermarket fruits and vegetables make camouflage nets when suitably decorated with small strips of tissue 'hessian'.

Some supermarket goods come in a plastic tray with a corrugated or chequered base for rigidity. Such material, depending on the form of the corrugations, can be used as simulated non-slip steel plate for tank floors, or another alternative for this is rectangular mesh net curtain glued to plastic sheet. This makes a good diamond pattern steel floor.

Modelling clay also has many uses. It is not easy to roll paper or cloth and make a realistic bedroll or rolled tarpaulin. The material lacks the weight to sit properly. If you make the required object in modelling clay and then cover with your material (tissue is useful) trim and then paint with two or three coats of styrene cement before colouring, it will look right. The knurled handles found on many small tools such as needle files can be rolled on to sandbags moulded from Milliput and the like to produce a simulated hessian surface. You can fit it in place before cement-coating to seat correctly. It is possible to fill pages with all the various items that can be used but perhaps this sample will give you ideas of your own.

Adhesives

A problem which will arise when using all these different materials is sticking them together. For instance, if you wanted to simulate one of the US Army post-D-Day tanks with heavy timbers fixed around the turret as added protection, styrene cement will not glue wood to plastic and the obvious material to simulate wood is wood itself. It is necessary therefore to know something about adhesives, but as this is a very complicated subject it is only possible to generalize.

Plastic is stuck together by using a solvent which dissolves the surface of the two pieces being joined and when brought together they bond and dry effectively as one piece. Wood or other fibrous material is glued by a substance which penetrates the fibres of both pieces and then hardens, while metal, glass and other non-soluble materials are glued by an adhesive which is capable of bonding to the smooth surface, such as solder, impact adhesive, or chemicals like cyanoacrylates. The strength of the bond depends on the strength of adhesive.

With plastic, it is obviously necessary to have a glue which dissolves both surfaces and this is normally no problem. However, in the case of, for instance, ABS styrene, such as is used for those useful girder and angle sections produced as Plastruct, or an acetate base plastic, or the soft plastic polythene used for many 'toy' figures, plastic cement sold for modelling will not dissolve them and so cannot glue such items to your model. Either a special cement must be used, or one of the surface adhesive glues.

Plastruct's own liquid cement *will* stick kit parts, but a better result may be obtained by treating the surfaces to be joined as follows: the Plastruct with Plastruct cement and the kit part with liquid styrene glue. Both surfaces dissolve and when put together the bond forms by the dissolved plastics mixing and setting as one unit.

Polythene with its slippery surface is difficult, but cyano or PVC adhesives can be tried.

Acetone-soluble acetates may be stuck by means of a mixture of acetone on the acetate and styrene cement on the kit, as for Plastruct/styrene joints. The impact adhesives are useful for sticking small parts to kit plastic, but the bond can break and a sufficient surface area for strength, or parts not likely to get touched, are the only cases where these can be used successfully.

White PVA adhesive or cyano will stick clear transparencies in place, as these are not usually made from a styrene plastic.

The experienced modeller has an armoury of several types of glue always available and learns which do the best job in each instance.

Research

There is another aspect of modelling which often becomes the really absorbing interest – research. It is quite acceptable to make, shall we say, a Tamiya Sherman as detailed on the box and give it every care in building and painting to result in a miniature work of art, but how much more satisfying to build the model as a tank, say, of the Guards' Armoured Division as it probably looked entering the battered town of Goch on a winter day in 1945.

To do this the first essential is a photograph. Many of the books on World War 2 have such photos and particularly those angled towards modellers' research. An appointment with the photo library at the Imperial War Museum or similar museums in most countries (write first) and you have thousands of prints from which to choose, all available as copies for a moderate sum.

Some of the model clubs have reference facilities and help members, or a letter to a model magazine can produce that vital information.

If you are really interested and methodical you will soon accumulate a well cross-referenced library of information. Some books are costly and it is worth searching the second-hand booksellers, especially those who specialize in military subjects. Old magazines are often invaluable and there are always new publications appearing. Be selective in what you buy as it is sometimes the case that a 'new' publication is a rehash of an accumulation of old material, by an 'author' who would not know a Panther from a Bren Carrier or a Hussar from a Cuirassier!

Finally, a word about drawings. The calculator and a metric scale can make drawings to the scale you require almost redundant, since a good model can be produced from any other scale drawing by simple transposition of dimensions. It will be found simplest to convert the scales to fractions; for example, 7mm to 1ft is 7:305, which reduces to 1:43·6. If a 1:35 model is required, each measurement from the drawing is divided by 35 and multiplied by 43·6, a very simple operation on the calculator.

Drawings are not always required for figures, but if you can sketch, even relatively badly, diagrams and notes made at a museum of uniforms can be a great help in getting details accurate and authentic.

War artists' sketches, made on the spot, can provide valuable research information. This drawing is by Clifford Saber, from his Desert Rat Sketch Book, *published in 1959 by Sketchbook Press, Franklin Square, New York. A novel twist is a model by Rusty Jenkins of the artist at work, based on the illustration and shown in the photograph.*

Single figure modelling

Single figures are the core of military modelling, since even massed battle scenes or vehicle dioramas rely on the accuracy with which men and uniforms are portrayed. Figures can be collected ready-painted, but most enthusiasts prefer to build and paint them from plastic or metal kits, or to convert commercial products to their own requirements or even, in some cases, to build completely from raw materials. Each of these approaches is described in this chapter, including the all-important aspects of painting and dress.

This axeman designed by Tim Richards shows how metal figures can be polished effectively rather than painted. Model from Phoenix Model Developments.

Plastic kit assembly

There have been large numbers of books and magazine articles written by various modellers stating the correct way to build plastic models and assemble plastic kits of model soldiers. In fact, there is no such thing as the 'correct way' or the 'wrong way', only the individual methods that enable different modellers to get the most out of their hobby. This chapter describes one way of making and converting plastic model soldiers and, although it may not be the best, or even the easiest, as the photographs illustrate, it works!

Basically there are two types of plastic used commercially for model soldiers – hard polystyrene and soft polythene. The polystyrene is that found in all plastic assembly kits and can be modelled fairly easily, whereas the other, polythene, is mainly found in toys, is unbreakable and almost impossible to glue. There are many different manufacturers of plastic assembly kits, but two of the best known are Historex and Airfix, each with their own advantages and disadvantages. Firstly, Historex are without doubt the finest as far as detail, moulding and spares are concerned, but can look somewhat stiff and unnatural. Airfix, on the other hand, are considerably cheaper and look very realistic when assembled, but lack the fine detail of moulding and range of spares, although with the introduction of the 'Multipose' series, the firm has increased the range of arms, packs, weapons, etc., considerably. As far as polythene products are concerned, there are dozens of different manufacturers throughout the world, although in this section mention is only made of those toys produced by Britains.

The French grenadier illustrated shows a typical assembly kit produced by Airfix on which no animation or conversion has been carried out. There is very little to say about the assembly of it which has not previously been said in the preceding chapter, except to emphasize the importance of removing all the moulding flash.

However, it does show how a comparatively inexpensive plastic kit can be transformed into an acceptable model with a little care in assembly and painting.

Simple conversion

Despite the availability of hundreds of different plastic kits, there are times when a modeller would like a figure with a uniform not yet available in kit form. Here one is left with no alternative but to make one's own model by conversion. The model of Major General Wolfe, the hero of Quebec, is a classic example of how a plastic kit can be completely transformed with a little skill and imagination. In fact, it was converted from the model of the French grenadier without alteration to the anatomy, as can be seen opposite. The first step was to remove the gaiters and replace them with leather boots, a very simple task, which was done by filing down the moulding of the gaiters and adding a strip of 10 thou. plastic card for each of the boot turnovers, filling in where necessary with body putty or versatile Milliput modelling compound. 10 thou. plastic card refers to the thickness of plastic card (metric equivalent 0·25mm), available at most good hobby shops, and body putty, also readily available, is produced by a number of different manufacturers. The American equivalent of Milliput is known as 'Green Stuff', and there are other clay-like epoxy compounds as well as body putty.

As can be seen from the diagram, the coat tails were removed and all the detail on the front of the model sanded down. The gaps left by the removal of the coat tails were then filled in with body putty, to the level one would expect on a human body, in order that the coat, when applied later, would hang naturally. The head came from the Airfix American Revolutionary kit, and after it had been glued into place, the visible hair was emphasized by scratching it with a hot needle. After the glue at the neck had dried hard, the collar was filed

Left The Airfix French grenadier built as supplied makes an attractive figure in its own right; the conversion to General Wolfe, in the right-hand picture, entails no major alteration to the basic pose but employs a head and an arm from other kits. Most of the conversion work consists of removal of the grenadier uniform and the addition of a coat and other details. The step-by-step illustrations opposite provide a simple guide for any modeller who wishes to attempt a reasonably straightforward conversion. 54mm models by David Hunter.

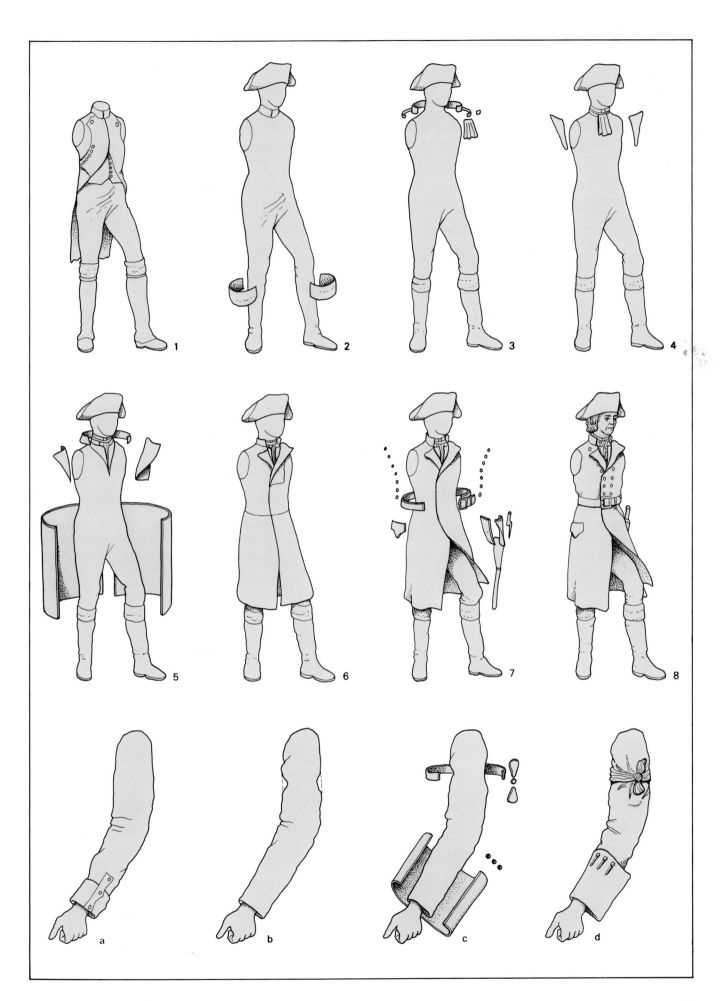

away and replaced with tissue paper to form the top of the shirt. As for the small part of the waistcoat which would be seen, all that was required to show it were two small pieces of 5 thou. plastic card placed as shown. The top front flaps of the coat and the collar were made in a similar manner, but using 10 thou. plastic card. The joins and gaps were covered over with body putty and when these had dried and been sanded down, the flaps were very gently heated and bent into the required shape; care had to be taken in order not to melt the plastic. The remainder of the join of the coat at the top was then carved into the plastic down to the waist.

Adding the bottom half of the coat looked at first to be a daunting task, but by following simple procedures it was relatively easy. Two pieces of 10 thou. plastic card were used and each was attached by cementing the top edge at the front and, after gently heating the plastic, wrapping it around the waist to the back. It was important to remember that, in addition to the centre vent at the back, there were also two pleats making it very full. When the cement had dried, the plastic was again reheated and suitable folds were worked in, giving it a more natural look. The joins were again covered over with body putty and the pockets added, out of plastic card. The waistbelt and straps for the bayonet were also made from plastic card, and a Historex buckle and Airfix bayonet added. Although the left arm was from the kit, the right one came from a Historex assorted pack, and both had large cuffs added. These were made from plastic card as sketched and each had three buttons added made out of plastic rod. The simplest way of making buttons is to take a piece of plastic rod, sand it round, then slice off the ends. The black arm band was made from four pieces of tissue

Opposite *A standard German officer kit from the Airfix 'Multipose' range of soldiers formed the basis of this 54mm Mannerheim figure by David Hunter. Details of how to construct the fur jacket and the hat are shown below and opposite.*

paper and added after a slight groove had been made on the arm, and the model was finished off by cementing the buttons to the front of the coat.

Variations

The models of Mannerheim and Foch (see photo on page 29) were both converted from the Officer in the Airfix 'Multipose' pack of German soldiers, and show two entirely different models made from the same kit. In each model the head, body and legs are the same and only the arms have been changed, taking advantage of the various different positions supplied by the manufacturer.

The first step on the model of Mannerheim was to cement the body and legs together, followed by the removal of the side pockets, epaulettes and insignia, as drawn. Although it wasn't necessary to be too particular, it was important to sand down any protruding edges, as will be shown later in the description. After having cemented the head on to the body, the top half was removed, as sketched, and a fur hat added. For this an odd scrap from the spares box was used, carved into shape, with the front and side flaps being made from plastic card. The whole of the surface of the hat was then worked over with a Pyrogravure to give it that fur look and, when completely satisfied with the result, a moustache was added, made from a piece of body putty.

The fur-lined coat was scratch-built from 15 thou. plastic card and, although like the previous model it looked difficult, it turned out to be fairly easy. The various stages of assembly are clearly shown in the diagram, the first being to cut a suitable strip of plastic card and cement the front edge on to the model. It was extremely important that the glue was only placed at about 1·5mm ($\frac{1}{16}$in) from the front edge, otherwise it might have run out and over the buttons at the front of the tunic. When the front edge had dried, the plastic was gently heated and slowly bent around the body. By fixing the coat in this way and by using polystyrene tube cement, as opposed to liquid cement, it was possible to obtain some natural folds in the material. When the

1

2

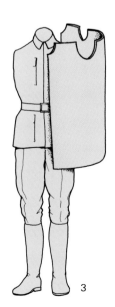

3

4

plastic coat was cemented into place, rather a liberal amount of glue was used at the waist, which had the effect of softening the plastic sufficiently for a piece of string to be tied round, pulling the plastic coat in at the middle in the same manner as a belt would have been fastened. After about two days, when the glue was completely dry and hard, the string was removed and all the joins covered over with body putty.

Fur edging was then added, using strips of plastic card, although the collar had to be built up in layers until a realistic look was achieved. Once again, when dry the fur edging was worked over with a Pyrogravure in exactly the same manner as with the hat. After the groove left by the string at the waist had been cleaned with a small file, the belt, a strip of 10 thou. plastic card, was added. Another groove was also filed across the shoulder where the cross strap was to be placed, although it wasn't as deep as that for the waistbelt. All too often modellers, even experienced ones, are inclined just to cement a belt on to a model without any thought to the fact that a fastened belt will pull into a coat or jacket, in particular a padded one like that worn by Finnish troops.

A suitable buckle for the waistbelt could not be found, but it proved possible to carve one from a scrap of plastic, although the cross strap buckle was a small one from Historex with the end replaced with a strip of plastic card as shown. The arms used on this model were the

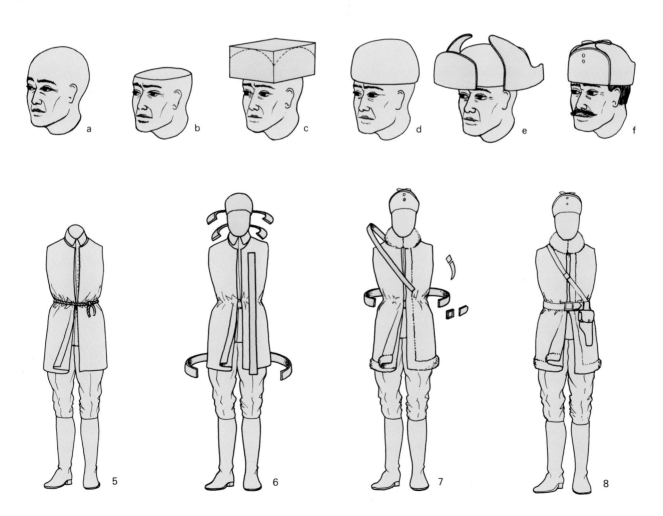

57

ones designed for the kit and were completely unaltered except for having the sleeve ends filed down a little, the reason being that they were elastic and fitted tightly around the wrists. The strap of the map case was made from paper but, unlike the cross strap, no groove was filed into the coat, as a map case is very light and would have made little or no impression. However, in order that the map case should hang naturally some of the protruding fur at the rear of the coat, under the spot where it was to rest, was removed. The pistol holster was then added with a strip of plastic card.

The conversion of the model of General Foch employed similar principles.

Some manufacturers turn out models of particular personalities, such as Historex with their range of Napoleonic marshals, but for the average modeller it can be extremely difficult to make up his own personality. The previously described generals go part of the way in modelling actual people, but the model of Custer (see page 26) is a good example of a personality who was easy to construct, as not only did he have a special uniform, but also a very unusual hair style. The basic model was made from various Airfix kits, but the hair and beard were made from body putty after the completion of the rest of the model. By using a needle, a little putty at a time was added until eventually it was built up to the required level. As it turned out, the moulding of the face in the Airfix American Revolutionary kit was perfect for Custer.

Polythene conversions

Cheap polythene toys can be turned into realistic models with a little care and imagination. The model of the Confederate standard bearer is a typical example of a model made from various parts of Britains' toy soldiers and a few odds and ends from Historex. The legs came from a cowboy in the Deetail range, the head from the 7th Cavalry range and the body from the American Civil War Swoppet range, now discontinued but still to be found in some shops. Although the left arm came from an odd model made by Britains, the other was supplied from an assorted pack of Historex arms. Despite the fact that polystyrene cement has only limited use in gluing polythene products, it was sufficient to hold the body and the legs together until the bottom half of the jacket could be glued into place. This was done by melting the plastic card on to the body and legs with the use of a Pyrogravure in a 'riveting' manner. The plastic was then gently heated, as previously described, and wrapped around the body, the holes left by the Pyrogravure being filled in with body putty. The join at the

Below left *This 54mm Confederate standard-bearer by David Hunter blends parts of various polythene toy soldiers with polystyrene additions.*
Below *More polythene figure work in a David Hunter diorama of the battle of Prestonpans with, opposite, details of the conversion of a 54mm Red Indian to one of the Highlanders.*

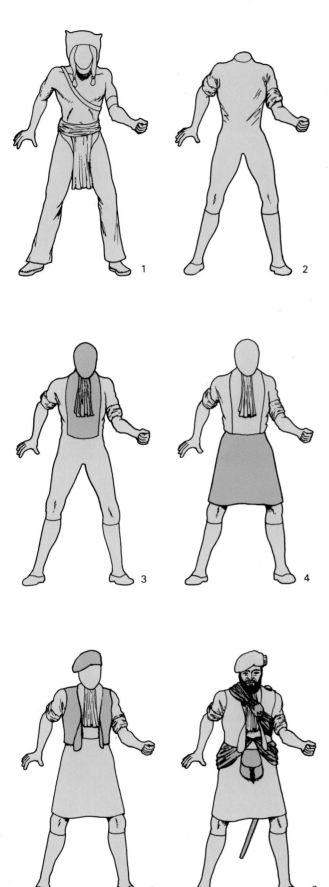

waist was also filled in and covered over with putty and, when it was dry and hard, the waist was carefully sanded down with wet and dry paper. Great care was needed as the polythene jacket would have frayed if it had been rubbed. The belt, buckle and pouch strap were then added using plastic card, with the ammunition pouch coming from the Airfix spares box.

The head was from a trooper in the 7th Cavalry, and after the hat had been removed, needed to be trimmed to fit into the hole at the top of the jacket. The rim of the hat was then removed and replaced with a piece of 10 thou. plastic card, and after it had been replaced on the head it was gently heated to give the rim that 'floppy' look. The joins were once again covered up with body putty and the arms added; after they had been glued on to the body to hold them in place, a hole was burned through the tops of the arms with a Pyrogravure, which melted the two plastics together. The holes were then covered up. The blanket roll was made from tissue paper soaked in polystyrene cement and, when dry but not yet hard, was glued to the body and given some natural folds.

There are a number of ways of making a standard, but on this particular model it was made from tracing linen, which is one of the finest cloths easily available, essential when one remembers that one is scaling down an already fine material, often silk. After having boiled out the wax coating, the linen was fastened to a piece of card and the design painted on to the surface with waterproof paint. Paint used on standards and colours should be flexible; since the design is painted on a flat form and the colour furled afterwards for a realistic effect, a non-flexible paint such as enamel runs the risk of cracking. Casein paint, such as marketed by Rose Miniatures, is excellent. Acrylic paint is not only flexible but will dry to a soft sheen, simulating silk. The procedure was then carried out on the reverse side, and when the paint was dry the cloth was fastened to a piece of plastic rod. However, the standard needed to be made natural and battle-worn, which was done by burning a few holes and generally fraying the ends. It was then sprinkled with a little water which made it more pliable and easy to bend into the required shape. After having positioned the standard on the model a pike was added, having come from a Historex lance. Finally, to finish off the model a sword, cup, pike and bayonet were added, all from Historex.

Tissue paper can be used as an alternative to plastic in the making of clothing and this is clearly shown on one of the Highlanders in the diorama of Prestonpans, 1745. The basic figure was a Britains' Deetail Indian with all the clothing removed, a new head added and the arms carved into the shape of rolled up sleeves. On the left is the construction in stages, but briefly the kilt (or belted plaid for the correct title) was made in three sections using good quality tissue paper. The first was the bottom half which was glued into place then coated with polystyrene cement (great care has to be taken as the paper has a tendency to tear) followed by the upper left- and right-hand sides. Each side was glued into position at the front and brought around the waist to the back, with the right-hand piece up to the left shoulder, taking care to create natural folds in the paper. Simple, yet effective.

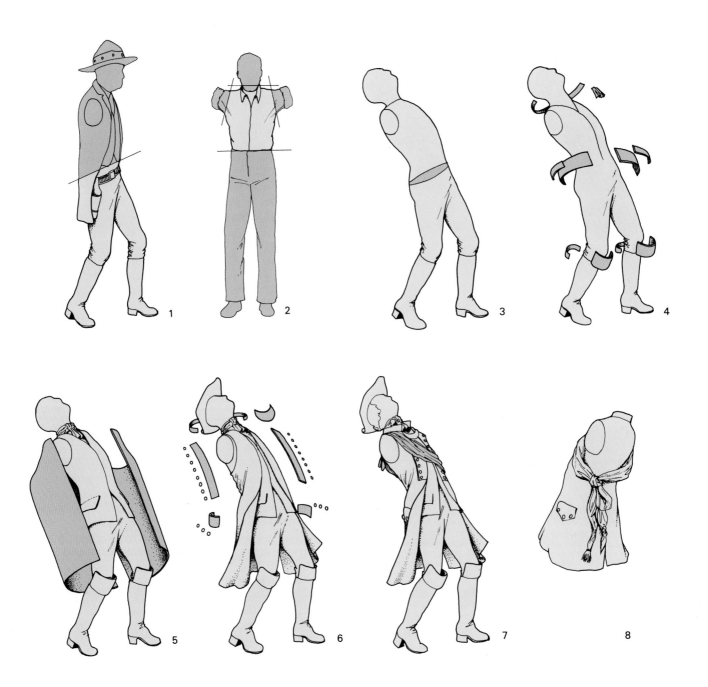

The officer in the diorama of Braddock's Massacre was also made from Britains' toys, but unlike the others, has been subjected to anatomical alteration. Above are shown the two figures, a cowboy and a farm worker, from which the basic model was made. The diagram also shows where the cuts were made on the figures in order that the pieces could be reassembled to give the effect of a dying man. The gaps between the sections were filled in with odd bits of polystyrene sprue, after which they were melted together with the use of a Pyrogravure. Not surprisingly, this left rather a messy join, but the excess plastic was trimmed off and the joins covered over with body putty. The top of the shirt was made from tissue paper and the hat added, as previously described, but in this instance body putty was required for the wig. The wig tail (or queue) was removed from the hat and replaced later after the collar had been fixed to the coat.

The waistcoat and the tops of the high boots were made from plastic card and melted into position with a Pyrogravure. As hard plastic had been used to fill in the join between the legs and the body, the plastic waistcoat cemented easily to the body. Although the coat was made in the same manner as that for the model of Wolfe, in this instance it proved to be a tricky operation and it took several attempts to get it right. The two halves were fixed at the front, one at a time, and fastened to the body with a Pyrogravure. They were then heated and slowly bent around into shape, making certain to obtain the correct folds and pleats. The joins were then covered over and the turnbacks added, also out of plastic card, together with the side pockets, collar and buttons. For the sash, tissue paper soaked in polystyrene cement was again used, for the gorget plastic card and for the sword sheath, plastic rod. Unlike the earlier standard-bearer model, the standard on

Opposite *Stages in David Hunter's fairly advanced conversion, using two polythene figures to create a mortally wounded officer in a diorama of General Braddock's Massacre in 1775. The effectiveness of the result can be judged in the photograph immediately above.*

Above right *Among larger kit figures is the 1:12 Aurora caveman, shown in the top picture as intended in the kit and, on the right, skilfully converted into a Confederate infantryman. Another large-scale and extensive conversion by David Hunter is illustrated on page 81.*

this one was made from paper, the reason being that the original was made out of a fine silk and that it needed to be half lying on the ground in a natural form. After the standard had been painted and fastened to a piece of plastic rod, it was soaked in water (hence the need for waterproof paint) and then shaped into the required position. Once the paper had dried it was again painted, only this time with a shading effect. The cords were made from cotton and the tassels came from Historex, as did the pike.

Larger figures

All those described so far have been 54mm figures, and it would be wrong not to mention briefly the larger figures, which in plastic seem to be confined to a scale of 1:12. There are several manufacturers and illustrated are two conversions, one from the Aurora kit of a caveman and the other from the Airfix kit of the showjumper. The problems in converting these figures are rather different from the others, primarily because they are hollow, as opposed to the solid plastic used in the

smaller kits. However, as has already been proved, nothing is impossible. All the clothing on the caveman had to be scratch-built, finishing up with a war-weary Confederate infantryman. The trousers, shirt and blanket roll were made from tissue paper in exactly the same manner as described for the Highlander, but the jacket and equipment were made from plastic card.

As for the model from the kit of the showjumper, which was transformed into a model of a hussar officer, the description would take a complete chapter by itself. A photograph of this model appears on page 81, from which an idea of the degree of conversion can be obtained. It was very complicated and took several months; the larger scale meant that different techniques were sometimes needed, such as for the fur on the pelisse, which was made from a piece of fine-quality sponge. All of the braiding on the jacket and pelisse was made from strips of plastic card and each button was individually fashioned. The sabretache was plastic card with 5 amp fuse wire for the rings and individually made buckles for the straps. The saddlecloth presented a problem, but this was overcome with plastic card and plenty of body putty. The important thing to remember with a large-scale model is that one has to be far more accurate as much more of the detail can be seen.

Finally a brief word about scenic bases. The idea of a base is to enhance the model, not to hide it. If one makes a base too scenic and interesting, then the model is apt to get lost, while if the base is poorly made then it will reflect badly on what could be an attractive model. In addition, always try to use natural ground wherever possible; the garden has a wealth of interesting material, such as twigs, moss, stones and so on.

Metal kits

The conglomeration of pastimes which we call, collectively, military modelling – tank kits, dioramas, fantasy scenes and the rest – is the ever-growing family of one original hobby. It did indeed all start with the model soldier and that soldier was made of metal.

Despite the meteoric rise over the past few years in the popularity of plastic kit figures, the metal model soldier still retains its prestige. While polystyrene armies have been filling shop windows, the development of the traditional medium has not stood still. Far from it; continuing experimentation to find the right blend of lead, tin, antimony and other metals has resulted in a crispness of detail and an exquisiteness of engraving quite impossible to achieve in plastic. Hand in hand with this has gone a near revolution in figure design, culminating in figures of such superb anatomical proportion and trueness to life that the hobby is now indeed an art form. Even the heavy weight is in itself suggestive of quality and value.

Admittedly a well-painted, good-quality plastic figure is preferable to an indifferently finished metal one, but the first rate, well-finished metal model soldier is the pinnacle of military modelling. As such it commands a certain collectability and accrues value with age in a way which its plastic counterpart generally does not.

Metal does have its drawbacks, especially for the beginner, and the first to be encountered is its cost, being several times that of plastic. Consequently the average modeller has to be very selective. If, having

paid a substantial sum for a figure, it turns out not to meet expectations, then the outlay is rather more than can be written off to experience. It pays to choose carefully, making sure before buying that the period, scale and general style of the figure fit in with one's personal taste. The really superlative kits are highly priced, but if one can afford it they are well worth the money. It must not be assumed, however, that quality is always commensurate with price. The high cost of the raw material is reflected in the price of all metal kits, whatever the quality. The standard of design and finish often makes little or no difference. It is important to remember also that the finish of each individual casting may vary. Examine several kits and pick the best one.

There is plenty of choice. The market has escalated from a handful of manufacturers a few years ago to a host, producing a range so varied in scale and subject matter that to catalogue them all would require several volumes the size of this book! Whether it be Greek hoplite or German paratrooper, Sioux chief or Napoleonic chasseur, if you want it you can probably buy it. However, if you require it in a particular scale or pose, you may have some reanimation to do.

The model soldier evolved from the true toy soldier and has inherited its standard size of 54mm, which has endured as the most popular scale for many years. The last decade, however, has seen the introduction and development of larger scales: 75mm, 80mm, 90mm, 100mm, some even 150mm and more. This trend has had significant effects on the hobby. Larger scale means greater opportunity for detail. What was a mere engraved circle in 54mm becomes a proper button in 75mm and may even have cotton holes in 90mm. Unfortunately there is also a reciprocal effect. Although the article as bought from the model shop is superior to its predecessors, the cost and the miniature's very excellence tend to discourage the modeller from trying his hand at a little innovation. We therefore find that collectors who practise the arts of animation and conversion, those cornerstones of the hobby in plastic, are fewer in number when it comes to metal.

Where the modeller wishes to construct the kit as designed with no attempt at animation the procedure is no different and certainly not more difficult than that for any plastic kit. Mould lines must be scraped away (this is best accomplished by drawing the edge of an old modelling knife blade along the raised portion of metal to remove it in a series of strokes). Flash (unwanted metal which has squeezed out between mould halves during casting) where it appears can be removed in a similar fashion, cleaning up finally with Swiss files – round and square section types are probably the most useful for this. One of the rapid setting 'super glues' or five-minute epoxy adhesives is ideal for gluing parts together and for figure kits it is advisable to construct

Left *The basic casting of the Sovereign crossbowman is in one piece; frequently figures have separate arms to reduce the overall depth of the mould for easier casting.*
Opposite above *A metal kit with the main body in two halves and small details packeted.*
Opposite below *These are actually Lone Star castings sold as toys, but are worth working on.*

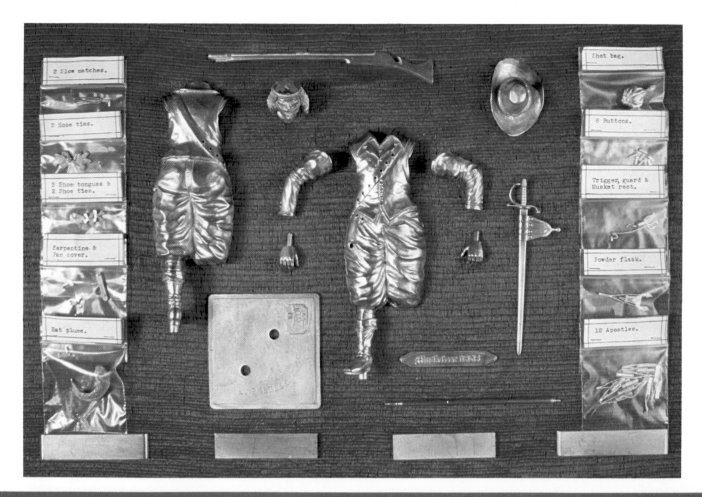

the model fully, leaving off only small items like swords, sabretaches and the like which can be attached when the main figure is painted. For mounted subjects it is best to treat horse and rider as two completely separate operations, painting them individually and uniting them only when each is complete.

It is essential to undercoat or prime white metal figures and best for this is an aerosol matt white which dries completely flat, thus revealing all of the cast-on detail to full advantage, and is also a perfect base for the modeller's choice of colour paints; artist's oils, enamels and even water-based types will paint perfectly over a matt white enamel primer coat.

Even a straightforward animation in metal requires a good deal of forethought. Let us say, for instance, that the object of the exercise is to move the left arm from a straight-at-the-side position to a hand-on-the-hip pose. In plastic we would probably need only to take the arm from the kit, apply a little heat at the elbow, bend it and glue it in position. In metal the procedure may not be so simple. The arm may not be a separate part; it may be joined to the body throughout its length and sawing it off could obliterate a lot of detail. The metal of which model soldiers are made varies with the manufacturer, but it usually has very limited pliability. Limb bending, therefore, may require a complete severing and rejoining process or the removal beforehand of a wedge of metal. This means the use of filler, followed by the reshaping of the limb and reworking of clothing folds. Rejoining the arm may, particularly in the larger scales, require drilling and pegging. (This is just one modelling task taken out of context and the job of the animator is littered with many.) As difficult as all this may sound, the beginner

Above *Components of a simple metal kit. Conversion will entail first sawing through parts.*
Below *Conversation in mess kit by Major Bob Rowe. Despite the difficulties with metal, each figure is differently posed.*
Opposite *One movable arm and a limited amount of bending can vary the pose of this Centurion figure. Painted example by Peter Wilcox.*

may rest assured that provided (a) each step is planned in advance, (b) it is realized that one anatomical change may necessitate others, and (c) the model is picked to suit the purpose, extremely pleasing and successful results are possible.

The business of choosing a model with an eye to the animation required is very important, even more so when it comes to a full scale conversion. It is manifestly silly, not to say expensive, to buy a model of an officer of the 11th Hussars and convert it into a Zulu warrior, destroying all the beautifully engraved lace, braid, etc., in the process. Wherever possible, conversions should be from simple to complicated, unclothed to clothed and from inactive to active. If a modeller wishes to make a relatively plain and unadorned figure, in informal dress, he should use another plain figure as a basis. Salient

too is the fact that as the scale increases the more exacting the modeller's task becomes. He needs to be more painstaking with detailing, folds in clothing have to be just right and anatomical exactness is of paramount importance.

The would-be animator/convertor is well advised to take note of the old 'run before you can walk' adage, working steadily through several simple projects before attempting anything radical or complex. He should also have the tools for the job. Modelling knives, needle files of various grades and sections, a junior hacksaw and a small drill are essentials. With these, a good modelling compound such as Milliput and a cyanoacrylate super-adhesive, the model soldier collector is all set for creative innovation; after all, this is the fundamental basis of the hobby.

Scratch-building

To the model soldier enthusiast the term 'scratch-building' means the complete construction of a figure from raw materials; sculpting in fact. On the other hand a 'converted' figure is one which utilizes commercially produced parts in ways not intended by their manufacturers. Between these two lies the half-way house, sometimes known as a 'composite figure', in which commercial parts may form the basis of the figure, the remainder being built up on this foundation.

Why scratch-build at all? After all, there are plenty of perfectly good figures available to suit all tastes and all purses. This is true, so far as it goes. There are, however, at least two occasions where it may be desirable. In the first place, there may not be a commercially produced figure available, or even one reasonably near enough to the desired result to make conversion a possibility; the amount of conversion work necessary may be so large as to make it more practical to start from basics. Secondly, large numbers of figures of identical, or nearly identical, poses may be required, e.g., for diorama work. Again, commercial sources may not have the particular models required; even where such figures may be bought the numbers involved may make it prohibitively expensive to do so. In such circumstances the only alternative would be to make the figures yourself by a combination of scratch-building and casting.

Materials

Having decided that you are going to take the plunge and sculpt your own figures, we come to the question of materials. What are they going to be made of? In order to be suitable for modelling purposes the material must be able to be shaped with reasonable ease, yet be strong enough to take some rough handling; at the same time

it should be capable of showing fine detail. Traditionally, sculptors have used such materials as clay, stone, wood and metal. To these the modern modeller can add products of the petrochemical industry, in the form of epoxy resins. All these materials have different working characteristics, each with its own advantages. Let us examine a few.

Wood and stone are best left out of our considerations; they lend themselves to large-scale figures, which are more likely to be found in museums. Metal has, of course, been used for making figures for several thousand years. The ancient Greeks, for example, cast figures in bronze (a mixture of copper and tin). For our purposes, however, a mixture of lead and tin (solder) is employed. Used by plumbers for joining piping, it can be obtained from building suppliers or hardware stores and can be melted over a domestic cooker for casting, although for younger modellers adult supervision is essential. The melting point of solder may be low by metallic standards, but it is much higher than the boiling point of water. Metal is, of course, hard and therefore difficult to work; it can really only be carved with the aid of power tools. It can, however, serve as a good foundation on which to build. Once a mould has been made from a master figure, metal replicas of the original can be faithfully produced.

Clay has the advantage of being easily worked and is capable of being shaped with ease and of showing much detail. It has two disadvantages: it requires firing to a high temperature and it is very brittle. The first of these may be overcome by using a modern synthetic clay such as DAS Pronto. This has all the working characteristics of potters' clay but sets without firing to a hard mass. The problem of brittleness remains, however, though it may be lessened to some extent by incorporating

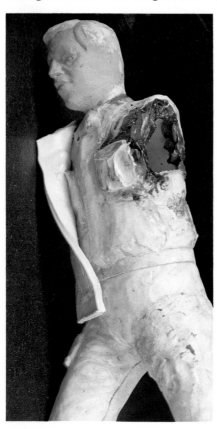
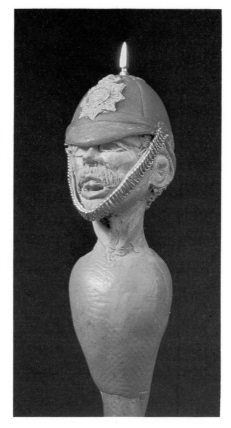
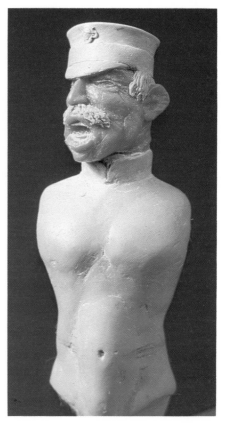

Opposite left *Thin-rolled clay can be used for clothing but the basic figure needs to have hardened off, as in this example by Mac Kennaugh.*

Opposite centre and right, and below *Three heads modelled by John Reagan in Milliput, shown several times actual size. The crispness of detail and excellent finish offered by this material are evident, as is the degree of skill exhibited in these very fine examples.*

Right *A large master figure of Charles, Duke of Orleans, at Agincourt in carved wood and Milliput by L. Martin Rendall from which moulds will be taken for commercial production. Flexible moulds and relatively low melting-point metals are used in the casting of most such figures. For more information about casting, see page 71.*

some reinforcement into the figure, an armature in fact. Plasticine is the most common type of modelling clay sold generally for use by art students and children. It never becomes hard, although it may be surface-hardened by painting with banana oil. An armature, an internal wire support, is essential to give figures some strength. Handling is impossible and Plasticine figures should not be stored in warm conditions because the clay will exude oil and lose shape. Nevertheless, the material is relatively cheap, it can be used over again and therefore is particularly suitable for practice in sculpting techniques.

Finally, we come to the more modern materials, the epoxy resins. These are chiefly used for the repair of objects and as fillers for car body repairs and are available under many trade names. They consist of a resin, to which a catalyst hardener has to be mixed. During setting the mixture will rise in temperature and pass through a sticky to a rubbery phase before finally setting

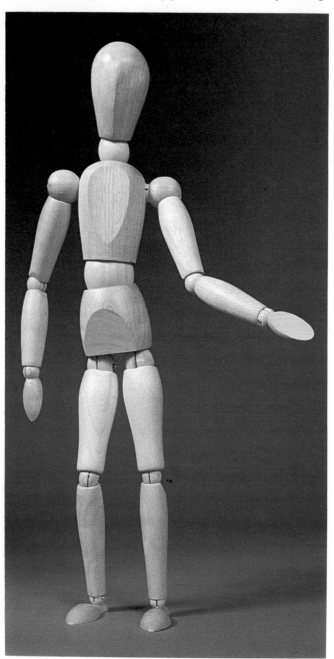

to a rock hard consistency, the whole process taking 10 to 15 minutes. The material will stick well to metal and is therefore admirable for filling in and building up. In the rubbery state it can be easily cut. When hard, it may be filed, drilled and sanded with ease. The rapid setting time, however, is a disadvantage in some respects as only small areas can be worked on at once.

An alternative is epoxy putty. In Britain this is commonly available as Milliput, while in the United States an equivalent is Brookstone's A & B Epoxy. In use, equal amounts of the resin and the catalytic hardener are kneaded together thoroughly. It passes through the same setting cycle as car body filler but over three hours. Also, before it sets it is water soluble. A figure can be built up in sections, or a metal manikin can be used as a basis for further additions. It can be worked much like clay, especially when in the rubber phase. Thin sheets can be pressed out and cut to the shape of garments. Once hard it can be carved, sanded, filed, drilled and polished easily.

Several materials could well be combined in the construction of a figure. Indeed, once the basic figurine has been constructed, other materials such as sheet lead, plastic sheet, perhaps cloth, etc., can be used to complete the model.

Human proportions
Before beginning to create your figure, however, you should be aware of the basic shape of the body. To begin with, your figures can be very simple. Later, as you acquire more experience, you can be more ambitious in your efforts. Simple or complicated, your models are going to represent human beings and therefore you must have a reasonably clear picture of what you are trying to do. Take a good look at yourself and those people around you. It is obvious that we are all built to a single design, although the size differs from person to person. In fact, the body is finely balanced, consisting of rigid pieces (the bones) which move upon one another by means of muscles. Take a look at page 70 on which is shown a sketch of the human form in the standing position. It can be roughly divided into quarters by lines passing (a) through the centre of the chest; (b) just above the point of division between the legs and (c) below the knee caps. Note also that the number of head measurements that will go into the height of the figure is usually seven. The arms extend to approximately mid-thigh while the elbow and knee joints occur at about half the length of the arm and leg respectively. In terms of width, the head is about one third that of the shoulders. If the body is looked at from the side, it can be seen that the head, neck and trunk do not form a straight line but that the neck is inclined forward. The trunk is supported by the backbone which forms a gentle curve, like an elongated 'S'. The pelvic girdle, from which suspend the legs, forms a sort of inverted wash basin. Similarly

Left Serious modellers may consider acquiring a fully articulated artists' figure which can be used as a guide to proportions.
Opposite Large-scale World War 2 figures modelled in Plasticine on wire armatures, by John Curran. Weapons and equipment are usually best made in wood, metal or plastic.

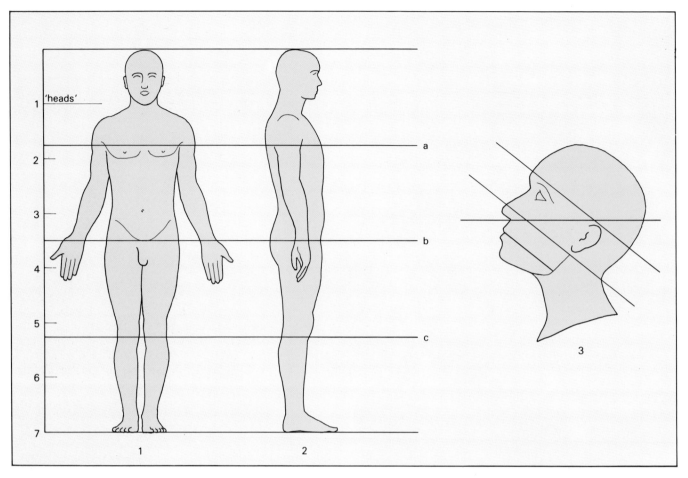

the arms hang from what can be regarded as a pair of coat hangers, in front and behind. If you take note of these features, then you can construct an armature for your figure from wire upon which your modelling material can be built up to flesh out the body.

Probably the most difficult part of scratch-building a figure is modelling the head and facial features. For a small figure, say in the popular 54mm size, this will not be too important provided that there is some indication of the presence of nose, eyes, ears and mouth, but for the larger figure, where obviously more detail will be visible, a correspondingly greater attempt will have to be made to model the facial features accurately. Large or small, the relationships between the various elements that go to make up the human head are important. Once again, take a good look at yourself in a mirror, or try and persuade someone to stay still long enough for you to examine them closely.

Look at the separate diagram of the head. Heads are rather like animated eggs; the only part that really moves is the lower jaw. Expression, resulting from the movement of muscles, is centred mainly around the eyes and mouth. Eyes are essentially balls in sockets and should be modelled in this way, adding upper and lower eyelids afterwards, rather than trying to carve these out of the head. Similarly, the cheeks and lips, together with the chin, can be successively built up with modelling material. The eyes are almost exactly on a line drawn across the centre of the head. The outer corners of the mouth are directly below the centres of the eyes. Seen from the side, the ear forms a good measuring point, especially for the eyes, nose and mouth.

Although we all have a body and see other bodies around us, few people ever pay much attention to proportions. There are some simple generalities: the head is about one seventh of overall height and half as wide as the hips, the leg from hip joint to ground is roughly half height, the lower leg and foot approximately equal the thigh in length and so on. Beware of applying such generalities to a woman; many apply, but while a man's shoulders are wider than his hips, a woman's are frequently narrower.

When the head is held level, the base of the ear is on a line with the base of the nose, the top part of the ear with the eyebrow. If the head is gradually tilted backwards, these relative positions change, until the top of the ear is on a level with the base of the nose. If the head is lowered, of course, then these positions are reversed. The ear is also useful in measuring the relation between the head and the rest of the body, thus when the head is held back the base of the ear is closer to the upper part of the shoulder than it would be if the head were held level. The line of the jaw is formed rather like that of the letter 'L', the point of which is almost on a level with the corner of the mouth.

Although all this may seem a lot to remember at once, bear in mind that you will be building up the model piece by piece. If your first efforts don't satisfy, take another piece of modelling clay and try again. All the while you will be gaining in experience and you will improve in time. Remember also that the basic shape of your figure is defined by the wire armature and you will be gradually adding the modelling material to this.

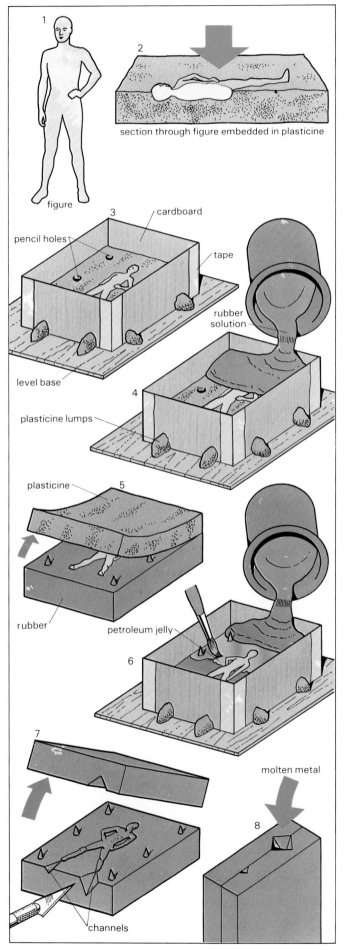

1

2

section through figure embedded in plasticine

3   cardboard

pencil holes

tape

rubber solution

level base

plasticine lumps

4

plasticine   5

rubber

petroleum jelly

6

7

molten metal

8

channels

Casting

This brings us to casting, a technique useful when a large number of copies of a figure are required. Casting can also be used to produce a refined master figure from a basic figure which has been built up with, for example, Milliput. To begin with, a two part mould of the master figure is made. Two common materials are used for making moulds; plaster of Paris and silicone rubber. The former is very cheap, but is soft and easily deteriorates with use, so only a few castings can be obtained. By contrast silicone rubber is very much more expensive, but greater detail can be obtained and the moulds will produce many castings. One word of warning. There are serious penalties attached to the copying of any commercial figures – so don't on any account be tempted to steal someone else's work! The accompanying illustrations should make the moulding and casting sequence clear, together with some added explanation.

Whether you decide to use plaster or silicone rubber, your master figure must first be embedded in a block of Plasticine to exactly one half its depth; there must be no gaps left between the clay and master and if the mould is to be made from plaster then undercuts must be avoided because the set plaster will be rigid and will break away when you try to remove the master. A fair amount of clay must surround the master, so that an adequate pouring channel can be cut. If the mould is too thin, it will deform under compression and molten metal may escape, not to mention distorting your casting. The embedding completed, a card retaining wall is erected around the master, deep enough so that the highest point of the figure will be covered to a depth of 1cm ($\frac{1}{2}$in). Finally, a pencil is used to make several indentations in the clay; these will later serve as keys to line up the two halves of the mould. The mould material is now mixed and poured into the mould so as to cover the figure to the required depth and the assembly is then put aside to set, after which the card wall can be removed and the modelling clay peeled away. To make the second half of the mould the card wall is rebuilt. Before pouring in the mould material, the exposed surface of the first half should be painted with melted Vaseline (petroleum jelly) to prevent the two halves of the mould from sticking together. Once set, the mould can be opened, and the master figure carefully removed. The final operation is to use a sharp knife to cut in a V-shaped pouring channel to the top of the figure and

Stages in simple mould-making. **1.** *The master figure is carved or sculpted.* **2.** *It is then pressed into a squared block of Plasticine to approximately half its depth.* **3.** *A card box is built, with tape corners and Plasticine blobs to hold it in contact. Keys are impressed with a pencil point.* **4.** *Silicone rubber is poured slowly at one end and allowed to flow over the figure; the box is tapped to drive out air bubbles.* **5.** *The Plasticine is removed and the exposed half figure cleaned.* **6.** *The box is reconstructed, melted petroleum jelly painted on the rubber and the second half poured.* **7.** *The halves are separated and runner and riser channels cut.* **8.** *The halves are reassembled with the keys located. Low-melt metal is poured in the runner, air escaping from the riser. The runner needs to be of adequate diameter for the free passage of the molten metal, since a quick, steady pour produces a better casting.*

air escape channels at the legs and arms. Note that with a plaster mould it is vital that, before use, it must be completely dry. Leave it for several days in a warm place, such as an airing cupboard. If you don't do this, when the molten metal enters the mould it will turn any moisture to steam, and this will explode the plaster.

In use, the two halves of the mould are clamped between two pieces of thin wood. If held in the hand be sure to protect yourself with a thick glove or cloth several times folded. The solder should be carefully melted in an old saucepan until the surface acquires a characteristic 'rainbow' effect. Use an old spoon to scrape aside surface scum before filling the mould, then bang the whole sharply on the table to drive in the metal. Allow several minutes to elapse before opening the mould and removing the casting. Snip off the pouring channel and return this to the pot. It may help to dust the surface of the mould with talcum powder or powdered graphite before pouring in the metal as this will make the casting easier to release.

A great deal of satisfaction is to be had from creating your own figures. Give it a try, you may surprise yourself!

Below left *It is something of an optical illusion, but this is an empty flexible mould for a Roman figure. The keys to locate the mould halves accurately together are clearly visible.*
Below *A casting from the mould; the angle of the chest strap and the arm are the most obvious reversals but of course everything is reversed left to right. The heavy runner and riser waste is still attached to the feet. Contraction of the metal in the mould on cooling can exert sufficient draw to suck additional still-molten metal from this waste.*

Figure painting

PAINTS

Today's modeller has never been so well catered for when it comes to choosing the right type of paint for his model.

The experienced modeller will have started to develop his own style and techniques, based on previous painting experience gained in the pursuit of his hobby. But for the beginner, the decision as to which paints he or she should buy must be given careful thought. The following notes divide the most popular paints into two categories, water-based paint and oils.

Waterpaints

For the beginner water-based paint is ideal, since it has good covering qualities and dries within minutes of application to a matt finish. When purchasing, always check that the paint dries waterproof, otherwise a medium should be mixed with the paint before applying to the model.

Acrylic colours such as Cryla, Flow Formula Cryla,

A 75mm Gladiator figure by John Tassel which looks bulky in plain undercoat but slims into proportion when painted. An undercoat is necessary to give a foundation that will accept paint. Plastic and metal figures must be treated in this way for water-based or oil paints.

and Acrylic Gouache (Shiva, Grumbacher and Liquitex in America) are water-soluble emulsion paints which will dry waterproof, and can be purchased from most artist shops. Cryla is a heavy medium-based paint and therefore requires a lot of thinning down to make it flow smoothly on to a model. Used straight from the tube it has several properties that make it useful to the modeller. It will fill in gaps in joints or build up areas to create folds in a uniform. Texturing can also be achieved by stippling or peaking the paint, but only do small areas at a time, since Cryla dries very quickly. Flow Formula has a thinner consistency and will flow more smoothly on to a model, but care must be taken to avoid brush marks. This paint also has the added advantage that it resembles oils when it dries to a slight sheen. Some of the darker colours in this range of paints, namely the blues and browns, tend to be translucent when applied over a light undercoat, and this can produce some pleasing effects, especially on horses. Acrylic Artist Gouache is the best of the group as it dries waterproof, can be used straight from the tube and will dry with a matt finish. It can also be mixed with Cryla or Flow Formula to produce different textures and finishes. A word of warning when using any of the Acrylic range of paints – always clean your brushes immediately after use, otherwise the paint will dry hard and ruin a good brush.

Above *Some uniforms are quite plain, as in this Russian example of 1905 from Sovereign Miniatures recalling the war between Russia and Japan.*
Opposite *Larger figures call for accurate painting of smaller details. The eyes of this Series 77 German Landsknecht of 1522, a 154mm figure by Dennis Green, are particularly noteworthy.*

Oils

Enamels are included in this section as, although they are only suitable for flat painting, they are the modeller's first step into oil painting. There are many ranges of model enamels to choose from, and some manufacturers produce a range of authentic colours, so eliminating the need for mixing specific shades. Care must be taken to ensure that the paint, which is supplied in small tins or bottles, is properly mixed before painting commences. This is best achieved by thorough stirring for about one minute with a cocktail stick, toothpick or the wooden end of an old paintbrush. If this procedure is not followed the paint, especially the matt finish type, can sometimes dry patchy or in glossy streaks.

Artists' oil paints have, for many experts, the last word when it comes to painting a military figure. They offer richness of colour and life found in no other paint. The rewards to the painter are endless, once the transi-

tion to oils is made, but, as always, it depends entirely on the painter's own ability to work with the paint and take control.

Like most paints, oils tend to vary from manufacturer to manufacturer, so always buy a good brand name and look for the word 'Artist' on the tube, as this usually signifies the best of the grades produced. Steer clear of the least expensive of the grades, such as students' oil colour, which do not have the permanence of colour or the smoothness of flow that can be expected from their slightly dearer companions.

A small selection of colours required to start off a collection of oil paints should include:
Large tubes
Flake White, Ivory Black.
Small tubes
Vermilion, Scarlet Lake, Burnt Sienna, Cadmium Yellow, Yellow Ochre, Cobalt, Prussian Blue.

Due to the extraordinary mixing properties of oil paint it would be virtually impossible to list the colour mixes that can be achieved by using the above-mentioned colours.

The range of mixes will be further increased by the addition of other colours to the list, as the painter becomes more proficient in the art of mixing. For the newcomer to oils the following suggestions for flesh tones, which always tend to pose a problem, show the flexibility of such paints:
White + Vermilion + Yellow Ochre + Burnt Sienna.
White + Vermilion + Yellow Ochre + Burnt Umber.
White + Indian Red + Yellow Ochre + Black. White + Scarlet Lake + Cadmium Yellow + Burnt Sienna + Black. White + Light Red + Yellow Ochre + Burnt Umber + Black. White + Indian Red + Yellow Ochre + Prussian Blue.

Oil paint can be applied straight from the tube, but this does not mean sticking the brush into the top of the tube to obtain the paint! Always squeeze a small amount of paint on to a clean dust-free palette, and draw the brush through the paint, then apply to the model. Be careful not to overload the brush as oil paint has a thick pigment that will clog the fine detail on a small model, and brush marks may also show up. Both these problems can be cured by cleaning the brush on a dry cloth, without the use of thinners or cleaning fluid, and then lightly brushing over the model and working the paint, until the excessive covering has been removed.

The thick pigment also gives oils the same properties as some of the Acrylic paints described earlier, in that it too can be used for building up, texturing and peaking.

Shading and blending of colours on a figure with oils is made easier due to the slowness of drying, which can be controlled to a certain degree by the addition of thinners or mediums. It must be noted that there is no definite rule as to the length of time involved, as certain colours, mostly the light shades, tend to take longer to dry. The temperature of the room in which the painter works, and the external weather conditions, will all play a part in the drying times; it is safer to avoid the use of driers such as terebine.

Whether the painter chooses oils, enamels or water-based paints, the quality of the finished figure will depend on the care and patience taken in assembling and painting.

Brushes

When buying brushes avoid the cheap ones because it will be found that many will not produce a fine point, or that the bristles tend to pull out from the ferrule when cleaning. Always buy the best that you can afford, such as a good quality sable. The brush should have long bristles protruding from the ferrule, a nicely balanced feel like holding a pen, and if dipped into water and flicked the bristles should form a point.

Brushes are internationally sized, so to start with one each of Nos 00, 1, 2, 4 and 6 are recommended.

No brush should be used to stir paint, and by this is meant with the bristle end, as nothing will remove the hairs more quickly. Do not let brushes stand in thinners supported on their bristles; always clean them by dipping into cleaning fluid and then stroke the brush across a clean, lint-free cloth. Avoid rubbing the bristles into the cloth. When clean re-form the point and store in a small jar or other such container with the bristles uppermost and above the top of the jar, free of anything that would damage or bend the bristles.

With care your brushes should give you good service but, although they will eventually need replacing, never throw them away. A good idea is to cut back the bristle length to produce a brush for stippling, or square off the end to use for drybrushing.

Airbrushes

As most of the figures to be painted are of such small scales, an airbrush is not really suitable. Modellers who own one will find them useful for undercoating a figure, prior to painting, or for spraying the base coat of paint on to a large model such as a 90mm horse.

Airbrushes will accept most paints, provided they are thinned down sufficiently, the usual ratio being about three parts thinners to one part paint. Check that the mixture is correct by spraying on to a piece of card before working with the model. The paint is thinned down to such a degree that more than one coat of paint will be needed to cover the model, but let each coat dry before respraying, otherwise paint runs will form.

THINNERS AND MEDIUMS
Household turpentine
Sold in large bottles in most hardware stores this thinner is too strong for mixing with or thinning down oil paints, but it is an excellent brush cleaning fluid.

Distilled turpentine
An ideal thinning agent for oil paints, and only a small amount is required to make the paint flow smoothly. The drying time of oils can be reduced by adding distilled turpentine, but care must be taken if painting over a previously applied coat of paint that has dried. With oil paint, the surface dries first, and any paint mixed with turpentine laid on top can reactivate the dried colour. This can cause the paint to lift from the model or blend with the coat being applied. Shading can be accomplished by this method, but it is not recommended for the inexperienced painter.

Distilled turpentine helps to relieve the high gloss finish of oils, although you can risk sacrificing the richness of colour if too much is added. Only practice and experience will tell the painter the correct amount to be added to achieve the desired effect.

Linseed oil
A medium that forms the basis of most oil paints, a thick but flowing liquid, binding the pigment of oil colours. It reacts in the opposite way to distilled turpentine, slowing down the drying time and producing a gloss finish when dry. A mixture of both combined with the paint will enable the painter to vary the finish of his model.

Copal oil
Use with oil paints to increase the speed of drying. Similar to linseed oil in use and finish; known as Copal Medium in USA.

Acrylic gloss medium
An acrylic emulsion that can be added to Cryla and Acrylic Gouache paints for thinning and glazing. Although milky white in colour it will dry colourless and waterproof, which makes it equally suitable for rendering poster and watercolours.

Acrylic matt emulsion
This medium has the same qualities that apply to the gloss medium, and should be mixed with the paint when a matt finish is required. Both can be combined together to achieve the right degree of gloss needed, or can be

Opposite *A hussar of the Lauzun Legion superbly painted by Graham Bickerton illustrates some of the techniques outlined in the text. From 54mm Historex plastic kit and parts.*
Right *British Lancer Officer, 1902–14, from Chota Sahib. By different painting this figure could represent any of half a dozen regiments.*

used by themselves, thinned with water, as varnishes. In America, Grumbacher Oil Painting Medium 1 or Dorland's Wax Medium can be added to oil paints to achieve a matt finish or control gloss.

PAINTING TERMS AND TECHNIQUES
Shading and highlights

This is the technique of adding depth and feeling to the model. One rule applies – the larger the scale of the model the more subtle the shading.

After the basic colour has been applied to the figure, a darker tone or black is painted into the creases or folds. Clean the brush and fade the edge of the paint until it has blended into the base coat. Highlights of a lighter shade are then painted on to the tops of the creases and treated in the same manner. This treatment is made easy if used in conjunction with oil paints, due to the slowness of drying. By changing the direction of

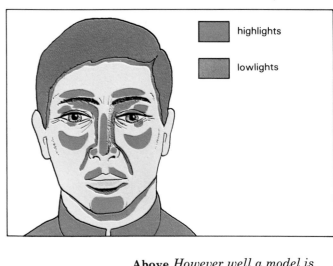

highlights

lowlights

Above *However well a model is built, painting determines its final success and the face is a vital part. Ten modellers with ten identical mouldings will produce ten different faces simply by variations of colour and technique. The basis of a well-painted face is the emphasis of light and shade by only small changes of colour; this drawing sets out the principles.*

the brush strokes the colours being blended either can be made lighter, by brushing the light colour into the dark one, or, if reversed, the opposite will occur.

Drybrushing

The technique used for picking out the highlights, mainly on large areas of raised detail such as ground work or the texture of a sheepskin saddle cloth.

The area to be treated is painted in a dark base coat and left to dry. A large size brush is then loaded with paint and drawn across a cloth or paper towel so that the brush fans out and only a small quantity of paint remains on the bristles. Lightly brush across the model so that the paint left on the brush catches the raised detail. A number of strokes may be required to achieve the desired effect.

Peaking

Both oil and acrylic paints may be used for this technique of representing feathering of a plume or the texture on a fur pelisse or sheepskin saddle.

Apply a thick coat of paint to the model, concentrating on a small area at a time. Before the paint dries, the point of a clean brush is used to lift the paint away from the surface to form a peak. Keep repeating this technique until the whole area is completed, before starting the next section. The paint will retain its peaks when dry, and then drybrushing will bring out the highlights.

Undercoating

Before painting is commenced, a foundation that will accept the paint must be applied to the model. Plastic and metal figures must both be treated the same way for painting, with water-based or oil paints. The only exception is enamel, which will take if painted directly on to the plastic.

The best medium for undercoating is a matt enamel, either an approximation of the final colours where dark tones are to be applied, or white in the case of light colours. Apply the undercoat thinly with an air-brush or a spray can, giving it several coats before putting it aside for at least 24 hours to dry thoroughly. One of the best undercoating primers is Floquil RA9 primer. Off-white, it is available in spray cans, and its extremely fine-ground pigment and self-levelling nature gives an excellent painting surface.

Another very good metal primer is made by Imrie/Risley. Medium Grey in colour, it will shrink into every crevice on a figure, forming a skin that holds every detail, no matter how minute. However, its surface is too slick to permit painting directly on it and a primed figure must then receive a thin coat of flat white enamel.

The model, whether a foot figure or a horse, should be temporarily glued to a base to facilitate handling while spraying and painting. In the case of a mounted figure the rider may be lightly stuck to a piece of dowel.

FIGURE PAINTING

When the figure is ready for painting a set procedure is followed and this will apply for any painting medium, whether oils or water-based paints.

The painter's task is to bring to life a piece of plastic or metal by adding colour and character. He must be

Initial stages of painting an undercoated part-scratch, part-conversion English Civil War trooper, by John Reagan. One of the best mediums for undercoating is a matt enamel. Using an airbrush is an ideal way to apply an even layer of undercoat quickly. To save time it is a good idea to undercoat several models simultaneously. Apply more than one coat.

able to visualize the finished figure even before he applies the first brush stroke of colour to the model.

It is best to start painting a figure with the face, for, if the face is badly painted, it can reduce a well-made model to the status of a toy soldier. A flesh tone is mixed as described previously, and applied to the face. Care must be taken to work the paint into the engraved features such as the eyes, nostrils and mouth.

Next, shade Burnt Umber into the eye sockets, around the nose, the bottom lip of the mouth and under the chin. When this colour has been blended the next and most important step is the eyes. White is applied for the eye-ball, then the iris is painted. Many modellers tend to paint the iris as a small dot surrounded by a sea of white which, in turn, gives the face a wide-eyed staring expression. In fact very little white ever shows in the eyes. A thin black or dark brown line is then painted along the bottom of the top eye-lid. The application of highlights to the eyes and the rest of the face is the next step. Add to the basic flesh-tone White and Yellow Ochre, then apply to the top and bottom eyelids, the bridge of the nose, nostrils, top of the cheeks and chin, blending in the colours as you work. The lips are painted with a mixture of White, Indian Red and Yellow Ochre, the lower lip being slightly darker than the top and highlighted with the addition of more white to the mix.

Finally the hair and any other details such as eyebrows and moustache are added by painting in the appropriate colour and highlighted by drybrushing with a lighter shade.

The painter's attention then turns to the uniform and here must be stressed the importance of historical research into the colours and details of the uniform. Most model kits come complete with an accurate painting guide, but it is still worthwhile to cross-check this information from the numerous books and cards available to the modeller.

Paint the uniform starting with the light colours first. Paint in smooth, even strokes, but take care not to overpaint on to areas to be painted later. Add shading and highlights as you proceed by applying darker shades into the folds and lighter ones to the top of the creases. When the light areas are completed the same treatment is carried out on the dark areas until the basic uniform is complete. During this stage the figure may tend to look displeasing to the modeller as certain areas of shading look too dark or light but, as the model progresses, they will blend together until the total overall effect is achieved.

The head-dress is the next item to be painted. In the case of a bearskin a base coat of black is worked into the engraved details and left to dry, before drybrushing with either grey or brown to pick out the highlights. For a metallic finish to a helmet as worn by a Dragoon or Cuirassier, the base coat is painted with enamels, brass, copper or silver. A thin wash of colour is then flowed across the surface and left to sink into the engraved details – for brass and copper a dark brown wash, and for silver a black one. The details can then be picked out, using a lighter colour, either by careful painting or drybrushing. Hat plumes may be textured by peaking with acrylic or oil paints before painting, first with a dark tone of the appropriate colour, then highlighted by drybrushing with a lighter tone.

Depending on the period of the figure being modelled, details such as personal equipment and weapons can now be painted. Some of these items, like swords and sabretaches, may have been omitted from the figure to ease the painting of the uniform. They can be fixed to the model now and painted, or left off until the model is finished, painted separately, then applied. It is purely a personal choice as to which method is employed.

All belts, buttons, turnbacks, epaulettes and any other details should be outlined either with a dark tone of the uniform colour or black, before painting in the appropriate colour. Any metallic parts of the uniform are best painted with enamels and shaded as previously described under head-dress.

The last two items to be painted are the hands and footwear. A flesh tone is mixed and applied to the hands or, if the figure is wearing gloves, an appropriate colour is used. Shade in between the fingers with a dark tone and add the highlights to the knuckles. When painting the figure's boots or shoes, use shading and highlights to resemble the polished sheen of the footwear. Do not be tempted to save time by applying a coat of gloss varnish over the paint, unless the figure is being depicted on the parade ground.

BASES

All that remains now is for the modeller to fix the finished figure, when completely dry, to a suitable base, the one supplied with the model or one made especially to show off the figure. The tendency here is to use materials other than paintwork to represent the ground features, such as sand, dyed sawdust or model railway gravel. Many kit bases do have ground work moulded on them and if used they should be given a coat of matt black enamel paint to act as an undercoat and basecoat. The colour of the groundwork is then drybrushed over the base, building up different tones depending on the number of applications or colours being used.

If care and patience has been observed throughout the painting of the subject, the modeller can now sit back and reap the rewards of a figure brought to life by his or her own painting skills. All modellers, whether experienced or just beginners, should always keep on striving to improve their work; there is always some lesson to be learnt from every model made, either in assembly or painting. Experiment with different paints, textures and finishes, and concentrate on finishing one figure before starting on another. If the paint is not producing the right effect or you find your concentration wavering, leave the model – put it aside, rather than force yourself to carry on painting – and wait until your enthusiasm returns. The finished result will depend entirely on your skill as a painter.

Opposite *An 8th Hussar figure (c. 1824) by David Hunter converted from the Airfix Showjumper kit. Many weeks of work were involved in the uniform and saddle details, which could have been wasted with hasty or careless painting. The fur on the pelisse was made from fine-quality sponge and the braiding on the jacket and pelisse from plastic card. (See page 61 for more details.)*

Uniforms

'Uniform – a dress or livery of the same kind for persons who belong to the same body . . .' This is a dictionary's definition of the clothing worn by a soldier. Why was such similarity of dress so essential, what were the reasons for the adoption of such a form of clothing and why, during the course of three centuries, did it evolve from a gorgeous, often gaudy and unserviceable dress, into the comfortable, highly sophisticated clothing of the present day?

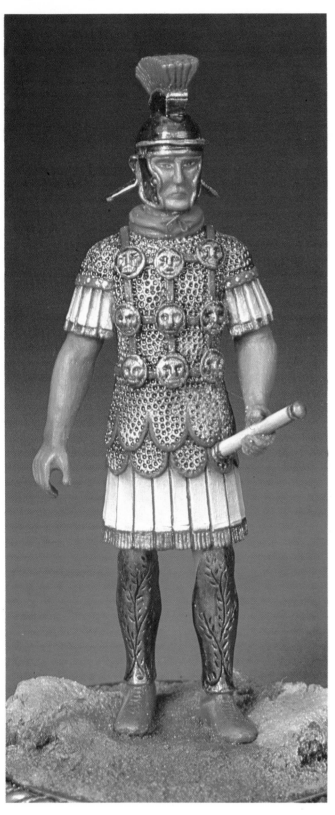

Before AD 1500

From earliest times it had been necessary to distinguish friend from foe by painting the body with various colours and designs attributable to one's own tribe, the blue woad markings used by ancient British tribesmen being a good example. The increasing use of more sophisticated weapons, other than flint arrows, spears and hatchets, made it important to protect all parts of the body with something more than animal hides, and shields of wood and leather were developed with additional protection for the head, chest and often the lower legs. The advent of bronze and iron and its use in the construction of weapons produced the need for even greater protection; consequently, shields became larger and reinforced with metal plates and studs.

The Roman Army attempted to achieve a degree of uniformity of armour, even to having the same type of shield in a unit as a form of recognition and economy. Personal protection covered more of the body, and ways of making stronger quilted and leather body armour were achieved by stitching on bone, metal plates and rings. Another stage in development was to encase the body as much as possible in metal armour, but skills and techniques needed to make fully articulated light-weight armour were still in the future, although plate armour was soon used in conjunction with boiled leather, padded and quilted clothing and later, chain mail. Obviously, the custom of painting the body as a recognition and identification sign was no longer relevant if it was covered by forms of protective clothing and such signs and displays were transferred to the next best thing – the shield.

Chain mail garments were becoming longer and made with hoods, and eventually the legs themselves were covered in this form of protection. To protect the wearer from the heat of the sun during the First Crusades, a long loose, linen garment was worn over the chain mail, which also protected the small metal rings from the worst of the elements. The head was now covered completely in massive enclosed helmets decorated with crests and plumes. Because the wearer could not be readily identified, the use of heraldic devices on shields, banners, surcoats, etc., became most important in battle. The knight's retainers and levees raised by him from hamlets on his estates began to be provided with coats bearing either his badge or a colour identifiable with his livery. The use of plate armour further developed and began to be worn as protection for knees, elbows, neck, etc., and by the end of the 15th century was being worn by the nobility of Europe, although among less sophisticated and nomadic peoples, animal hides and furs still formed the basis of body protection.

Left *Early armour often consisted of metal plates stitched to a leather or cloth tunic, as on this Roman Centurion in parade dress from Sovereign. Metal greaves for the legs were a Roman introduction.*
Opposite inset *Woad was used by Ancient Britons, and others such as this Pict javelineer by Peter Wilcox, partly to look fearsome but also for rapid identification in battle.*
Opposite *Another Roman from Sovereign Miniatures, a 2nd century cavalry auxiliary wearing an early chain mail tunic but without leg protection.*

16th and 17th centuries

One of the first examples of 'uniform' as we now know it was worn by the personal bodyguard raised by Henry VII and expanded by Henry VIII. The Yeoman of the Guard still exists to the present day and since 1509 the style and colour of their uniform has changed surprisingly little. The use of coloured surcoats, cassocks, etc., for various bodies of troops as well as retainers had by Elizabethan times become an accepted practice but, although red was much in evidence among English troops, there was still no uniformity of colour.

The introduction of gunpowder began to render personal defensive armour obsolete and by the first half of the 17th century, only nobility wore a form of protection identifiable with the old plate armour, in a much modified form. Although heavily armoured cavalry was still preferred on the Continent of Europe, in England types of light cavalry, known as 'shot on horseback', had been used since the latter half of the 15th century. The English Civil War in 1642 saw a much greater use of the light cavalryman, but two regiments of heavily armoured cavalry formed part of the Parliamentarian Forces. Such armour consisted of a plumed open helmet, cuirass and armoured thigh guards ('tassets') etc., under which a thick hide coat was worn, the legs being protected by high, thick, untanned leather boots. Generally speaking, cavalry on both sides wore little armour, favouring manoeuvrability and speed.

Infantry of the period started the conflict dressed mainly in civilian attire, except pikemen who wore a 'morion' or pot helmet, breast and back plates, and, occasionally, 'tassets'. Distinctions were made in the form of emblems stitched to clothes or pieces of paper, leaves, etc., which were placed in hats as 'field signs'. In some cases, coloured scarves were worn about the body, either around the waist or over the shoulder, and coloured ribbons were added to the hat; the scarves generally settled as two predominant colours, red or orange for Royalists and Parliamentarians respectively. It did not take long for commanders to realize that more distinctive forms of clothing would have to be adopted and whole regiments began to be clothed in coats of the same colour on both sides, red and blue predominating, but also grey, green or yellow: not only did this imbue regiments with *esprit de corps* but it was far more economical for colonels to procure the cloth in bulk, finance being, as now, a major consideration. Upon the formation of Cromwell's New Model Army, the coats of British soldiers began to be standardized with red as the chosen colour. In Europe similar changes were occurring.

Upon the Restoration of Charles II in 1660, a number of elements of the old Parliamentarian Army were absorbed into the standing army of the new monarch. Cavalrymen were still clothed in a similar style to that worn during the latter days of the Civil War, a large, soft felt hat, with a high crown and panaches of feathers (the Cromwellian 'pot' helmet being worn only in action), buff coats, cuirasses, coloured sashes and high riding boots. Infantry were still divided into musketeers and pikemen, but pikemen had shed the tassets altogether; musketeers wore short, buff leather coats with loose slashed sleeves allowing arms freedom of movement; beneath these they wore jackets with red pantaloons and stockings. The equipment was a sword slung from a baldric over the right shoulder and powder and shot for the musket suspended in twelve wooden containers (the famous 'Twelve Apostles') and a leather bag from a wide leather baldric.

Senior officers of all armies still dressed in virtually what they liked and the civilian fashion of the time saw the increasing use of metallic lace on coats and waistcoats, particularly along the seams, coat edges and around the buttonholes, which had the dual effect of reinforcing and decorating the garment. Gradually, the buttonholes of coats of private soldiers were also decorated with woollen braid looping. At about the same time the linings of the coats, folded-back cuffs and skirts, were faced with a contrasting colour cloth which made regimental distinctions. This custom, which had started in the latter days of the Civil War, developed as units increasingly began to use uniformly coloured coats.

About 1670, a new type of soldier began to emerge on the European battle fields – the grenadier. The development of gunpowder had seen the introduction of projectiles and it was not too long before hand thrown explosive missiles were invented. To use these weapons, called 'granades', specially selected infantrymen of good, strong, physique were formed into bodies of so-

called 'grenadiers' within infantry regiments. The broad brimmed head-dress of the time became an encumbrance when slinging the musket across the shoulder and throwing the fused grenades, and a close-fitting cap with a hanging cloth body encircled with fur was introduced. The grenadier was also differently equipped, having a lighter musket or 'fuzee' with a strap attached; he also carried a slow burning fuse, a sword, hatchet and a pouch for carrying extra grenades.

Concurrently, new types of cavalrymen were making appearances, the dragoon and hussar. Employed primarily as mounted infantry, the dragoon was not as heavily clad as heavy cavalrymen, emphasis being given to speed and manoeuvre. He often wore a cap similar to the grenadier. Muskets were shortened and supplied with straps to enable them to be slung across the shoulders. The only armoured protection for these troops was an iron skull worn beneath the head-dress; boots were lighter and less cumbersome, to facilitate ease of movement when fighting dismounted. The hussar originated in Eastern Europe; riding strong, small horses, he was lightly clad and equipped, armed with a brace of pistols, a musket and heavily curved sabre. His dress consisted of a cloth cap often encircled with thick fur, a short, richly ornamented jacket, tight breeches, short soft leather boots and he carried an animal skin around his shoulders as protection from inclement weather.

The hussar was used as a scout or skirmisher ahead of or on the flanks of an army; Frederick the Great of Prussia turned these colourful characters into highly organized cavalry regiments capable of charging home as normal cavalry. The romantic dash of hussars caught the imagination of most armies and they soon became useful adjuncts to the cavalry arm. Their dress was gradually modified and stylized, the cap becoming higher using more fur, the cloth crown hanging over the side as a bag. The animal skin cape now became a short, fleece-lined coat (pelisse) in its own right, decorated in similar style to the jacket or dolman and when not in use slung from the shoulders by retaining cords. Breeches remained tight and were not furnished with pockets; the original hussar carried a large purse from his waistbelt which literally evolved into a portable writing desk and despatch carrier known as the sabretache. The sabretache gradually became less functional and more a gorgeously decorated item of dress for hussars of all nations.

Part of a splendid English Civil War diorama by K. M. Yuill, photographed at a leading modelling exhibition. Every figure is carefully researched.

18th century

A universal pattern for uniforms was now emerging throughout Europe; in common with civilian head-dress, the crown of the hat became lower, the brims less wide and usually turned up. Coats were fashioned without collars, were long and full in the body and sleeves; the custom of turning back the cuffs displaying different coloured linings as distinctions was now firmly entrenched. Buttonholes were now reinforced and decorated with gold and silver lace for officers and woollen braid for men. In a few years these distinctions were going to play an important part in the identification of regiments, especially in the British Army, each having their own particular facings, buttonhole spacings, pattern and style of lace, etc. Officers' dress became more distinctive and sashes, plentiful metallic lace, and bunches of ribbons worn on the shoulders all became important adjuncts to an officer's dress.

The introduction of the grenadier had forecast further changes of equipment and head-dress for other units of an 18th century army; the introduction of fusiliers, initially formed to guard trains of artillery and armed with flintlock fusils, gradually saw the demise of pikes as a weapon. Also to become obsolete were the last vestiges of armour, except for iron skull caps, breastplates and gorgets; the latter had been the armour worn about the neck to protect the area between the breastplate and helmet. This gradually became smaller until it became the symbolic distinction of an officer. The gorget developed differently in various countries, some becoming small and quite plain, others highly ornate and used as a part of dress uniforms both in Russia and Germany as late as World War 1. In Britain, the last trace can be seen on the collars of General Officers in the form of small coloured tabs and buttons, forming a representation of how the gorget used to be attached. The 'Ringkragen' of standard bearers in the old German Army and Wehrmacht was also a reminder of this piece of armour.

The pike was retained by sergeants and in various forms of polearm by officers as indication of rank.

By the middle of the 18th century the style of military coats began to change. Lapels had been introduced to button across the breast in bad weather and the front and rear of the skirts were made to button back to give greater freedom of movement when marching. Hats were now turned up at the rear and both sides to form the well known tricorne and the grenadier cap now became stiffer, higher and more decorative. As the century progressed the utilitarian purpose of lapels and skirts declined and they solely became more decorative, the skirts being permanently turned back and stitched. The coat itself became even more ornamentative, cuffs developing in various national styles, and breeches and stockings were protected by thick, thigh-length gaiters, although these were shortened as time passed.

On the continent of North America, British and French armies and colonial settlers in America and Canada had to develop a new style of fighting in the vast primeval forests. To a large extent the French regiments and their Canadian settlers had already adapted to these new conditions, but British regiments still fought in clumsy clothing and rigid formations. Experience deemed it necessary to dress and equip selected troops in clothing and equipment better enabling them to fight in the backwoods environment. Coats were shortened by cutting off skirts, the brims of hats were adapted by making them smaller or removing them altogether, and some regiments had their head-dress replaced by specially made, close fitting leather caps. Equipment was made more functional, knives and tomahawks substituting for swords. Long gaiters were made shorter or Indian style leggings or cloth overall trousers substituted for normal leg wear. Out of this conflict the light infantry arm was created and eventually adopted by most armies of the time. In the latter half of the 18th century uniforms changed little until, in the years just before the turn of the century, coats generally became tighter, closed across the body and coat tails shortened, except in the French and some other Continental armies where long-skirted coats cut high over the breast were retained; collars, which had developed as folded down items, were fashioned in a standing style.

Opposite *A French infantryman of 1720–57, by John Tassel.*
Below *Continental Marine, American War of Independence, 1775.*

19th century

The middle European shako replaced the old cocked hats and trousers were introduced for campaign purposes during the Napoleonic Wars; thereafter breeches and gaiters were reserved for parade dress. Each major European power had selected national colours for the uniform coat. There appears to be no hard and fast reason for this, other than favouring the colour of their flags and sashes worn before uniform was developed, or possibly the availability of stocks of cloth of certain colours at the time; the Prussians had a rich dark blue, the Austrians and French, white (the latter changed to blue during the Revolution, then back to white for a short period, and then to blue once again). The Russians had green and the emergent army of the United States favoured blue, sometimes grey; the British retained their familiar red.

The more peaceful years following the Napoleonic Wars saw an explosion in sartorial elegance in civilian and military dress. Head-dress became larger and more ornate, long tails to coatees began to reappear, the coats became even tighter, collars were made higher and stiffer; trousers became rather loose and in many countries were trimmed with coloured cloth stripes or metallic lace. Officers' accoutrements became less functional and more showy; in fact the whole emphasis was now on parade-ground elegance, a situation which lasted until the middle of the 19th century when British and French armies went to war with Russia, the British especially suffering appalling hardships in the Crimea due to the inadequacies of their clothing and equipment. This campaign caused such an outcry that, among

other reforms, British uniforms underwent major changes; the tight, long-tailed coatee worn by all arms, with its lack of protection for the lower abdomen, disappeared, giving way to a long, full, loose fitting tunic with a low collar, copying very much the French uniform style. This influence held sway in military fashion for the next few years until the Franco/Prussian War of 1870, when victorious Prussia took the next lead in the field of military dress, particularly in the form of their spiked 'picklehaube' head-dress which many armies adopted in some form or other.

The army of the United States was also much influenced by France in her military dress, but the Civil War of 1861–65 soon found a need for more functional uniforms and many colourful volunteer units who entered the war dressed as French colonial zouaves ended it in a simple jacket, trousers and kepi.

Climatic influence
From this period on, sweeping changes began to affect the dress and equipment of all armies. Colonialization and the need to keep large armies in often hot, unhealthy climates, fighting savage and cunning natives in their own familiar terrain found the need for lightweight, comfortable clothing. Lightweight materials had been used for the uniforms of British soldiers in

Tangiers in the late 17th century, but an established hot weather clothing took many more years to become reality. Until the middle of the 19th century the only concession to the sun were hats made from straw, linen breeches and stockings. Even the French Foreign Legion, long used to campaigning in hot climates, wore a dress more suited to temperate zones. The United States soldier, fighting American Indians in equally inhospitable terrain, shed his coat, fought in shirt sleeves, and adopted a wide-brimmed hat.

Opposite top *Converted from a 1:12 scale Airfix figure by Bernie Harris, this is an officer of the Sapeurs Genie of Napoleon's Imperial Guard in the year 1813.*
Opposite bottom left *Another 1:12 conversion of an Imperial Guard figure by Bernie Harris, this is a trumpeter of the Grenadiers à Cheval of 1810.*
Opposite bottom right *The Imperial Guard, a 1:12 Airfix figure and Bernie Harris again combine in a splendid conversion, this time a Chasseur à Cheval of 1807.*
Below *Major Bob Rowe produced these Confederate soldiers at rest for Cavalier Miniatures of New York. The careful addition of some foliage around the figures sets the scene and makes the diorama look more attractive and convincing.*

Disappearance of colour

Running concurrently with the need to adopt specialized clothing for hot climates was the need to make the European soldier less conspicuous when fighting in deserts, jungles, bush and mountains in his vivid coloured clothing, often against skilful aboriginal warriors who were completely at home in their environment. It was necessary to find a serviceable, inconspicuous dress for service conditions and in this field Britain led the rest of the world.

During the American War of Independence, two regular British units were dressed in brown or green coats and many Ranger units wore green clothing, if not adopting the hunting shirt of the American woodsmen. It was not until 1846, however, in India, that a serious attempt was made to provide a uniform which would blend with the surrounding countryside. Raised initially to police and combat the wild tribesmen of the Northwest Frontier, Sir Henry Lumsden's Corps of Guides were dressed in white cotton clothing stained with river mud; the resulting shade was called 'khaki',

a Persian or Urdu word meaning 'dust'. Such was the success of this unit that some regiments involved in the suppression of the Indian Mutiny in 1857 also stained their white hot weather clothing a light brown or grey. In 1868, the British Army mounted an expedition against King Theodore of Abyssinia and all the infantry involved in the march to Magdala were ordered to be clothed in khaki.

By 1880 most Indian Army regiments and British troops serving on the Indian Continent were dressed in khaki hot weather clothing; the lower legs of troops were also wound in cloth wrappings or bandages called puttees, a fashion that reached its peak in nearly all the armies of the world up to the outbreak of World War 2. Khaki, however, was still not properly uniform and the colour was not as we know it today, varying from light brown, ochre, pink to a buff/grey, depending on the material and substance used for the dye. It was not until 1884 that a fast reliable dye was found and, in 1902, a khaki service dress was issued to the British Army and the old colourful scarlet, blue and green

coats were gradually laid aside, thereafter only to be worn for parades or walking out.

The new drab-coloured clothing had not gone unnoticed either in Europe or America. The American soldier wore a mixture of blue and drab during the Cuban campaign and German colonial troops wore hot weather khaki clothing. By 1910, Germany had begun to clothe her army in a subdued uniform for service, the now familiar 'field grey'. France, however, though one of the first to experiment in the quest for a subdued uniform, still adhered to scarlet and blue until 1915, when the French soldier was issued with a 'horizon blue' service dress. By the middle of World War 1, all combatants were clothed in subdued-coloured uniforms.

World War 1, with its accompanying horrors of trench warfare and massive artillery bombardments, the greater use of the machine gun, etc., saw an ever increasing need for specialized clothing and equipment and we come nearly full circle with the adoption of forms of body armour. The air-burst shell and shrapnel caused many needless head wounds on all sides and once again the soldier was equipped with a form of metal casque as a protection. At first these were worn only in the trenches and passed on to relief when going to the rear areas for rest periods, but it was not long before steel helmets were issued to all officers and men and worn at all times unless well away from the front line. Each country developed its own particular style of steel helmet which became almost as readily identifiable as the vivid colours of the old dress tunics. German snipers were also equipped with a form of body armour, but it proved so heavy and unwieldy it was rarely worn.

Battle dress

Uniforms were never the same after the Armistice; armies retained their service dress for all occasions, although better tailored and considerably smartened, and the old colourful uniforms were laid aside except for special honour guards or displays. However, the quest for greater comfort never diminished and by the end of 1937 a new form of utilitarian uniform was adopted by the British Army which again was to have a major influence on the dress of most world armies – 'Battle Dress' had arrived. By the end of World War 2, most armies were wearing this in some form or other. It consisted of a short, waist-length blouse, the front fastening by a row of small flat buttons covered by a cloth fly, the cuffs buttoning at the wrist; it had breast pockets, folded-down collar fastening at the neck with hooks and eyes, and a cloth strap on either shoulder. Puttees were dispensed with and trousers with a patch pocket on the front of the left leg and another smaller pocket near the waist on the right-hand side containing a field dressing were worn with ankle-length webbing gaiters.

The decline of the use of the horse and development of mechanization resulted in the need for other forms of specialist protective clothing, some virtually becoming a parade dress in their own right; two good examples are the black berets and black tank overalls worn by British tank crews prior to World War 2 and the black, double breasted, short waisted jacket worn with black trousers gathered at the ankle, plus beret with its leather protective skull worn beneath, of the World War 2 German tank regiments. Originally designed to

avoid snagging on the vehicles, with black favoured as the colour least likely to show oil stains, they came to mean much more to the men who wore them. The same may be said of the parachutists' smock, now the mark of élite troops and worn as parade dress in many countries.

Opposite left *Colour was still to be found at the turn of the 19th century. This German officer of the 13th Dragoons of about 1900 wears a field-grey manoeuvre cover over his 'picklehaube' helmet.*
Opposite right *Full dress uniform of a British Army Medical Officer, c. 1900, featuring a Home Service Pattern Helmet.*
Below *Olive green for jungle fighting gradually replaced khaki in British uniforms after World War 2; this example as worn in Brunei and Borneo, c. 1962–3. Note the canvas rubber-soled boots.*

Combat dress

We have described how, during the past century, the soldier has been issued with a number of combinations of dress for specific purposes, i.e., hot weather or tropical clothing, subdued service dress and parade or full dress, a single uniform no longer sufficing for all duties. The latest creation, born out of necessity, is the multi-purpose combat dress. World War 2 saw the adoption of smocks and jackets in both lightweight and shower-proof materials, and garments supplied with detachable or reversible linings. Often manufactured in coloured, broken camouflage patterns, they have been tried and proved successful throughout the world. The soldier dressed in his disruptive patterned combat clothing is a familiar sight in most countries.

Combat clothing and battle dress have served well, but the drabness and austerity of uniforms since World War 2 has resulted in an urge to return to smarter walking out and parade dress. Since 1945, forms of full dress have gradually emerged in most countries, some based on the old time full dress, others of a completely new design.

Above *An Unterscharführer of the German Waffen-SS, 1941. With camouflage smock and helmet cover, this figure is a good illustration of how combat dress became less colourful but far better suited to battle conditions. Note how the simple addition of a broken wall gives the model a more realistic setting. Model by B. William.*

Left *Riot control or public order dress of the British Army of the 1970s, including a flak jacket worn over the standard disruptive pattern jacket, a long baton and a transparent shield and helmet visor made from Makralon.*

Opposite *World War 2 US infantryman, part of a diorama by Don Skinner. Authenticity of uniforms of the last 50 years or so often comes under the scrutiny of veterans who actually wore them.*

Above *A Lancer of Skinner's Horse, formed in 1803
and becoming the 1st Duke of York's Own Bengal
Lancers in 1899. Mounted figure by Sid Horton.*
Above right *A Chasseur à Cheval of the Imperial
Guard, 1807, as converted from a 1:12 plastic figure by
B. Harris.*

Head-dress

Brief mention has been made on the subject of head-dress, but to elaborate further on this important item of a soldier's apparel is not within the scope of this section on the evolution of uniform. Suffice it to say that the development of military head-dress from the 17th century to the latter days of the 18th century was, generally speaking, one of gradual change, although the head-dress of the light cavalrymen began to differ with helmets of leather frequently being adopted besides the fur cap. In the hundred years spanning the 19th century, there was a great acceleration embracing a host of styles of hats, shakos and helmets, developing along nationalistic lines. The passing of the felt cocked hat, with its many permutations of setting up the brim culminating in the bicorne, saw the heavy cavalry of many countries developing their own forms of head-dress, at first made mainly from leather and then metal;

light cavalry, however, other than hussars, in many countries favoured the shako until they, in turn, developed their own forms of helmet.

Although the lance had been used for many centuries, its popularity waned as a weapon of war from the latter half of the 17th century, except in Eastern Europe, where it was still successfully employed as an offensive weapon by some light cavalry. Prussia, under Frederick the Great, expanded the use of the weapon, and Napoleon Bonaparte employed regiments of Polish lancers with such brilliant success it fired the imaginations of most European armies, with regiments of light cavalry being converted to use the weapon or new regiments of lancers being raised. Britain was rather late in acquiring her lancer arm, four regiments of light dragoons being converted in September 1816. As the hussar had done nearly a century before, the lancer was to do now, influencing the dress of a particular type of soldier. Each country developed the lancer uniform in its own particular way, but the short-tailed, plastron-fronted jacket and the four-sided cap or czapska, based on the cap worn by the peasants of Poland and adopted by Polish cavalry, were to remain the distinctive characteristic of the lancer in most armies until the eclipse of full dress uniform.

Below *The colour and romance of the medieval period are embodied in this 54mm knight.*
Bottom *Historex include this 54mm Napoleonic Line Dragoon Officer in their extensive range of figures. Model by Edward Pollard.*
Right *A model of the famous Sioux chief Crazy Horse, winner of a major award for maker Terry Smith.*

CRAZY HORSE - OGLALLA SIO

Identification by insignia

The disappearance of the old armoured knight and his retinue did not see the demise of military heraldry. When standing armies became established throughout Europe, regiments were first clothed and equipped by their colonels, many coming from the Royal Households, nobility or aristocracy. The individual's family coat of arms was carried on regimental colours or standards and on the fronts of the grenadier caps. In the case of the Guard units responsible for the protection of monarchs, the colours of the royal livery were generally worn on their coats. Senior regiments of the British army carry reminders of these early devices on their regimental cap badges to the present day. Heraldry in other forms was also adopted when large armies began to dress their men in similar fashion and colours; the Union Army of the American Civil War adopted cloth and metal badges in various geometric shapes which were worn on the head-dress, identifying their brigades or divisions, a reminder of the old 'field marks'

of earlier days. When the British Army adopted khaki hot weather clothing in the latter days of the 19th century, there arose a need to identify units regimentally. The simple expedient was adopted of cutting shoulder straps from old red coats with their regimental designation and stitching them to the side of the tropical helmet. It was not long before more elaborate 'flashes' were used and specifically designed for that purpose. World War 1 saw a proliferation of this form of identification either painted on the helmet or worn as cloth insignia on the tunic. The American Army adopted this idea on her entry into the war until finally whole divisions, brigades and armies, were identified in a similar fashion; the practice reached a zenith in World War 2 when even small specialized units had their own particular cloth emblems or signs. The system is still very much a part of the American serviceman's dress today and can also be found in use in a number of world armies.

What will future students of military uniform see in

Typical World War 2 insignia:

Far left *US General Staff badge worn by staff officers.*
Left *American nurses' badge shown above the medical award for 60 days' front-line service.*
Far left, below *Insignia of the US 4th Armored Division.*
Centre below *US Medical Corps badge on shirt collar with a unit distinction badge on jacket lapel (usually worn on pocket).*
Below *German insignia. Golden party badge worn by members of the Nazi party is shown above an Iron Cross First Class. To the left of this is an army assault badge (the figure 50 refers to the number of assaults taken part in). Directly underneath the Iron Cross is a wound badge.*

years to come? It would appear that uniforms have progressed as far as they are able, but who knows what future fashions or special contingencies may influence the soldier's dress? One thing is certain, the modern soldier wearing a protective flak jacket, helmet, and visor, plus a riot shield carried for use when engaged in public order duties, does not seem far removed from his ancestors of centuries ago. However, the soldier in times of peace is ever a peacock, quick to display honourably earned distinctions, and we can rest assured that all soldiers will continue to use small patches of coloured cloth, their specialist badges, regimental and unit devices, insignia of rank, etc., and no matter how drab his basic uniform may be, he will always endeavour to provide himself with a smart and attractive parade or walking out dress when the need arises.

More World War 2 insignia:

Top left *A German sports badge.*
Top right *A German artillery officer's breast eagle. An eagle insignia was also worn on the front of Wehrmacht officers' caps. Waffen-SS had a variation of this insignia on the left sleeve.*
Centre left *A German officer's collar patch (called Waffenfarbe). The red background denotes the artillery branch of service.*
Centre right *US Armored Division insignia shown above a US Army Combat Infantry Award (marksman) and two rows of medal ribbons.*
Above left *A German artillery officer's epaulette (rank, Oberst Leutnant).*
Above right *A German sports badge shown above the Volunteer Fire Fighter's badge.*

Weapons, equipment and mounts

A major attraction of military modelling is the opportunity to show developments in arms and equipment. Another which has very wide appeal is the modelling of horses, associated with soldiers from earliest times down to ceremonial occasions today. This chapter details the histories of hand weapons and personal equipment and sets out how to go about making and painting convincing models of horses.

Charles, Duke of Orleans, at Agincourt. 90mm carved wood and Milliput figure by L. Martin Rendall.

Hand weapons

Weapons of early man – 6000 BC–AD 500

Man's first weapons consisted of rocks, wooden clubs and pointed sticks, but over the centuries he learned to use more effective materials such as flint, bronze and eventually iron; the knife, spear, axe and, although rare, the sword gradually evolved as standard hand weapons. Protection was afforded by skin-covered wood frame shields, and missile weapons were the bow, sling and javelin. The pattern thus established remained basically the same until the introduction of firearms. Chariots carrying bowmen were used by the Hyksos during their Egyptian invasion in 1680 BC, and chariots remained popular until 300 BC.

The highly disciplined Roman army was the most efficient of this period, its legionnaires being equipped with short thrusting swords, javelins, large shields, metal body armour and helmets.

Anglo-Saxons and Vikings – AD 500–1066

Anglo-Saxon arms were the spear, small shield and scramassaxe (long bladed knife); only chiefs carried short swords. The Vikings and Norsemen (AD 800 onwards) possessed greatly superior weapons due to their technological advances in metallurgy, using swords, long-handled axes and powerful bows, and they wore metal helmets, occasionally ring mail, and the hauberk, a padded coat on which were sewn metal rings. Their swords had long, well-tempered blades, the hilts of which were capped with distinctive Brazil nut or cocked-hat shaped pommels.

At Hastings in 1066, the Anglo-Danish army consisted of regular troops (Housecarls) equipped with metal helmets incorporating protective nose pieces, tall kite-shaped shields, long hauberks, two-handed axes and swords. Supporting levies (the fyrd) possessed inferior arms and protection but inflicted many casualties with the bill, a curved heavy blade on a pole.

Below *Early weapons almost certainly evolved from hunting implements and relied on stones or flakes knapped from flints, bound with animal thongs to wood hafts and shafts.*
Bottom *The basic English longbow and some typical polearm heads. The designers of these sought to produce thrusting, pulling and chopping edges, and frequently incorporated notches to entrap, or shapes to deflect, opponents' weapons.*
Opposite *A Peter Wilcox model of a Celtic warrior of about 1290 BC.*

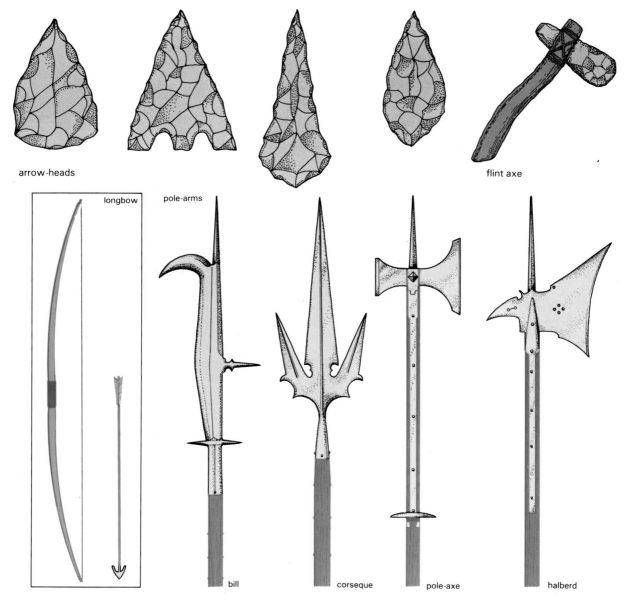

arrow-heads

flint axe

longbow

pole-arms

bill

corseque

pole-axe

halberd

The Norman Army included contingents of archers and cavalry; the latter also wore the hauberk and helmet but wielded ash pole spears, maces, and long, clumsy double-bladed swords with heavy counterweight pommels. Their long, kite-shaped shields were supported by a strap over the right shoulder and held on the left arm.

Evolution of cavalry – 300 BC–AD 1200

Light cavalry was employed by Alexander the Great during his campaigns (336–323 BC), and by Hannibal in the second Punic War (218–202 BC); Hannibal also used elephants upon which were mounted wooden towers containing archers. However, it was not until the high war-saddle and stirrups (invented in China about 3000 BC) were adopted that European/Middle Eastern horsemen achieved shock power. The Romans increased cavalry units to compensate for declining infantry standards and to give better army mobility, but a united army of Huns, Goths and Alans employed mounted archers to defeat them at Adrianople in AD 378. Byzantine cavalry of about AD 650 wore light mail and carried a small shield, axe, curved sword and bow. Cavalry became the supreme Continental arm during Charlemagne's empire (AD 771–814), in which leading soldiers (knights) were given semi-independent control of territories which they protected with cavalry contingents. Genghis Khan achieved immense conquests (AD 1206–1227) using light horsemen equipped with helmet and bow and lance-wielding heavy cavalry protected by helmet and mail armour.

Domination of armoured cavalry – AD 800–1420

After Hastings, armoured cavalry dominated warfare. European knights rode powerful warhorses, using a second steed to transport baggage and the hauberk/mail mounted on coat-hanger shaped frames. Greater protection was constantly sought: helmets eventually completely encased the head, ring-mail suits replaced the hauberk and were later superseded by steel plate armour. By 1400, the knight was completely encased with high-quality plate which, although very heavy, was remarkably flexible. Shields were discarded and the lance replaced the spear. Horses were also armoured, but the increased weight necessitated the employment of massive steeds such as the Percheron.

Decline of armoured cavalry

Cavalry declined because heavy armour reduced mobility, the helmet restricted vision, and infantry adopted the following efficient weapons and tactics.

The crossbow. The first mechanical infantry weapon was a trigger-operated bow, mounted on a stock, with windlass drawbow string. It could fire three bolts, or 'quarrels', every two minutes, with considerable velocity which easily penetrated mail up to 100m or so (120 yd), and sometimes plate armour at short range.

Polearms. The various categories were all similar to the bill but with more sophisticated and elaborate blades. They were effective when used by drilled and disciplined infantry, such as the Swiss phalanx, because they presented a hedgehog formation of bristling blades which were impenetrable in defence and irresistible in attack.

Longbow. The 5–6ft (1·5–1·8m) longbow was introduced in Wales about 1130 and was the standard English army missile weapon by 1250. Made from elm or yew, it accurately fired five or six aimed arrows per minute, the arrows being about one yard long (cloth yard) fitted with various patterns of head, all of which could penetrate mail, and in certain cases plate at short range. The longbow, superior to the crossbow in range and rate of fire, decisively contributed to cavalry decline by winning Crécy (1346), Poitiers (1356) and Agincourt (1415).

Utilization of gunpowder to weapons – 1320–1780

The first hand-held firearm was a handgun introduced about 1320, consisting of a wooden stock to which was fastened a simple, hollow tube which was filled with a powder charge and missile, and ignited with a hand-held brand at the touch hole. Later, a heavy two-man firearm was introduced which enabled the firer to support the weapon and simultaneously take correct aim while a second man ignited the charge. Soon, crude mechanical ignition systems were introduced which enabled one man to aim at the target and fire the weapon at the same time while holding it with both hands. Eventually, these improvements were incorporated in the matchlock-operated arquebus, a fairly efficient shoulder-firing weapon. Firearms made armour obsolete because they could penetrate it, and, furthermore, they made the weak, untrained man equal to the most valiant warrior – no longer would warfare be the prerogative of a highly trained élite.

By the 1500s cavalry had adopted the wheel-lock pistol and employed it in the formal caracole or wheeling attack tactics. However, Gustavus Adolphus reorganized his cavalry (1615) into three-rank formations trained to charge together with the sword, using shock power to achieve success.

Sword patterns changed: heavy, knightly swords were replaced by more slender and manageable patterns. Cavalry used robust basket-hilted swords with

Left *A 3rd century Persian clibanarius by Peter Wilcox, interesting and attractive with its leather and metal crescent horse armour.*
Below *John Tassel's model of a 1st century Southern Gaul Spearman, 75mm metal. Horned helmets were intended to be intimidatory.*
Opposite below *Stacked muskets and scattered equipment in a small part of a diorama by François Verlinden suggest the aftermath of a battle. Note how the modeller has sunk the butts of the muskets slightly in the ground to make the scene more convincing. Small touches like this all contribute towards an effective diorama.*

either straight or curved blades, and sword rapiers; the rapier, a favourite civilian weapon, was constantly altered during the 17th century, gradually becoming lighter, shorter and more flexible.

By the end of the 16th century infantry was a mixed force of musketeers and pikemen, but firearm improvements and the cartridge enabled musketeers to increase their rate of fire, causing pikemen to become obsolete, though their function was retained in the bayonet. During the early 18th century, the matchlock was replaced by the flintlock-operated musket. Constant foot and weapon drill was essential to achieve disciplined volley fire, the prerequisite to battle success.

Napoleonic wars – 1790–1815
Infantry weapons at this time primarily consisted of the smooth-bore, flintlock musket and the bayonet, the British using the famous Brown Bess with a calibre of ·75in (19mm) and an accurate battle rate of fire of two rounds per minute at up to 50m (60yd). An important, accurate new weapon was the Baker rifle used by some British units at Waterloo. Cavalry normally employed either the heavy sword or sabre and pistol or carbine and, although French light cavalry favoured the lance, their heavy cavalry (cuirassiers) used a straight, heavy sword and wore breast-plates. Uniforms were colourful to provide instant recognition and enhance the soldier's ego, tall headgear and packs worn high increasing their formidable appearance.

Modern firearms – 1820–1914
Industrialization caused many firearm improvements, particularly the replacement of flintlock mechanisms by the percussion cap. Metal and paper cartridges were

invented, enclosing bullet, charge, and percussion cap, discharged with a firing pin. Important early rifles were the Prussian needle gun (1840) and the French Minie muzzle loader (1851). Rate of fire was increased by the magazine, a box containing a store of cartridges resting upon a spring, which enabled rapid feeding of the breech. Rifles clearly demonstrated their effectiveness in the American Civil War, the Franco–Prussian War and the Boer War.

By 1914, bolt-operated rifles could achieve accurate, rapid fire at long ranges, and the Germans with the Mauser and the British with the Lee Enfield finally proved that massed troops could not stand up to modern firepower. Effective machine-guns were introduced by the French with their Reffye mitrailleuse, with 25 rotating barrels firing 75–125 bullets a minute. Maxim introduced the first fully automatic gun in 1885.

World War 1 – 1914–18
Fire from large machine-guns, rifles and high-powered artillery forced armies underground into a trench warfare stalemate, and cavalry became obsolete until it re-emerged in its new form, the tank. Light mortars, some of great accuracy, were much employed because their bombs could penetrate trenches.

Short-range weapons such as the hand or stick grenade and sub-machine-gun (SMG) such as the Italian Villar Perosa and German MP18 were adopted. Flame-throwers and poison gas were employed, the latter causing the gas mask to join the steel helmet as standard equipment issues. This war also saw the introduction of the first one-man operated light machine-gun (LMG), the American Lewis.

1918–45
Between the wars standard weapons were the bolt-action rifle and bayonet, an LMG per section and medium machine-guns. During World War 2 the principal change was a proliferation of automatic weapons, particularly by the Americans and Germans. The latter used large numbers of SMGs (9mm MP40), MG 34, and automatic rifles plus medium machine-guns.

Modern weapons
Infantry of leading military nations today are equipped with automatic rifles/bayonets, SMGs and general purpose machine-guns and protected with steel helmets and nuclear, biological and chemical (NBC) warfare suits. Mechanized infantry are transported into battle in armoured personnel carriers and they deal with tanks – their main enemy – with anti-tank guns, wire-guided anti-tank missiles and rocket launcher teams.

Contemporary hand-held weapons are accurate, rapid firing, versatile and destructive. Despite their extreme sophistication, however, they will be superseded in due course because weapon development history clearly illustrates that more effective and devastating weapons are constantly developed.

Accoutrements

Accoutrements are the personal equipment the soldier needs to live and fight, and vary according to whether he operates on foot or mounted. A foot soldier requires the means to carry his ammunition and side arms, together with his rations, water, spare clothing and articles to keep him warm and dry; the mounted man can transfer much of this burden to his mount so his equipment is reduced.

In the 17th century, when standing armies began to be maintained, infantry consisted of musketeers and pikemen. Because of the musket's unreliability and slow loading, the musketeer had a sword for his personal protection which he suspended in a leather belt slung over his right shoulder. Over his left was a bandolier, another leather belt from which hung 12 powder charges, a priming flask, bullet bag and, when not in use, a slow match.

The pikeman had a similar sword belt but was also accoutred, for a time, with an iron helmet, cuirass and steel plates known as tassets to protect the upper thighs. Provision of the means to carry his immediate necessities was the soldier's responsibility. By the early 18th century the pikeman's armour had been abandoned and the introduction of the bayonet in the 1680s made his function obsolete. The musketeer carried his bayonet in a frog attached to his sword belt which, by the end of the 17th century, was being worn round the waist. The latter part of the 17th century saw the arrival of a third type of infantryman, the grenadier, who was furnished with a leather pouch slung over his left shoulder to carry his grenades.

In the early 18th century, with the advent of the cartridge containing bullet and charge, a similar pouch replaced the bandolier. Although the shape of the pouch and the width of its belt would vary over the years, the practice of suspending the infantryman's ammunition container over the left shoulder to hang near the right hip would continue for about 150 years or more.

As the 18th century progressed, the bayonet joined the sword in a double frog attached to the left of the waistbelt which by the middle of the century was more usually worn under the open coat. Soldiers were now issued with articles to carry their necessities: a knapsack, usually of some animal hide, and a water container slung over the right shoulder and a canvas haversack for rations over the left. The infantryman might also be burdened with other impedimenta such as tent poles and cooking pots.

Cross-belts

During the latter half of the 18th century it became the practice to transfer the bayonet belt, the sword being discarded by some armies, from the waist to the right shoulder. By the 1780s this had evolved into the cross-belt equipment, two belts of equal width crossing on the chest, where in some armies they were secured by a decorative plate, and suspending the pouch and bayonet at the right and left hips respectively. From the 1760s these belts were generally kept clean with white pipeclay. During the campaigns in America infantrymen had adopted the Indian method of supporting the knapsack, now more rectangular in shape and made of hide or canvas, by straps over both shoulders so that it rode

high on the back. Blankets or greatcoats were rolled on top. Except for a few modifications such as the use of black leather by light troops, these types of accoutrements, with haversacks and wooden or metal water bottles slung separately, remained in general use with most armies throughout the Napoleonic Wars and well into the 19th century.

Three 1:12 Airfix Imperial Guard figures by B. Harris. The Voltigeur or skirmisher of the 29th Infantry, 1809, illustrated opposite shows the position of the bayonet scabbard and pouch, attached to cross-belts as on the Grenadier 'à pied' below. The Artilleryman 'à pied' on the right shows pouch, sword and bayonet, knapsack and blanket very clearly.

Waistbelts

In the middle of the 19th century, the cross-belts began to be replaced, first in the Prussian and French armies, by a waistbelt to which were attached a bayonet frog and one or two ammunition pouches, the weight being supported by braces over both shoulders. Knapsacks, now of a more rigid construction and often with great-

coats and camp equipment attached to them, were secured by their straps to the braces. Haversacks and water bottles either hung from the waistbelt or were slung separately. The chief material remained white, black or brown leather. Variations on this theme were adopted by all armies from about 1860 onwards and were continued by most, with certain modifications, until World War 2.

Webbing
Experiments in the United States with webbing cartridge belts and British experience in colonial campaigns led, first, to the reintroduction of the bandolier as an ammunition carrier with individual cartridge loops or small pouches, and subsequently, in the decade before World War 1, to the use of webbing equipment in one assembly, with small pouches containing rounds in clips for the magazine rifle, by both British and US armies.

World War 1 saw the readoption of protective helmets and even, in some armies, body armour, which today is still used but in the more sophisticated version of the bullet-proof jacket. In World War 2 the widespread use of magazine-fed, automatic weapons required larger ammunition pouches. Since 1945 most armies have followed the British and American lead by adopting lighter equipment in webbing or modern fibres, with the weight distributed evenly over the shoulders and hips, rather than on the back. Nowadays, with infantry driven to battle in armoured vehicles or flown there by air, the foot soldier has most of his burden carried for him.

Officers
In the 17th, 18th and much of the 19th centuries, most infantry officers had their personal kit transported and so had only their swords to carry. The method of suspension evolved from the mid-17th century embroidered baldrick worn over the shoulder to the waistbelt with frog worn under the coat. From the late 18th to the mid-19th centuries this was generally replaced by a shoulder belt, either with frog or slings, though some officers retained the waistbelt. Throughout the latter half of the 19th century a waistbelt with slings was most customary, to which a revolver holster was attached in due course. In some armies officers carried their own knapsacks, in others only haversacks and water bottles, while extra items like binoculars, compass and map cases were added. The brown leather belt with brace, designed in about 1860 by a one-armed Indian Cavalry officer, Sam Browne, to carry his sword and revolver, was subsequently adopted in one form or another by most armies. The unsuitability of the sword for modern warfare and the need, in both World Wars, for officers to assimilate their appearance to that of their men, led to their gradually adopting the same accoutrements.

Below *'Bringing up the rations' by R. Philpott; two Tommies of World War 1 struggle through the mud with an ammunition box. Puttees and chest pouches are typical of this period. Scratch-built.*
Opposite *A scratch-built 60mm Roman Legionary in marching order, by Peter Wilcox. The forked stick coped with all the impedimenta.*

Cavalry

The cavalryman carried only his weapons and ammunition on his person. From the 17th to the mid-18th century his sword was suspended from either a shoulder or waistbelt with frog, and the carbine, when not fastened to the horse, was attached to a steel swivel hanging from a broad belt over the left shoulder. In some cases the ammunition pouch was slung from a separate shoulder belt, in others it was joined to the carbine belt, a practice which became general in the later 18th century. The lobster-tailed helmet of the 17th century was finally abandoned by the early years of the 18th, but the cuirass was worn by some heavy cavalry up to the late 19th.

For most of the 18th century the sword belt was worn round the waist under the coat. The regiments of hussars raised by Austria in the late 17th century carried their swords from slings attached to a waistbelt, from which also hung a sabretache, originally a bag for the hussar's personal kit. By the Napoleonic Wars the sling waistbelt, and in many cases the sabretache, had been adopted by all cavalry, although the chief purpose of the latter, now highly decorative, was to protect the horse's flanks from the loosely hanging sword. If the horse was over-encumbered, the haversack and water bottle were both slung over the man's right shoulder to leave the sword arm free.

The combined carbine and pouch belt and sling waistbelt remained in use for most of the 19th century, the latter usually being worn under the tunic by light

Above *A French Napoleonic cavalryman endeavours to extricate his horse from swampy ground. This model by W. Lascom uses Historex 54mm parts and demonstrates that horses need not be shown in a formal pose.*
Opposite *The Samurai are a rich part of Japan's history and form elaborate and colourful subjects for figure modellers. This superb model of a Samurai of 1600 by Daniel McKay carries the usual vast assortment of weapons and typical fighting headgear.*

cavalry. By 1914 the sword and carbine had generally been transferred from the man to the horse and the cavalryman carried his ammunition either in a bandolier or pouches of infantry pattern. When the horse was superseded by the armoured fighting vehicle, the mounted man only required a skeleton equipment to carry a few rounds for his personal weapon, first a holstered revolver and more recently a machine-carbine.

Cavalry officers' accoutrements generally followed those of their men but without carbine attachments. When the revolver replaced the pistol, formerly carried on the saddle, its holster was attached to the sword belt. Until the adoption of more serviceable clothing and equipment for field use, the officers' belts were always more ornate than the men's white or black leather, being covered with gold or silver lace.

Horse artillery accoutrements resembled the cavalry's though without carbine belts, while foot artillery and engineers usually had infantry equipment.

Samurai

Horses

The history of the horse can be traced back as far as 2000 BC and since then man has cherished the horse as his servant and friend in both peace and war. Of the many models produced by today's manufacturers, mounted figures depicting this relationship throughout the ages account for about 60 per cent of the market. Therefore at some period in his hobby the military modeller, unless devoted to the foot figures, will attempt a mounted model.

Metal kit horses
Metal models of horses are the simplest to assemble, consisting of approximately six main parts – head, left and right body halves, tail, stirrups and reins. The bridle and saddle are usually moulded on to their respective parts.

File off any casting lines and check the fit of the parts before assembling the model. Use one of the epoxy or contact adhesives for fixing the parts together, but leave off the stirrups and bit rein until the model has been painted.

Metal horses do not lend themselves easily to conversion or animation work, being designed as a model intended to be built as shown in the kit instructions. Conversion work *can* be carried out on metal horses, but as this usually involves major surgical work, due to the number of items such as the saddle being moulded integrally with the body halves, it is best left to the experienced modeller.

Animation of the legs, head and tail can easily be accomplished by gently bending the part to the desired position. A small vice would be useful to hold the model secure, as would a pair of pliers to ease the bending of the limbs and a hacksaw blade for making small cuts in the legs at the knee or hock. Remember that the weight of the horse and rider will have to be supported by the legs after animating them, so that if it is necessary to cut right through the leg to reposition it, holes should

be drilled into both parts and a small pin inserted to strengthen the limb. A cut may also be made in the throat to help move the head to the required position. Fill in saw cuts with a suitable body filler and build up any muscle that may have been destroyed; check the rest of the model for any gaps in the joint lines and fill these also. Use a small file to remove any excess filler, then wet and dry paper to smooth and blend the filler into the model. The model is now ready to be undercoated prior to commencement of painting.

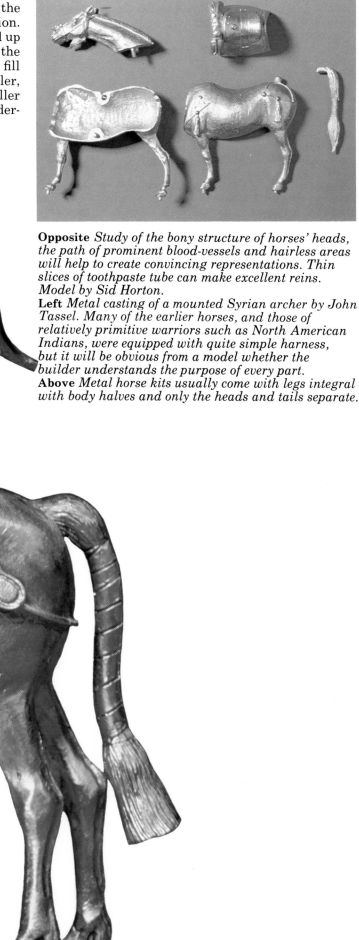

Opposite *Study of the bony structure of horses' heads, the path of prominent blood-vessels and hairless areas will help to create convincing representations. Thin slices of toothpaste tube can make excellent reins. Model by Sid Horton.*
Left *Metal casting of a mounted Syrian archer by John Tassel. Many of the earlier horses, and those of relatively primitive warriors such as North American Indians, were equipped with quite simple harness, but it will be obvious from a model whether the builder understands the purpose of every part.*
Above *Metal horse kits usually come with legs integral with body halves and only the heads and tails separate.*

Plastic kit horses

Here one manufacturer stands supreme, Historex. They have about eight standard horses in their range and each one comprises two body halves, head, mane, forelock and tail. All the parts are interchangeable with their respective counterparts, so producing an endless number of combinations. The saddles are moulded separately, usually in two main halves, and will fit on to any of the horse combinations. When purchasing a Historex mounted kit, it is possible to choose the horse position that you require, or alternatively select and purchase the parts from their comprehensive range of spares. Due to the range of parts available and the ease with which plastic can be cut and worked, conversions may be attempted by the inexperienced modeller if care and patience are exercised. Excellent horse models in a variety of scales are also produced by US companies like Breyer of Chicago, Squadron/Rubin and Series 77 of California – the last two firms offering metal castings, Breyer's products coming in tough plastic.

Animation can be performed following the same procedure as that used for metal, but applying heat to the area of the joint to be bent, either from a flame (with care) or from a flameless source such as a soldering iron or a Pyrogravure. Take care, as only a small amount of heat is required to soften the plastic and make it workable. Another idea is to cut the horse halves into quarters along the saddle girth line, giving different combinations of leg positions when used with other Historex horses. Always check that the pose of the horse retains its natural appearance after animating.

Above *A hussar of the Elite Company, French 5th Regiment, about 1812. A Historex conversion by Graham Brown.*
Below *Plastic horses as supplied in kit form.*
Opposite *Major-General Montcalm by David Hunter.*

Assembly

Clean off all the moulding lines before assembling the main components. Start with the two body halves, checking that the legs, if all four are on the ground, are square when stood on a flat surface. The head and neck along with the ears are the next parts to be cemented in place. After the cement has dried, fill any gaps in the joints with body filler and file to a smooth finish.

Parts of the bridle are already cast on the head but, depending on the figure being modelled, various other straps will have to be added to complete the bridle. Plastic card cut to the correct thickness and length is used and cemented in place with one of the liquid cements. Extra buckles and bridle ornaments are all supplied with the kits and these, along with the bits, are cemented in place. Leave the reins to be added when the completed horse and rider are united after painting.

When assembling the model to the stage of painting, some modellers prefer to divide the model into three items: horse, saddle and rider. Slight disadvantages can be encountered with this method, especially for the beginner, when the saddle is fitted on to the horse, in obtaining a proper fit and alignment of girth and breast straps.

The alternative is to assemble the saddle, check the fit on the horse and, if necessary, carve or file away the underside so that a correct sit is obtained before cementing in place. Add the surcingle, girth, crupper and breast straps, made from plastic card or thinly sliced metal from an empty toothpaste tube, but not the stirrups, which are again fitted after painting.

The mane, forelock and tail as supplied with the kit are cemented in place and many modellers tend to roughen up the texture of the hair with a pyrogravure or a heated needle. Some even discard these plastic parts and use fine, coloured nylon 'hair' to represent the mane and tail, which must be added after the horse has been painted; it is a personal choice as to which method is employed.

If the horse is modelled with one of its legs raised, a V-shaped cut is made in the rear of the hoof, opening out towards the heel. Horseshoes from either the spares box or made from plastic card are fitted, the open end of the shoe pointing towards the rear.

Opposite *Graham Bickerton was responsible for this splendid trumpeter of the Orleans Cavalry of 1724, a 90mm model built from a Poste Militaire kit. The figure won first prize at the 1979 Northern Militaire exhibition in England.*
Left *The unfinished head of L. Martin Rendall's rearing horse in carved wood and Milliput is remarkably expressive, mixing fear and hatred. Shiny finishes on horses are common, but the only time a horse shines is when it is terrified. The normal coat has only a little sheen; exertion darkens it without increasing gloss.*

115

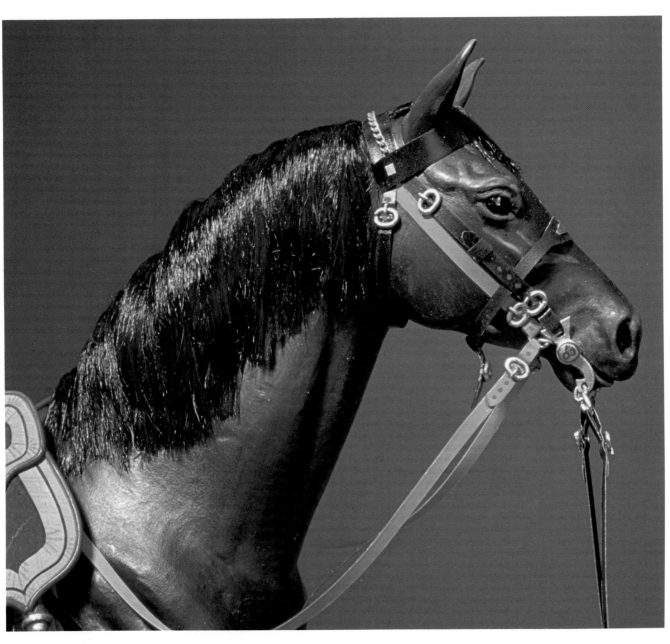

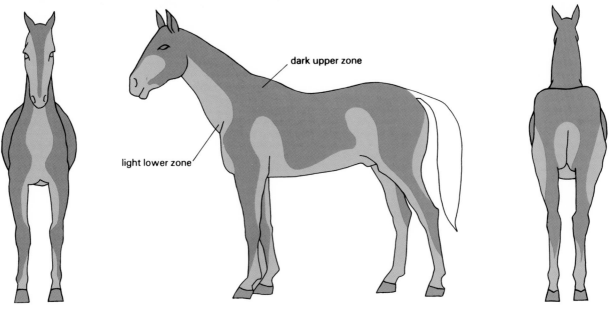

dark upper zone

light lower zone

Painting a horse

Both metal and plastic horses have now reached the stage where they are ready to be undercoated prior to painting. Research the intended subject thoroughly or you could end up with Napoleon mounted on a piebald that would have done justice to Geronimo! Cavalry regiments tried to keep a uniformity of colour throughout with their horses, the heavy units mounted on dark bays and blacks, the lighter units preferring to monopolize the paler colours such as the light and cherry bays, although on campaign this trend would be hard to uphold. Trumpeters, as a rule, were mounted on greys, but again there were exceptions.

Undercoat the horse with a matt finish enamel of an appropriate colour. Most modellers prefer oil paints when it comes to painting horses, due to their richness of colour and the fact that oil paint will dry to a slight sheen, simulating the natural faint gloss of a real horse. Paint the horse in its base coat, following the direction of hair growth with the brush. The coat of a horse is rarely a uniform colour and to help with this, the horse should be split into two sections, upper and lower. Basically the upper zone is of a darker tone, achieved by the addition of black to the base colour, which is carefully blended in. A rich light tone is then applied to the lower zone and into the muscular depressions at the top of the legs.

Any distinctive markings such as a blaze on the face or socks at the base of the legs can now be added. If the horse is shown with a number of white socks the hoofs should be painted a light greyish yellow, whereas hoofs without socks tend to be a dark grey or brown.

When painting the eyes, hardly any white should be visible, and what there is should be limited to the corners only. Emphasize the eye with deep shadows and highlights along the lids; with some of the greys, the eyes were surrounded by a marked area of black.

Opposite Larger models of horses can use combed nylon manes and tails successfully, as an alternative to pyrogravure engraving. Model by Bernie Harris.
Below *Light and shade and hair growth direction illustrated.*

The muzzle skin is hairless, as are the lips and nostrils, and should be painted a pinky grey shade. Sometimes these areas had distinctive markings, so check on any illustration references you have.

Subtle shadows are painted into the muscle depressions and then highlights are added. Any dappling that may appear on the horse is also applied at this stage, with the point of a small brush and following the coat of the horse. Reference must be made for the colour of the mane and tail, due to the various colour combinations that occur. A light grey horse will not necessarily have the same colour mane and tail – it can be black, golden yellow or pure white. Paint the mane and tail in a darker tone of the intended colour, then drybrush over with a lighter shade to pick out the highlights of the hair.

Paint the harness and straps in the appropriate colour and depict the leather finish by adding touches of highlights, not by using varnish, which would give a high gloss finish. Enamel paints are used for the buckles and any other parts of the harness fittings.

All that remains is to paint the saddle, adopting the same techniques as those used in figure painting, before adding the completed rider along with the stirrups and reins. Plastic card, paper, or the lead foil previously mentioned are just some of the materials that can be cut into strips to represent reins; care should be taken when fixing them to the rider's hands, as riding styles differed from country to country.

An additional touch favoured by some modellers when painting a cavalry mount in the field, such as in action in dry conditions, is to make the legs seem dusty. After the completed horse is thoroughly dry, dry brush a thin coating of dull ochre oil paint over the legs. This should be thin enough not to obliterate the leg colour or any detail – simply a very subtle, dull dusting. The 'dust' may be extended on to the boots of the rider.

It is advisable to build a small reference library of colour pictures of horses, either inexpensive or moderately priced picture books on horses or magazines for horse fanciers. Another excellent reference source, which includes a number of colour pictures, is the latest Historex catalogue.

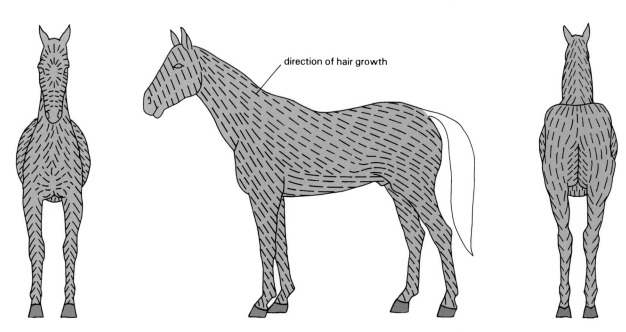

direction of hair growth

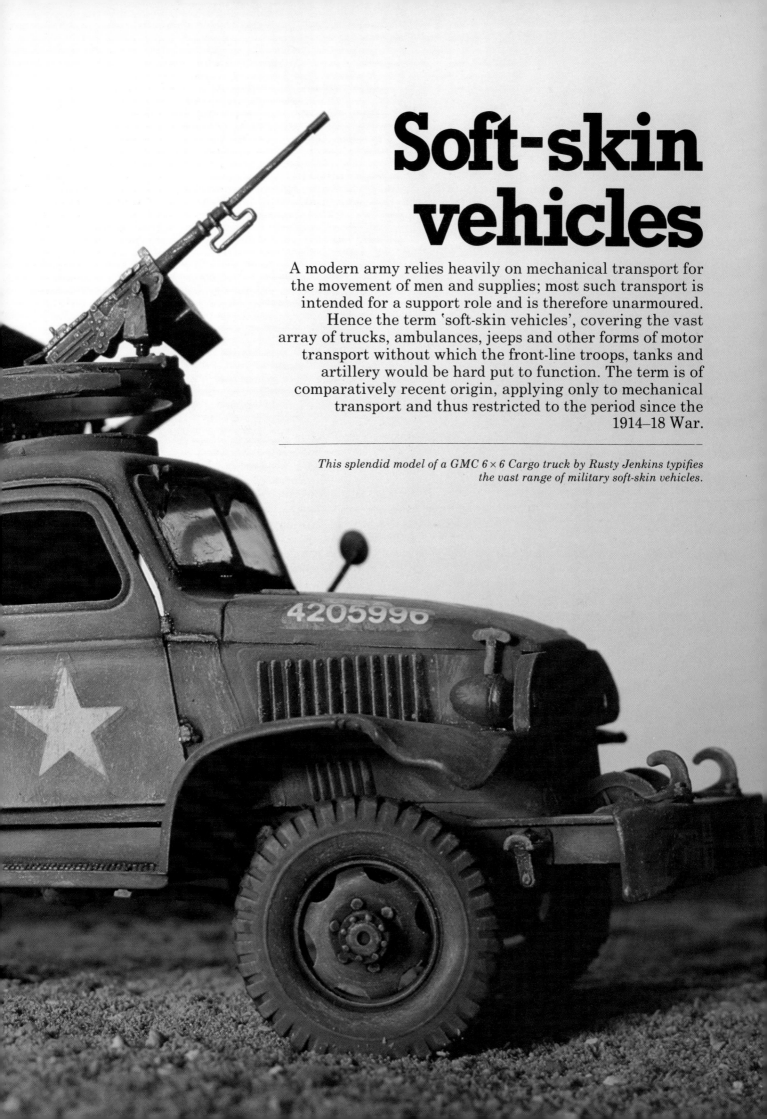

Soft-skin vehicles

A modern army relies heavily on mechanical transport for the movement of men and supplies; most such transport is intended for a support role and is therefore unarmoured. Hence the term 'soft-skin vehicles', covering the vast array of trucks, ambulances, jeeps and other forms of motor transport without which the front-line troops, tanks and artillery would be hard put to function. The term is of comparatively recent origin, applying only to mechanical transport and thus restricted to the period since the 1914–18 War.

This splendid model of a GMC 6 × 6 Cargo truck by Rusty Jenkins typifies the vast range of military soft-skin vehicles.

Introduction

'Soft-skin' vehicles – in other words, non-armoured – have, until recently, been less popular as modelling subjects, due mainly to the lack of suitable kits from which to work and perhaps also because of the undeniable glamour that surrounds the 'hardware' – the armoured fighting vehicles. The kit manufacturers have naturally placed greater emphasis on producing models of tanks over the years and only recently have they turned to the humbler trucks for their new releases. It is perhaps worth remembering that, however glamorous the tanks may be, they would not get very far without the continual flow of supplies which are brought up by the trucks, so they are both equally important in their respective spheres.

Regrettably, there are still comparatively few kits available of pure *transport* military vehicles, and consequently a high degree of kit conversion or complete scratch-building will be required to build up a collection of representative military transport vehicles. Nevertheless, the few kits of trucks that are available are good quality products that will result in a satisfactory model if built straight from the box, but, as will be shown, the addition of careful extra detailing and painting can turn them into the 'supermodel' class.

Superdetailing

As far as extra detailing is concerned, this largely depends on the scale. Obviously, as for any model, the larger the scale the more detail that can be incorporated. However, a surprising amount of detail can be added to even 1:76 scale models, and in the final analysis it all comes down to the preferences – and level of dedication – of the individual modeller.

Cab interiors

Most kits provide a fair amount of detail inside cabs or drivers' compartments, and in most cases the extra detailing will cover small items such as switches, brackets, straps, etc. Even in 1:76 scale seats, steering wheel and perhaps gear lever are supplied, and in some models this is all that can be seen anyway. In this case the degree of detailing has to be tempered with common sense – there is no point whatever in adding items that will not be visible in the finished model.

It is, of course, important to *know* what you are adding to your model. There is no point adding what you think *might* be there – a situation which applies to any model. If you are not sure what the interior fittings are, the best idea when practicable is to examine a preserved vehicle at a museum or military vehicle rally. There are a number of such rallies held in various locations and from past experience the owners will usually let you examine their vehicles if you ask nicely and take care.

In 1:35 scale or larger, the cab interior is a much more important part of the model. Even on models with a full cab, a lot of the interior will be visible through the windows and it is worthwhile making this area look as authentic as possible. Opposite is the sort of detail that should be added in a 1:35 scale model. Some of it may look insignificant, but it all helps to make the model look authentic.

In some kits the foot pedals may be moulded in relief on the floor or bulkhead. If this area is not very visible in the finished model, this deficiency can be covered up with careful painting, but if they can be seen it is worth removing as much of the mouldings as possible and replacing them with made up items. Handbrakes and gear levers can often be improved by adding more

Opposite *A Chevrolet 15cwt truck by Mac Kennaugh in 1:35 scale from Japanese Max moulds, now produced and marketed by Airfix.*
Right *An SAS Jeep of the type widely used by the British for special missions in the North African deserts during World War 2. A condenser was fitted ahead of the radiator grille and as many cans of fuel and water as possible were stowed. Weapons varied, but twin Vickers and a Browning machine gun were common. A Tamiya 1:35 scale model by Don Skinner.*
Below *Interior cab details that could be added to a model. Many of these items can be made from plastic card or stretched sprue.*

effective gaiters from scraps of tissue paper. In most kits the moulded instruments are quite reasonable and only require careful painting, but switches and knobs tend to be moulded in relief and these will look much better if they are cut off and replaced with made up items. (Making simple knobs from plastic rod using a heat source such as a candle is shown on page 123.)

The addition of internal body construction also depends on final visibility and also the kit construction method. If a cab door is moulded 'solid' whereas the full

size is actually an outer skin over a framework, then it might be worth replacing the door with an item built up from plastic card. This particularly applies if the model is to be displayed in a diorama setting and the door will be fixed in an open position. One final area to be considered in a cab interior is the roof. In most military trucks the roof is just a skin over a simple framework, but there are occasionally details that can be added, particularly the hipring (not fitted to *all* military trucks) if this is not included in the kit (see page 123).

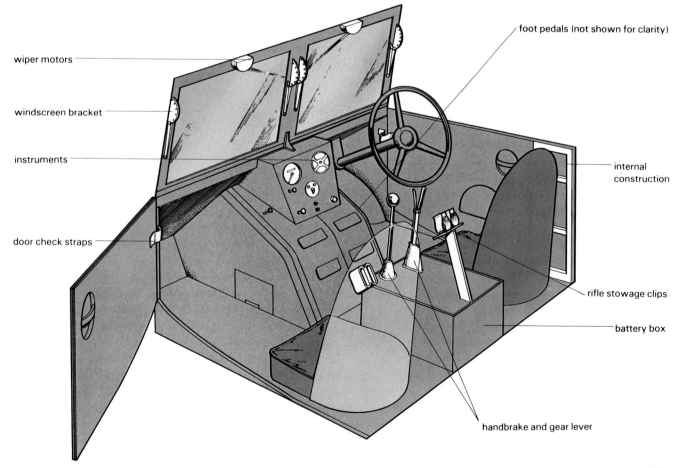

wiper motors

windscreen bracket

instruments

door check straps

foot pedals (not shown for clarity)

internal construction

rifle stowage clips

battery box

handbrake and gear lever

Detailing chassis and wheels

The chassis is a visible part of a truck model and should be treated as such. The detail included in most truck kits is usually quite adequate to show the major assemblies and the most important task is to ensure that all mould lines are filed and sanded away and all parts are cemented together correctly so that the model sits squarely on its wheels. The removal of mould lines is particularly important in such items as springs, where it is desirable to create the correct effect of flat leaves clamped together by U-bolts and clamps. Page 123 shows a few of the details that can be added to the chassis around the front axle, if they are not already included in the kit. Track rods are included in most of the larger scale truck kits, but the steering linkage is usually not. On some military trucks this can be seen clearly at the front of the vehicle, and the addition of the linkage will improve the appearance of the model immensely.

The final detail on the chassis that must not be forgotten is the tow hook at the rear. The leaf-sprung drawbar on British military vehicles, for example, was a standard WD pattern, and so this component should look the same on most models of British trucks. Page 128 shows this drawbar, and note that it was not in fact a complete fixture but was merely located in the slots in the end brackets (attached to the chassis side frames) so that some movement was allowed.

Wheels in most kits are generally quite suitable to be used as they are, but occasionally there is scope for some extra detailing on such items as wheelnuts and tyre valves. Tyres are not likely to require any detailing, but their appearance can be improved by 'scuffing' the tread to present a more realistic 'used' appearance, as in the photos. Hold the wheel in one hand and sand around the circumference quite heavily so that the mould line is removed and the sharp corners rounded off a little. There will be a build up of waste plastic 'dust' in the treads, and this can be attended to by brushing on fairly liberal quantities of liquid plastic cement, taking care not to let any of it mark the actual wheel.

Detailing the exterior

This depends very much on the scale of the model and also the type of vehicle – some trucks are fairly neat and smooth in appearance, others appear to be festooned with assorted brackets, hooks, handles, etc. Even on a 1:76 scale model a considerable amount of extra detail can be incorporated, including detail supplied in the kit that can be replaced with items of finer or more scale-like appearance. This particularly applies to such things as ladders, which are invariably far too chunky in appearance due to limitations on fineness of moulding. Building a ladder in this small scale is a tricky undertaking requiring the use of a jig, but the result will be well worth it. (See opposite.)

Below *A simple basic chassis and two methods of making scale-appearance springs, with a close-up showing the spring in position with the axle.*
Opposite *Typical exterior details of vehicles and some easy ways of producing them in plastic using styrene rod and fuse wire.*

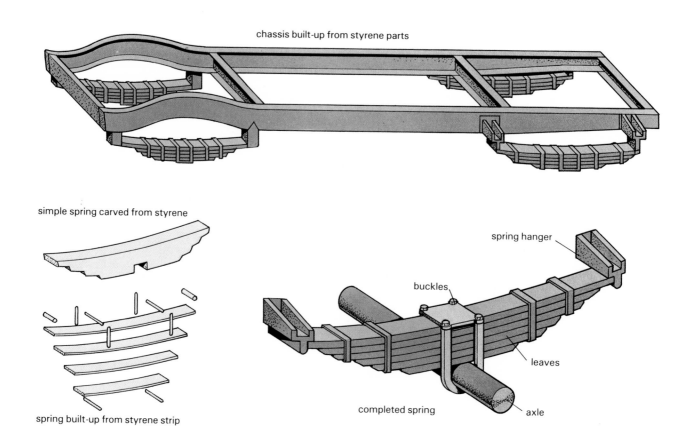

chassis built-up from styrene parts

simple spring carved from styrene

spring built-up from styrene strip

spring hanger

buckles

leaves

completed spring

axle

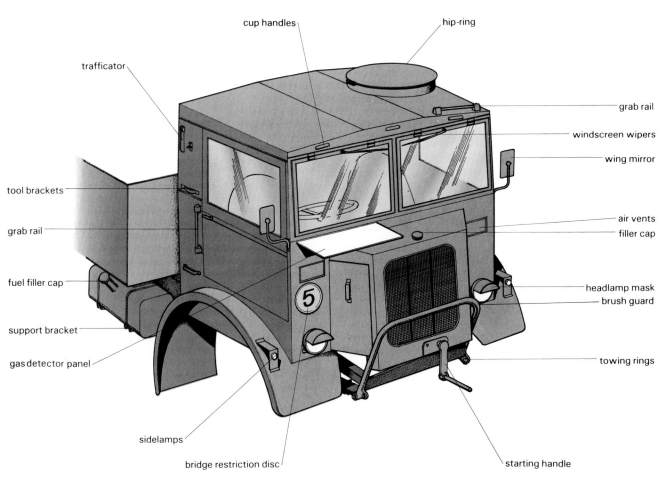

trafficator

cup handles

hip-ring

grab rail

windscreen wipers

wing mirror

tool brackets

grab rail

air vents

filler cap

fuel filler cap

headlamp mask

brush guard

support bracket

gas detector panel

towing rings

sidelamps

bridge restriction disc

starting handle

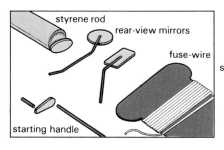

styrene rod

finished gear-stick

twist rod in candle flame

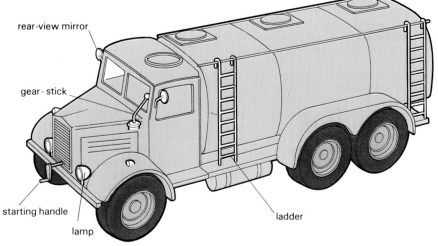

rear-view mirror

gear-stick

starting handle

lamp

ladder

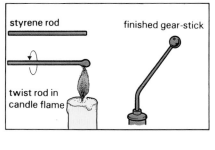

styrene rod

rear-view mirrors

fuse-wire

starting handle

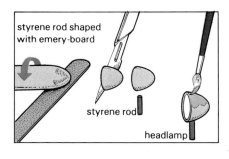

styrene rod shaped with emery-board

styrene rod

headlamp

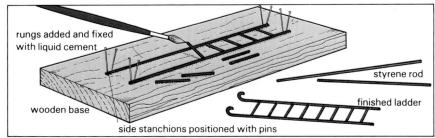

rungs added and fixed with liquid cement

wooden base

side stanchions positioned with pins

styrene rod

finished ladder

The larger the scale, then of course the greater amount of detail that can be shown, and in 1:35 scale it is even possible to incorporate working hinges for such items and tailboards and spare wheel carriers. This can be done quite easily using plastic rod. Some kits make an attempt at these working features anyway, but the results do vary in strength.

Illustrated on page 123 are some of the items that can be added to the front of a model. Extra details such as grab rails, tool brackets and brush guards can all be made from plastic card, microstrip, plastic rod, etc., and should not cause any problems. Starting handles and lamp brackets are just a little trickier and care should be taken to see that they are fitted in the correct position. Even if the parts are supplied in the kit it is worth checking to ensure that they are fitted where they should be – for example, the starting handle on the Bandai 1:48 scale Austin K5 is intended to be mounted on the centre line, but in fact the engine in the K5 is offset a few inches towards the nearside, and the starting handle should be repositioned accordingly.

References for extra detail that could be added around the rear end of a model truck are easily found. Planking and framing might well be already moulded on the kit parts, as in the Hasegawa G.M.C. kits, for example, but these can still be improved by the addition of small but significant extras. The rubbing strip along the lower edge of the body is fixed to the outer edge of the framing and consequently there is sometimes a gap between the strip and the body side proper. The correct duplication of this feature will improve the appearance of the model significantly. Mudflaps, even when sup-plied with the kit, could well be replaced with thinner items from plastic card, with the stays added from microstrip. Tailboards on trucks invariably had one or two pairs of cut-outs which acted as steps to help the troops climb aboard when the tailboard was hanging down, and the positions for these should be carefully checked from plans or pictures.

Below *One of the boxier-type bodies was that of this Austin ambulance. Don Skinner has added a lot of small detail to this 1:76 model from the Airfix HO/OO series.*
Bottom *Tamiya offers a range of 1:35 scale soft-skin vehicles; this is a Chevrolet as used by the British Long Range Desert Group in World War 2. Model by Don Skinner. Other Tamiya kits include a Kübelwagen, a BMW R75 and sidecar, a Willys jeep, a Horch and a lwb Land Rover ambulance.*

Constructing tilt hoops and covers

On general service (Cargo) trucks and some other types, the load was protected from the elements by a tilt cover. This usually consisted of a large one-piece canvas sheet draped over a simple framework and tied down to the hooks on the body sides. The correct duplication of this feature is essential for the appearance of a model, whatever the scale. On page 126 is a typical tilt frame arrangement with three transverse hoops and seven longitudinals. This arrangement was fairly standard on three-tonners, but larger vehicles might have a greater number of transverse hoops, whereas smaller vehicles would still have three hoops but would not have any longitudinals.

On a model the hoops can be bent to shape from plastic rod, warming the plastic and using round-nosed pliers to give the correct corner radius. Most round-nosed pliers are supplied with tapering jaws, and the plastic rod can be gripped in the jaws in the appropriate position to give the required radius. The hoops should be glued in place on the model first and allowed to set before the longitudinals are added. Check that the hoops are set square and upright and are not twisted, and also that the hoops sit in line with each other viewed from the end. On a 1:76 scale model the tilt frame can be simplified – if the cover is being fitted – by leaving out two or three of the longitudinals, but the number of

transverse hoops should *never* be reduced.

The tilt cover should preferably not be fitted until the remainder of the model has been painted, and tissue paper is probably the most convenient material to use. The tissue should be cut to a rectangle of the correct size, taking the dimensions off the model and allowing for the tilt to come down to about a scale foot below the top of the body sides. For fixing the tilt in place (see next page), the use of liquid cement is advised. Lay the tissue over the frame, making certain it is centrally placed with equal amounts projecting at the sides and ends. Now wrap one side down and fix by applying small amounts of liquid cement with a brush through the tissue, so that it adheres to the points of contact underneath. Now wrap down the other side, pulling it reasonably tight and repeat the process. The ends should be folded in just like a parcel – top first and then the side flaps – and again fixed with liquid cement. For a touch of variety the rear end could be left hanging open, in which case the tissue must be teased into a series of vertical creases to make it look as though it is hanging naturally.

On the full size vehicle, the tilt is retained by ropes laced through eyelets along the edge of the cover, pulled tight over the hooks on the body sides. Page 128 shows a typical arrangement. On a 1:35 scale model it is possible with care to duplicate this arrangement correctly using cotton thread, but of course the hooks on the body sides must be made as proper hooks, as shown on page 128. In 1:76 scale the ropes can be painted on using a fine brush – the effect is quite sufficient in this scale.

Below *Civilian vehicles were adapted in World War 1; this US Balloon Tender was a stake truck. 1:35 scale model by R. Wright. The rest of this prizewinning diorama is shown on page 181.*

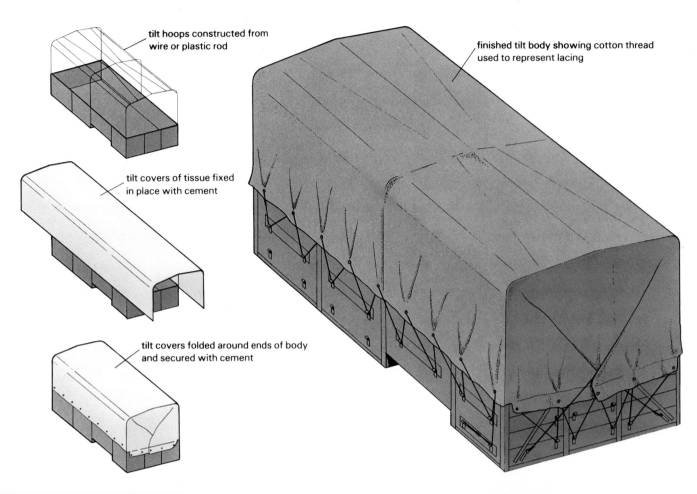

tilt hoops constructed from
wire or plastic rod

finished tilt body showing cotton thread
used to represent lacing

tilt covers of tissue fixed
in place with cement

tilt covers folded around ends of body
and secured with cement

Simple conversions

There are innumerable simple conversions that can be carried out on the available truck kits, a change of body being the most obvious. Perhaps the simplest of all in 1:76 scale is to make a Bedford QL GS by fitting the body from the Airfix Matador straight on to the QL refueller cab/chassis from the Airfix Refuelling Set. The body will need shortening by removing one bay from each side and trimming the floor by a corresponding amount, but this is virtually the only extra work involved. The resulting GS body style is not strictly accurate for QLs, but nevertheless it does make an ideal first conversion for beginners.

The many and various body types that were fitted to military vehicle chassis were generally built as simple as possible, with very few double curvatures or similar features that were undesirable in wartime production conditions, and consequently are quite easy to simulate in model form. A Cargo body in particular is basically just a box, and so even the beginner will find these a simple introduction to the art of plastic card construction. Some Cargo bodies had shallow wheel arches for the rear wheels, others were completely flat floored. Box bodies (usually known as 'house type' in military parlance) are a little more involved, the curved roof requiring the most attention (see page 130).

Even in 1:76 scale the floor should be cut from 60 thou. plastic card, as this is after all the main structural component. For the walls 20 or 30 thou. will be sufficient, and do not be tempted to fall into the trap of using thinner plastic card just because it is easier to cut. Butt joints will be most suitable at corners, etc.; mitred joints should only be used where special circumstances arise. For the curved roof there are two methods to choose from – laminating or moulding. Laminating involves cementing two or more sheets of thick plastic card together and then carving and filing to shape *after* the glue has set thoroughly. Moulding involves using a heat source to produce a shaped part over a prepared wooden mould, and the method for this is shown in detail below. All minor details on these simple conversions are added just as already described in earlier paragraphs on superdetailing.

Advanced conversions

Having gained useful experience in plastic card construction on simple conversions, the modeller can now extend this logically by trying conversions which are a

Opposite above *Realistic tilt covers are simple.*
Opposite below *Canadian Military Pattern cab on a 15cwt Chevrolet, a 1:32 Airfix model by David Jane.*
Below *Moulding of plastic parts is not difficult, though a little practice is necessary to judge the right degree of heat. When held in front of an electric fire, or above a radiant hot plate, the styrene will suddenly appear floppy, at which point the male mould should be pressed against it. For a deep draw as illustrated rewarming may be needed; if only the front section of the pattern is required, as drawn, a smaller female plate could be used. The moulding should be 8–9mm (⅜in) deeper than necessary so that any buckling which may occur can be cut away to leave a distortion-free part. Acetate sheet can be similarly moulded.*

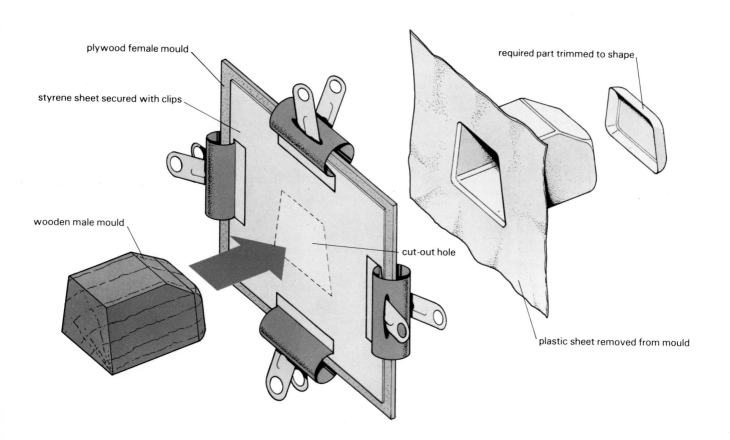

plywood female mould
styrene sheet secured with clips
wooden male mould
required part trimmed to shape
cut-out hole
plastic sheet removed from mould

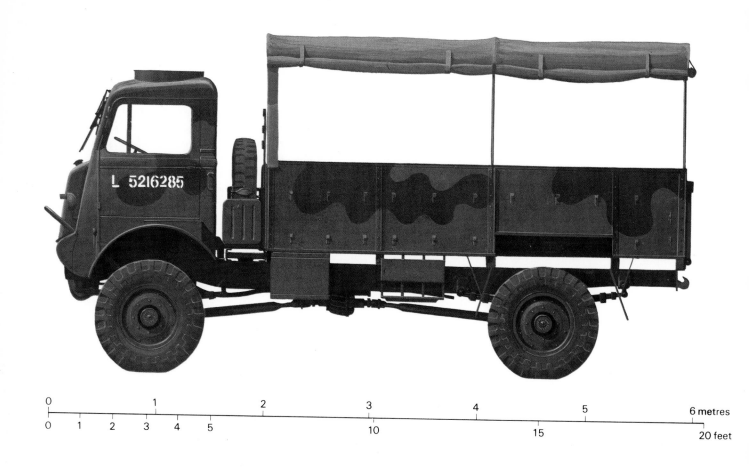

Opposite *The Bedford QLD 3-ton GS truck. The exposed chassis and simple box body are typical of military vehicles. Note the leaf-sprung drawbar and hooks for tilt lacing.*
Above and below *A Dodge ambulance from a 1:35 Max kit, with some conversion work, by Rusty Jenkins.*

little more involved. This can vary from just lengthening the wheelbase to model a longer version of the same truck, right up to altering the kit vehicle to an entirely different type, with perhaps a new cab as well as body. At this level the dividing line between conversion and scratch-building becomes rather fine. However, as a rough guide, if a kit chassis is still being used as a basis, then the model is a conversion: if the chassis is a handmade structure then the result is a scratch-built model, even if parts such as axles and wheels, which are difficult to construct from scratch, are still being taken from suitable kits.

Body structures will be obviously the same as discussed earlier, and the difference between 'simple' and 'advanced' in this case is merely in the work that the modeller feels capable of putting into the model, according to his experience. The significant advancement in this section will come from having to construct new cabs which are obviously much more involved structures. Fortunately from a modelling point of view, most military vehicle cabs are very utilitarian, boxy structures with few curves to worry about and are therefore a relatively straightforward modelling proposition. Sides, front and rear should be marked out on 30 thou. plastic card and the windows cut out before separating the sheet into individual parts. The task of cutting windows out can be made easier by drilling the corners very carefully first and then connecting with careful knife cuts. Once the waste is removed, the apertures can be cleaned up with needle files. Glazing can be a tricky problem if not tackled carefully and the most important point to note is that, if the cab sides are more than 30 thou. thick, the glazing must be cut to fit *within*

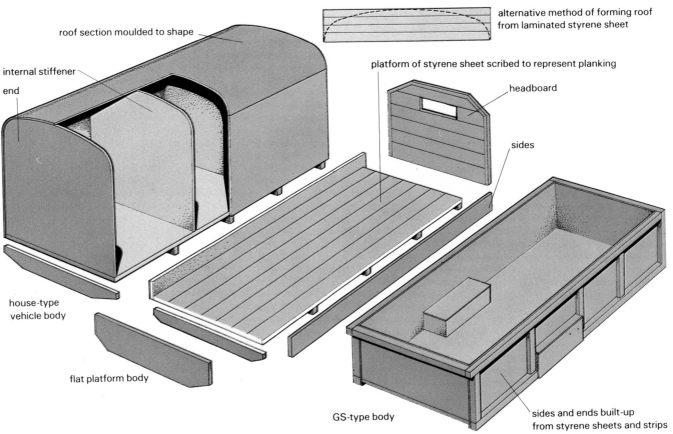

roof section moulded to shape

alternative method of forming roof from laminated styrene sheet

internal stiffener

end

platform of styrene sheet scribed to represent planking

headboard

sides

house-type vehicle body

flat platform body

GS-type body

sides and ends built-up from styrene sheets and strips

Above *Despatch riders are quite common in dioramas, adding perhaps a sense of urgency, but their machines are usually in small scales. This is a 1:9 model of the Triumph 3HW solo 350cc bike from an Esci kit, built by Frank Cook. Sadly motorcycles, particularly military ones, are somewhat neglected by kit manufacturers. However, Tamiya produce in 1:35 scale the rather curious German Kettenkraftrad motorcycle half-track and a US military police set.*
Left *House type, platform, and General Service (GS) or Cargo bodies with constructional suggestions. Note how it is advisable to scribe the styrene sheet to represent planking where it is visible.*

the aperture, not just glued behind it, otherwise the scale effect will look wrong.

Cab roofs can be constructed from either the laminating or moulding method, the latter being preferable, especially in 1:35 scale where the cab interior is more visible. There are some military vehicles – the AEC Matador for example – that have simple roofs without double curvatures, and these will obviously be easier to construct. At the other extreme, those military vehicles that were based on contemporary commercial types – early Chevrolets being a classic example – had cabs that were formed almost entirely of pressings having double curvatures, and these will be far harder to duplicate, necessitating in some cases the entire construction being of moulded panels in almost the same way as the full-size vehicle.

Scratch-building

When the stage is reached of having to construct new chassis as well as cabs and bodies, then the model can be regarded as a 'scratch-built' one, and to many modellers this is the most satisfying stage of all. There are still some parts that are very difficult to construct and may be taken from suitable kits – engines, wheels and axles being the obvious examples – but there is a definite sense of achievement in knowing that your model started life as nothing more than a sheet of plastic!

Chassis frames may look awesome at first sight, but in fact will be relatively easy to construct. Most military vehicle chassis are constructed on the ladder frame principle with side frames that generally are parallel in plan and usually of constant depth, although they may taper upwards at the rear in side elevation on some types, and there may also be some upsweep over the axles, usually at the front. In 1:76, a suitable assembly of 40 or 60 thou. strips will be sufficient, but in the larger scales some attempt at the correct section is desirable. Most chassis frames are channel section and this can be represented by cementing flanges to the upper and lower surfaces of the side members and cross members, or by using commercial strip sections (e.g. Plastruct) if the appropriate size can be found in your model shop.

Springs can be made quite simply as shown on page 122, either by laminating strips of thin plastic card or by cutting the shape from a block, the former method being preferable. Note that each strip, or 'leaf', should have its correct curve imparted to it by pulling the strip between finger and thumb. The spring brackets, and the various other brackets, flanges, etc., that may be found on a typical chassis frame can be represented by suitably shaped pieces of plastic card.

Although wheels can be taken from appropriate kits for use on a scratch-built model, this may be regarded as a rather expensive method, as the remainder of the kit is therefore more or less unusable. One way around this is to mould a series of wheels using a master wheel as a pattern. There are various ways of doing this, the simplest being to press the wheel into a block of Plasticine up to its centreline and then remove it, leaving a perfect female mould of a half wheel. This mould is then filled with an epoxy resin mixture and left to set. The result, hopefully, is a perfect reproduction of the half wheel. The inner half of the wheel is then reproduced in the same way and the two halves joined together. This method is only suitable for a very few repeats, however, and a more suitable method is to produce the female mould in one of the silicone rubber preparations that are marketed for this purpose. These moulds, once prepared, will last almost indefinitely and therefore a mini production line of useful sets of wheels can be set up quite easily.

Once the modeller has mastered the joys of plastic card construction, moulding techniques, etc., then to a certain extent he will no longer need to read instructional books, because modelmaking is such an individual pastime that no two enthusiasts will work in exactly the same way and each modelmaker will naturally develop his own shortcuts and techniques as his modelling interests develop.

13 Pounder 9cwt QF Anti-Aircraft Gun
on
Mk 4 Motor Lorry Mounting (Peerless)

Opposite *Two close-up views of G. Doorman's scratch-built model of a World War 1 13pdr 9cwt QF anti-aircraft gun on a Peerless Mk 4 motor lorry mounting. Kits of World War 1 vehicles are virtually non-existent, so scratch-building is the only answer if you want to model in this period.*
Top *The prime mover or gun tractor for the 5.5in gun shown on page 171. Model by M. C. Baskerville.*
Above *A steel-bodied version of the Morris Commercial C8 extensively used by the British in World War 2. This superb small-scale model was constructed by David Jane.*

Painting notes

The first thing to be considered is ease of painting – it is no use completely assembling a model and then finding that you cannot reach some parts of it with the paint brush, and this particularly applies in 1:76 scale.

The answer is to build the model as a set of sub-assemblies which can be finally put together when painting is complete. The cab interior should obviously be painted before the roof is fitted in place, and if glazing is being added it is usually best to fit this before painting the exterior; if the model is being airbrushed, the glazing can be masked with Scotch tape, masking tape or one of the liquid masking solutions (e.g. liquid frisket or Maskol by Humbrol).

The most convenient model sub-assemblies will usually be chassis, cab, body and wheels. These can all be painted without any undue difficulties at this stage. Painting the wheels and tyres can be made much easier by mounting each wheel on a small stem of wooden dowel rod. The rod should be carved to a taper suitable to be a tight push fit in the wheel, and a separate rod fitted to each wheel; with firm fitting mounted wheels can be held in a scrap block of balsa wood, or even a lump of Plasticine if this is more convenient. The wooden stem can be twirled between finger and thumb against a stationary brush to make painting even easier. Fortunately the wheels in most kits have a clearly defined rim, and it is best to paint the wheel disc first and when this is dry paint the tyre colour up to the rim edge.

If the model is being airbrushed, then of course the main colour of the vehicle will be taken care of, but any subsidiary camouflage colour, such as the black 'Mickey Mouse Ear' pattern on late-war British vehicles, will almost certainly have to be brush painted. Airbrushing is not suitable in this case because, apart from the intricacies of the actual pattern, there will be too many awkward corners and details to mask effectively. The best way is to pencil in the pattern lightly on to the model (making sure that the base colour is thoroughly dry first) and carefully fill in the area using a good quality soft brush.

On most military models matt paint will be the most suitable of course, but there are occasions when a semi-gloss finish will be required, especially on postwar vehicles – for reasons of 'scale effect' however a high gloss finish should never be used. There are few subsidiary colours to worry about in military models. The cab interiors are usually the same colour as the exterior, or a closely allied colour, and this applies to seat material also. The bridge classification disc on the front of the vehicles should be painted yellow, and for the gas detector panel (which was only fitted to British vehicles in the early part of the war, incidentally) a sickly, green-yellow shade is required – Humbrol HD.4 'Zinc Chromate Primer' is ideal for this. There is a strong school of thought that black paint should never be used for tyres, but a dark grey shade should be used instead. This is good advice if the tyre is to remain in an 'unweathered' state, but if it is to be weathered the distinction is not so vital, as the weathering process will automatically take care of the colour shade. Humbrol No. 67 is a suitable dark grey shade to use without having to resort to mixing.

Decals should always be applied carefully, bearing in mind that the adhesion is likely to be poor on a matt surface. It is vitally important to trim away any excess carrier film from around the edge of the decal symbol, as this will otherwise remain clearly visible.

Weathering
This is the term given to any treatment that gives a model a 'used' appearance – for example mud splashes, dripped paint, exhaust stains, etc. – and which should always be applied in a correct sequence if it is to look most effective. Try to imagine the life history of a vehicle – it will start looking obviously smart and new. The engine and chassis will soon acquire streaks of grease, oil and fuel, and this will in turn encourage the adhesion of mud, dust and other road muck. If the vehicle is not washed this travel staining will slowly advance up the vehicle, so that there is a strong film of grime around the lower half of the vehicle, which is particularly thick on the back due to the suction effect when travelling (take a look at your own car in winter to get an idea of the effect!). Careless filling of water and fuel will result in streaks running down from the filler caps. Due to constant use the paint starts wearing away and bare metal appears on cab steps, floors, rails, and other areas of regular contact. In an extreme case rust patches start appearing at significant points. This, then, is the life story of an average truck in hard, constant service, and it will be an advantage to bear it in mind when you contemplate weathering your model.

Right *The German Opel Maultier (Mule) half-track which was a conversion from the Blitz 3-tonner. Model by John Wylie.*
Below *A Krupp Protze used as a troop carrier by the Germans in World War 2. Model by Tim Simmonds.*
Opposite *A close-up of a 7th Armoured Division Bedford QL 6-pounder 'portee' from an Airfix (Max) 1:35 scale kit. Model by Mac Kennaugh.*

There are two basic techniques involved in applying weathering to any vehicle with a paint brush – wet brushing and dry brushing. The first involves sloshing fairly liberal quantities of what should be more dirty turpentine than thinned paint, so that it lodges in the cracks and crevices to help highlight the shadows. The second involves applying the minutest quantities of paint to highlight edges and corners.

Following the sequence mentioned above, the first part of the model to be attended to is the chassis. On a palette, a scrap piece of plastic card, or a plastic coffee can lid, put a blob each of matt black and matt earth colour. Dip the brush in the turpentine (use an old brush for this) and then on to the palette, mixing just a little of the black, then apply this thin mixture to the chassis, working the brush quickly but carefully. Thicken up the paint content here and there to increase the black, thin it even more in others. The effect to aim for is one of generally dirty and oil-stained mechanical components. The wheel discs can get the same treatment, using a thinner mixture. Now mix in a little of the earth colour and apply it in random areas, also applying a well-thinned earth mixture to the tyres so that it lodges in the treads and produces a dusty or muddy effect.

The body can now get a dose of the same treatment. Apply the thinned earth mixture fairly liberally over the model, remembering that it must be very thin – just a hint of earth and occasionally black. Streak it along the vehicle so that the effect of movement is apparent.

Ensure that small areas such as radiator grilles are dealt with in the same way as this helps to accentuate detail. When the effect looks satisfactory, put the model aside to dry thoroughly, preferably overnight.

Now the dry brushing can start. On the palette, mix a shade which is a few shades darker than the model colour. Now just touch the brush to the colour so there is only the minutest amount on the end, fan the brush out on a rag or tissue, then apply it to the model. The idea is to work the brush to and fro very gently so that the ends of the hairs just touch the surface. You will soon see a very faint darkening occurring at the points of contact, which will be on corners and edges, and on raised details. Then repeat the entire procedure using a colour that is a few shades lighter than the original model colour. The final result will be to heighten the effect of light and shade and give the model a surprising quality of depth. This dry brushing technique takes a lot of practice and it is advisable to try it on old models first to get the hang of it.

To get the effect of worn paint with bare metal showing through, the dry brushing technique can be used again, this time using silver paint. Here even less paint should be used and the effect should be to introduce just the merest suggestion of metal showing through on edges, etc. It is imperative not to overdo this silver dry brushing, as if too much is applied the model will just not look right. A lot of models are spoiled because the builders do not wait a sufficiently long time for the paint to dry completely.

Armoured fighting vehicles

Although armour has a long history, reference to an armoured fighting vehicle is accepted as meaning a protected self-propelled machine, and as such its history is generally held to have started in the 1914–18 War. In keeping with other 20th century innovations, development has been both rapid and extensive; the mechanical aspect tends to attract a different type of modeller from figure builders, though interests frequently overlap. How to tackle model AFVs, whether from kits, as simple or difficult conversions, or from scratch, is dealt with in this chapter.

A British Matilda II tank captured by the Germans. A 1:35 scale model by John Wylie.

Above *A German Sd Kfz 232 armoured car made from a 1:35 Tamiya kit by Don Skinner.*
Right *Armoured cars were the first protected vehicles and are still widely used today. This scratch-built Humber by John Tassel is typical of World War 2 cars. An interesting touch on this model is the fitting of German jerry-cans, quite a normal wartime procedure.*

The armoured fighting vehicle is a modern solution to the age-old military problem of a balance between offensive power, protection and mobility. Such a vehicle became a practical proposition during the late 19th century but it was not until the middle of World War 1 that the concept of a mobile heavily armed and armoured machine emerged in a definitive form.

If the history of armoured vehicles is studied, the distinct impression is formed that fighting vehicles were forced upon a very hidebound military leadership. The first actions fought by tanks were not a success, but they showed the value of these machines and gave practical experience as to how they would best be employed, and within a very short time it was realized what a valuable machine the tank was.

The military virtues of a tank are obvious; here is a vehicle which can use its mobility and protection to enable its direct-fire weapons to be brought to bear upon the enemy. Once the tank had established itself with the military it began to spawn a host of supporting vehicles, all of which needed the tank's attributes of protection and mobility. Tanks themselves began to evolve into specialized vehicles intended for different roles such as infantry support and reconnaissance, as well as general purpose types. Today tanks are main battlefield weapons, but the other services now largely operate with armoured vehicles. Thus, in addition to light and main battle tanks, much artillery of all types is self-propelled, infantry are carried by armoured personnel carriers, and armoured engineer and recovery tanks abound, as do many highly specialized types such as supply carriers and command vehicles.

The first true armoured fighting vehicles were armoured cars, and this type of vehicle is still an important item of equipment with most armies. One type of vehicle which was very important during the massive battles of World War 2 was the half-track, a combination of wheeled and tracked vehicles with front wheels and rear tracks which in its armoured form was mainly used to transport infantry. This compromise type of vehicle has now been superseded by fully tracked or wheeled types.

The impact that the armoured vehicle has made upon the art of warfare is reflected in the amount of modelling material available. The range of models is truly immense, with all types and scales being covered. The two most popular scales are 1:76 and 1:35, which roughly correspond with the two main figure scales. 1:76 is the

most favoured small scale, frequently used for war-games. In armoured vehicles this scale gives a good standard of accuracy, detail and finish, allied to small overall size and relatively modest purchasing costs, and is ideal for those making a start at AFV modelling. 1:35 scale is something of an anomaly, as 1:32 (or 54mm) scale had been established for AFV models. However, the Japanese concerns who began to manu-facture in 1:35 scale had no model soldier tradition on which to base their new military modelling industry, and they thought 1:35 scale gave a nice-sized model which could be conveniently packaged in kit form. Many of these early models were motorized.

At first it was difficult to take this scale seriously, as the models could only at best be regarded as 'model toys'. However, the Japanese manufacturers improved

their models to the extent of making them, quite simply, the best AFV models available in terms of scale accu-racy, attention to detail and general appearance. When it was discovered that many modellers used these vehicles in conjunction with traditional 54mm figures, but were uneasy at the slight but noticeable difference in scale, figure sets were produced by the same firms at competitive prices. Continually improved, these figures can now stand comparison with the best available.

Obviously other scales exist, from tiny metal-cast items of 1:265 scale, with which it is feasible to fight a battle upon a table top, to huge 1:16 scale machines within which can be installed full motorization and a radio control unit. Smaller models tend to be static, al-though from about 1:90 scale on most models at least feature elevating main armament and a traversing

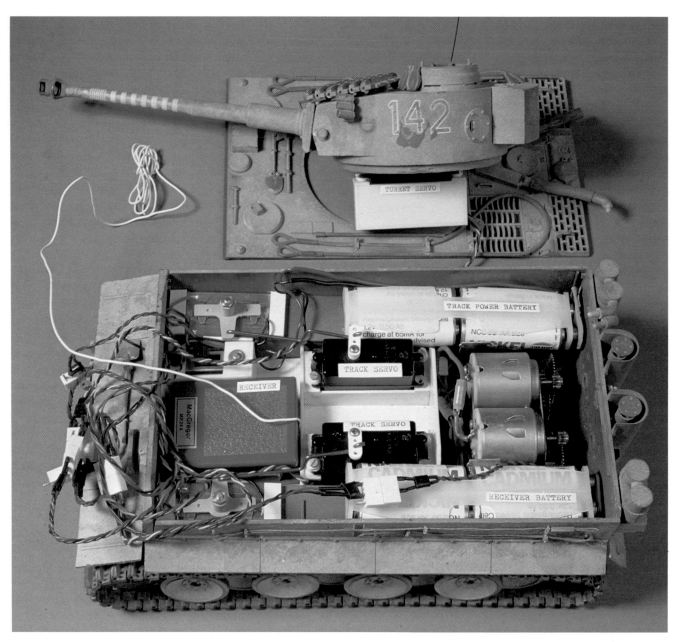

turret is possible on virtually any scale of model. Some 1:76 scale kits used to feature allegedly moving tracks, but unfortunately this was abandoned in the interests of scale accuracy. There were also some rather crude models with friction motors, in the best toy tradition, but these are no longer available.

True motorization becomes possible at 1:48 scale, but is not featured in many models, and, in fact, usually starts at 1:35 scale, many models having this feature as an option. As mentioned, the first 1:35 scale kits were motorized, but then scale accuracy tended to be subordinated to performance. The running gear was usually kindly described as 'semi-scale', while the tracks were simply detailed rubber bands, giving, on balance, a very good automotive performance. However, scale accuracy rapidly proved a much stronger selling point than 'play value', and as accuracy improved so motorized performance fell off. Some models have two motors and gearboxes, one per track, so that they can be guided by a trailing wire to a control box; as there is a fair degree of power, with fresh batteries

installed their performance is quite satisfactory.

From about 1:25 scale and larger motorization becomes a really viable feature. Models in this scale are superb items, usually with working suspension and tracks built up from individual links. These features make the models extremely effective from the motorization point of view, indeed some may have a power-to-weight ratio similar to the prototype vehicles. This scale is also about the minimum size of model which can properly take a radio control installation, but there are some big 1:16 scale kits intended specifically for this purpose.

There are model AFVs in scales to suit any modelling purpose, from that of the wargamer who wishes to fight tank battles on the dining-room table to large-scale examples of miniature engineering upon which the modeller can lavish all the care, skill and patience he can muster.

Tools
Regarding tools, the AFV modeller is served by the same

items as the figure modeller, with the addition of a steel rule and a setsquare (triangle in the US). If modelling is a major interest with a good rate of production, then an airbrush becomes an excellent investment, the cheaper types such as Morris and Ingram's 'Badger' or Humbrol's 'Studio 1' being perfectly adequate. However, more expensive Morris and Ingram products and makes such as Paasche and De Vilbiss are extremely useful and most versatile precision instruments which amply repay the fairly high initial investment.

References
There is a great deal of specific reference material available. Just as there are books documenting, for example, the Napoleonic Imperial Guard there are volumes covering the Tiger, Sherman, etc. As the interest grows, so does the knowledge of the subject, and researching a modelling project can be every bit as enjoyable as the constructional aspect. As with model soldiers most reference collections begin with the specialist magazines and from them it is possible to find out precisely what references are available. MAP Ltd, the publishers of *Military Modelling*, produce an excellent range of AFV plans in the major scales, and these are ideal as 'first' specific reference material for AFV modellers.

Kits
The huge range of AFV kits available accurately reflects the main areas of interest, with World War 2 German equipment out in front, followed by other World War 2 subjects, and then modern items. World War 1 vehicles are virtually disregarded, while the period between the wars is, in effect, ignored. Modern kits are so well designed and manufactured that they fit together very easily and produce near perfect miniatures.

All types of plastic kit are constructed working to the same principles, and these are amply described elsewhere. Since AFVs are no exception to the rule, they should be carefully made up bearing the basic guidelines in mind.

However, AFVs are rather different from figures in that they require a more rigid discipline in construction, and there are some special points to consider when assembling them. When the road wheels for, say, an armoured car are removed from the runners they usually have a mould line centrally round the tyre. On occasion this can be correct, as the rubber tyres of the full-size car are themselves moulded, but after a few miles of running this wears off and the rubber changes,

Opposite *Radio-controlled working tanks are occasionally seen. This one is converted by John Wylie from a 1:25 scale Tamiya kit of a Tiger 1, in which there is adequate room for the equipment. A servo is mounted in the turret of this model to allow the gun to be elevated as well as traversed; steering is by stopping one or other of the tracks.*
Below *Reference material on tanks is not difficult to come by. The Matilda in the photograph is based on an Imperial War Museum photo of a captured vehicle given hasty German markings. Many military books contain drawings of tank colour schemes.*

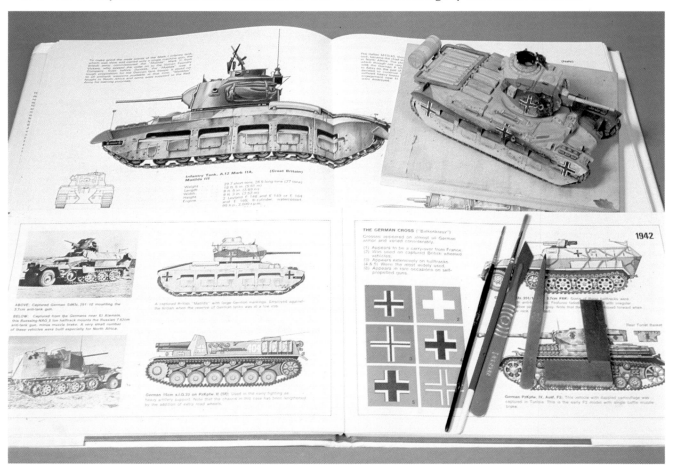

very quickly, from a smooth surface to a rough, cracked and pitted one. To achieve this effect remove the mould line using the coarse side of an emery board and simply leave the tyre fairly rough; do not sand perfectly smooth with a finer grade.

One-piece cylindrical parts, such as short gun tubes, should have the mould lines gently scraped away to remove the line only and *none* of the 'essential' plastic. Too vigorous a sanding or scraping on such areas produces a distinctly visible 'flat'. Large cylindrical parts such as fuel tanks, long gun barrels, and exhausts are often moulded in two pieces. When they are joined a distinct line shows and if sanded this can also produce a flat area. To overcome this problem, scraps of plastic sprue are dissolved in liquid cement to make a runny plastic solution; each butting edge of the cylinder is coated with a thick layer of solution and then joined. Some of the dissolved plastic will be squeezed out, and when dry, this can be sanded down, thus preserving the perfect roundness of the parts as well as filling any gaps there might have been.

Moulding dimples tend to occur on fairly large solid parts. Of course, they should be filled and the filler sanded smooth, but frequently they appear in the most awkward places, such as centrally within a circle of bolts on a drive sprocket. In an instance such as this it is very easy to make a sanding tool on a rod end. Tools like this can be simply made for any purpose where a file, emery board or piece of abrasive paper is unsuitable. If a moulded rod type of aerial is supplied, discard the rod and replace it with one made from stretched sprue. Finally, machine-guns always look much better if the ends of the barrels are drilled out, easily done by fitting a long pointed blade to a craft knife and drilling out the ends with a simple twisting motion.

Painting

On balance, modern AFV kits are flawlessly designed and the illustrated kit instructions are excellent. If assembled carefully, bearing in mind all the basic principles involved, a model of excellent quality is the rule rather than the exception, but no matter how well a model is made, if it is badly painted it looks dreadful. A model with a neat, plain paint job looks merely indifferent. On the other hand, a model which looks as if it might have seen active service looks very realistic indeed; in fact good painting can, and frequently does, cover up a mediocre assembly. Prior to painting,

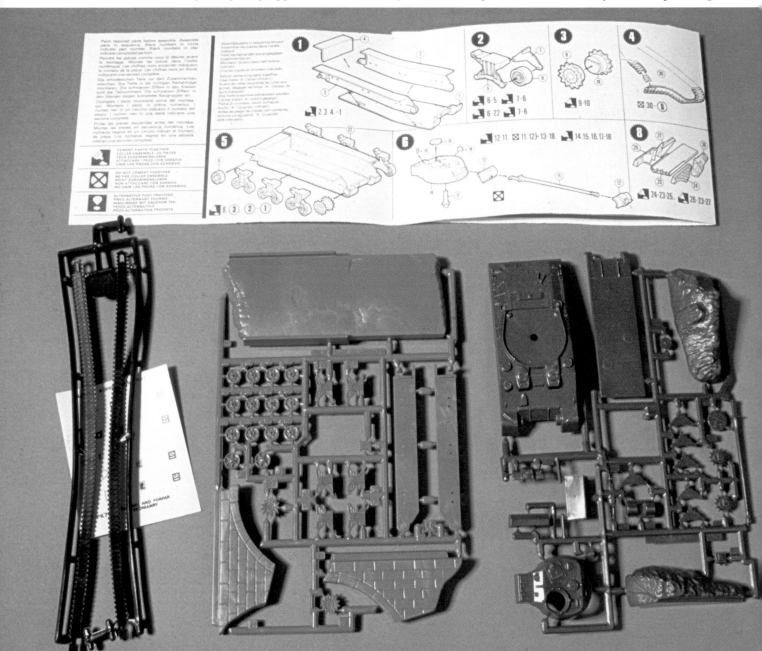

Opposite *Diorama builders favouring the broad sweep find that many available tank kits are too demanding on space. Fortunately there are smaller scale kits such as this Matchbox Sherman Firefly in 1:76 scale, four of which require roughly the same space as a single 1:35 model.*

Above *Another tank kit manufacturer is Airfix, using 1:32 scale. The three photos showing stages of construction are of an Airfix Grant tank; Monogram also have a kit of this vehicle, as do Tamiya, a finished example of which is shown (made by Rusty Jenkins). Differences in the representation of the tracks caused quite a famous controversy in 1979. (The Grant is very similar to the Lee which was the variant mainly used by the US.)*

let the model stand for at least 48 hours to allow the cement to dry, and make sure it is dust-free by giving it a quick blast over with an empty air brush or, if you do not have one, gently dust it with a dry soft brush. The first coat is then applied, of the correct base colour, completely covering the model so that no plastic shows through, yet thin enough not to obscure any fine detail. An airbrush is the ideal instrument with which to apply this base coat, using well-thinned paint (not cellulose) sprayed lightly from the recommended range for the gun, covering the model completely but without risking

runs. It is not always necessary to ensure an exact match to the real colour, as frequently a dark colour such as Panzer Grey or Olive Drab overpowers a small-scale model. On a full-sized vehicle the light which hits the considerable area gives the effect of the colour being brighter than it in fact is. Thus on Olive Drab it is best to add a little yellow to the 'authentic' colour and with Panzer Grey a little light blue works wonders. This also gives the effect of a somewhat faded and therefore realistic base colour.

There are several styles of painting, i.e., 'apply the basic colour(s) and leave it', the 'artistic' style which looks very pretty and is at present very much in vogue but is losing ground. Then come the 'cover every square millimetre with mud, dust and grime' brigade and the 'play it by ear' approach which is a combination of all these and really the only one to consider. Painting a model AFV is very much a compromise between realism and the natural desire to produce an attractive model. Realism can dictate a tank which is so covered with mud it looks like a tank-shaped mud sculpture, or an immaculate parade vehicle. The desire to produce an attractive model, however, may mean mud only in areas where it does not overpower the model, i.e., it is still easily identified and paintwork, markings, etc., are not obscured completely.

Above *Bill Evans' Panzer IV F1 from another Tamiya 1:35 kit; German tanks are by far the most popular among modellers. Tracks are never bar-taut and, being extremely heavy, always droop between the rollers at the top, an essential modelling point for correct appearance.*

Equivalents for plastic sheet

thou	inch	mm
40	·040	1
30	·030	·75
20	·020	·50
15	·015	·375
10	·010	·25

The Panzer IV F1 was used during the early days of the Russian campaign and in the desert. In either area its blue/grey surface would quickly become covered with a thick layer of dust. Tanks were frequently used in their European colours in the desert if there was no time to repaint them before they were needed in action. The dust would be thickest about the trackwork and front and rear plates. The model illustrated was sprayed blue-grey, the wheels painted Panzer grey (much more realistic than black), the machine-gun silver, which when dry was overpainted with thin black, and the exhaust in a mix of rust and grey. Unfortunately, the turret decals provided in the kit could not be used as they would not be flat over the vision flaps, so they were traced and the tracing transferred to the relevant position on the turret where it acted as a painting guide for the numbers, which were carefully painted in with matt white. On the real vehicle, paint would be worn away where there was a metal to metal contact, e.g., tracks and driving sprocket, or crew access areas in hatches, trackguards, etc., and a black/silver mix was applied to these areas using a dryish brush; they were then high-lighted using pure silver paint and a very dry brush.

Low grade metal fittings such as hinges would quickly rust, so they were dry brushed with rust on coloured paint. A 50/50 mix of Sand and Dark Earth was next prepared and the chassis sides, trackwork, front and rear plates liberally dry brushed with it. The whole vehicle was then dry brushed with Sand paint rather more lightly, but heavily enough to show a definite layer. The Sand was lightened with a little white and the whole model very lightly dry brushed with it, just enough so that some paint lay on hard edges and raised surface detail. All the engraved detail such as hatches, vision slots and suchlike was lined in with a sharply pointed soft lead pencil.

Finally the model received a light overspray of water to which a few drops of matt black ink had been added. The tracks were oversprayed in rust on the outer surfaces, followed by a layer of Sand. The outers were then dry brushed in silver/black and silver. The inner surfaces of the tracks were dry brushed silver. Jerry-cans were painted dull green with white crosses. The end result is attractive and realistic without looking over-done, and this should apply to all models.

Interiors
Many available kits are of open-topped types such as self-propelled guns, troop carriers and reconnaissance vehicles. Obviously this means that the interior will be seen and it must show signs of having been lived in. The 1:35 scale Tamiya Sd Kfz 223 light armoured car was chosen to illustrate this type of vehicle modelling. It is a splendid kit and comes with a mass of stowage to give

Opposite below *A normal colour scheme for a Panzer IV. In service, colours faded, but looked darker in wet conditions, so that a colour specification must be regarded as an intention rather than a fact.*
Below *A Tamiya 1:35 Sd Kfz 223 light armoured car, employed as a radio reconnaissance vehicle (the frame is in fact a radio aerial). In remote areas, individuality was shown by car crews in respect of equipment carried and how it could best be stowed. Model by Bill Evans.*

a typical 'cluttered' look. There is considerable scope for improving the stowage provided in the model, even though it represents the highest quality of plastic moulding available. The excellent illustration on the box top also shows a normal but interesting colour scheme of a hasty coat of Sand paint over the dark blue/grey base.

The radio operator figure was cleaned up and painted, then the radio and other small interior pieces were fitted into the hull chassis. A coat of light buff paint was applied to the interior. The radio was painted dull green and the dials picked out in black with tiny white markings. Seats were normally a grey/green canvas. The turret was made up next, minus the machine-gun and overhead mesh screens. Obviously the floor would be well scuffed, so it was dry brushed with gunmetal and lightly with silver, the guard rail around the radio receiving the same treatment. Interiors should look fairly 'lived in', but normal weathering techniques are rather overpowering; the best method of reproducing the desired effect is simply to rub the interior with fingers which have not been near a wash basin for a couple of hours. This produces a very realistic effect!

The rest of the model can be built up following the excellent instruction sheet which is a feature of Tamiya kits. Flat areas were sanded into the tyres where they would come into contact with the ground, giving an impression of weight. Once the basic model was made up minus the accessory parts, the interior was masked off with paper to preserve the painted surfaces and the model given an overall coating of Panzer blue/grey. Working from the box art, the areas of grey

showing through were masked with Humbrol Maskol and the model sprayed with Sand, leaving the chassis and areas under the mudguards blue/grey. The model was then dry brushed with Sand paint to which 30 per cent white had been added, then, rather less heavily, dry brushed with the same mix to which another 20 per cent white was added. When dry, the Maskol was rubbed off, revealing the grey undercoat. Gunmetal dry brushing was applied to the wheel rims, turret edge, mesh screens and the 'bedstead' aerial. Rust was applied sparingly where necessary. The jerry-cans were replaced with superior Italaerei items held in position with paper straps.

A new tarpaulin was made up as shown in the drawing, while the camouflage net was simply cut from a ladies' hair net and fitted with paper straps. Paper straps were also fitted to the helmets and water bottles, which were suspended from a length of thin fuse wire tied between the nearside aerial supports. Tyres were painted in Panzer grey to which a little Khaki was added, with the treads on all but the spare picked out in light grey. The chassis was then weathered by dry brushing with a 50/50 mix of Panzer grey and Sand. The commander's figure was assembled, adjusted, painted and fitted, then finally a German national flag, made up from soaked bank paper, was added.

The M5 Light Tank
In north-west Europe, it was felt that the armour on most American vehicles was too thin and many expedient forms of protection were fitted, the most popular being sandbags. The M5 Light Tank almost always

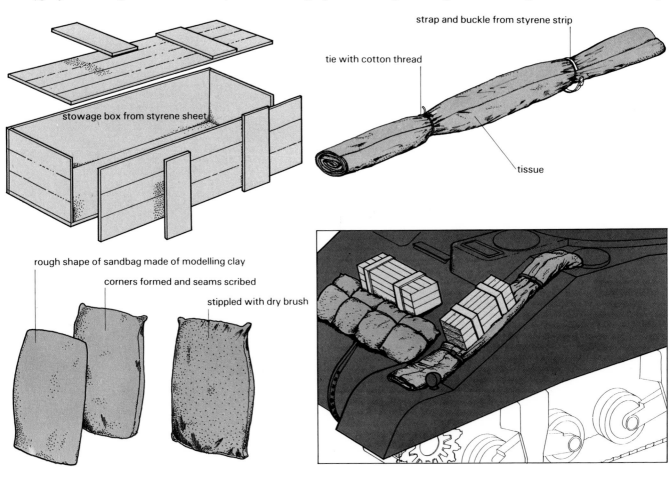

stowage box from styrene sheet

tie with cotton thread

strap and buckle from styrene strip

tissue

rough shape of sandbag made of modelling clay

corners formed and seams scribed

stippled with dry brush

Opposite *Accessories to fit individual models are simple to make and add tremendous atmosphere.*
Above *An M5A1 Stuart made by Bill Evans. The gadget at the front is a Cullin hedgerow cutter, invented by an American sergeant for use in the bocage country of Normandy, and the swept-up extension on the right-hand side of the turret is protection for the machine-gunner, whose gun is shown elevated.*

had sandbags piled over the glacis plate to protect this rather fragile area. The trackguards (supplied with the kit) were normally 'lost' or discarded in the field, as they were flimsy and frequently fouled the tracks if damaged. The side pieces were deleted from the model and the front portions, moulded integral with the hull top, were sawn off, reshaped by rounding the outer edges and the fitting plates scraped and sanded off. The sandbags were modelled as shown in the drawing and moulded on to the full front while still pliable, then allowed to dry. When dry they were removed and glued in position.

A stowage crate seems to have been almost a standard fitting on M5s and one was made from 20 thou. (0·5mm) plastic sheet, pre-scored as in the drawing. Making up small items such as these is fairly easy and self-explanatory, as well as being good practice before tackling conversions or scratch-built models where much work in sheet plastic is required. A tarpaulin was made and the box pushed into it as in the drawing, when it was fitted. Finally the sandbags were tied down with brown thread to give their distinct stability on the

model some link with the laws of gravity. Finished in Olive Drab, this model is most interesting from many angles, yet is rather bland in appearance from the sides, so a crew figure helps the overall effect no end. The white stars on the vehicle proved to be a good aiming point for enemy anti-tank gunners, so they were usually painted out and, as this paint was fresher than the base coat, it would show as darker patches. Weathering was similar to the Panzer IV, except that a rather darker basic weathering shade was used. Note that the trackwork is by far the most heavily weathered.

The M3A1 Half-track

Open-topped vehicles expose their occupants to the elements, so covers are usually provided. With half-tracks, these covers were left on during most of the winter, and it is a fairly easy matter to convert the Tamiya M3A2 to the much more widely used M3A1 as shown in the instruction leaflets. Tilt hoops (the canvas cover is a tilt and the supporting stays are known as hoops) are easily made from plastic rod bent to shape, and the 'canvas' is cut from wet-strength tissue glued in place on the painted model with white glue. The best way to ensure a snug fit is to use the age-old and infallible method known as trial and error! Once the tilt is fitted it is painted with a mix of one part white glue to eight parts water. This wrinkles the tissue in a realistic manner and serves as an excellent undercoat for modelling enamels. Strapping is made from paper and the buckles are simply small squares of 20 thou. plastic sheet. A photo of the model appears on the next page.

Above The M3A2 half-track in the Tamiya range can easily be converted into the A1 shown here. Adding a tilt cover is straightforward but it should be given a faded look. Model by Bill Evans.
Above right Track damage on a Panzer IV by John Wylie reflects a common cause of incapacitation.
Right Battle damage on a Russian T-34/76 includes deformed plating and splinter marks. Model by Bill Evans.

Battle damage

An AFV is designed to resist damage and frequently does so successfully, although a destroyed AFV is a common sight on a battlefield. However, a wrecked AFV is possibly one of the most difficult projects to complete successfully. Moderate battle damage is fairly easy to depict, as on the T34 shown, where hits have failed to pierce the main armour envelope but have left some fairly spectacular scars. Near-misses have thrown up dirt over the vehicle, which is fairly muddy in the first instance. The nearside trackguard was cut through where the front and upper portions meet, then moved about over a birthday cake candle until the plastic was soft. Treat flame/plastic combinations with *great* care! When the plastic was soft, it was deformed as shown, as if by blast. Shell holes were put in with a large nail heated up just enough to melt into the plastic (practise first); the nail was bound to a wooden handle. The heavy splash marks were put in using the tip of the nail. A new stowage box was made from 15 thou. sheet minus the lid and front end, heated and deformed as for the trackguards, and cemented in position. Splinter marks were made using an old knife blade heated to a dull straw colour; note that they go right through flimsy parts such as trackguards and the stowage box. Colour scheme is very dark green, which lightens considerably when weathered. The 'mud' was a mixture of Dark Earth matt enamel, coarse black pepper and flour applied with an old soft brush. The areas about the blast were heavily dry brushed with black and the fresh damage picked out in pure silver.

Conversions

AFVs are usually modernized during their service life and an early model frequently bears little resemblance to the final version evolved after, say, three years of warfare. Specialist vehicles such as SP artillery and recovery vehicles are usually converted from a standard type of armoured vehicle, almost always the tank or armoured personnel carrier. Conversion in modelling terms is the same as in real life, and this means that a collection of AFV models can be extended. A conversion can be as simple as a few detail changes or as complex as virtually completely rebuilding on little more than the kit chassis. The two examples included represent the middle/extreme conversion possibilities, as simple ones will probably suggest themselves during the construction of basic kits.

When Tamiya produced their M3 light tank, many modellers thought that they had brought out the wrong version. The M3 won fame as the 'Honey' in 8th Army service in the North African campaign, pitted against the vaunted Afrika Korps. The British Army received many of the early M3s with octagonal turrets as opposed to round ones. The sponson machine-guns were deleted, stowage revised and sandshields fitted. These changes applied to the round turreted version, as in the kit, but the turret is, in fact, too small, so a new one improves the appearance of the model.

Begin by assembling, painting and weathering the kit chassis, fit and paint the tracks. Cut a length of 20 thou. plastic sheet the width of the trackguards and pull a length of this under a ruler until it assumes a

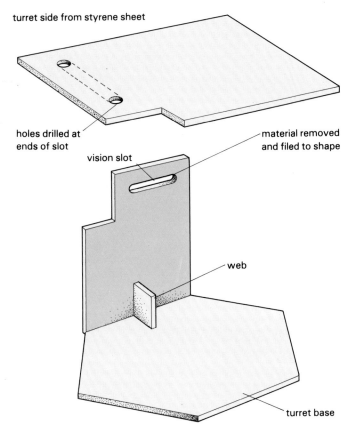

turret side from styrene sheet

holes drilled at ends of slot

material removed and filed to shape

vision slot

web

turret base

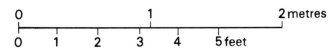

Above *Details of making a new turret for the M3 'Honey'.*
Below and opposite *Drawings of the converted M3; dimensions may be taken direct from these.*

6

T27978

curve (see drawing); working from the plan fit the front portions of the sandshields, from this strip, to the front of the trackguards. Cut out the sandshield sides from 20 thou. sheet and fit them, then attach the ends of the sandshields, fit the hull top to the chassis, then the inner portions of the sandshields and allow to dry. Assemble all the hull, but delete the stowage boxes and cut away the mountings for the two sponson machine-guns; cap the holes left on the front sponsons with thin slices cut from the kit sprue. A long stowage box across the hull, a smaller regular oblong one for the nearside rear and a fuel can box must now be made from 20 thou. sheet and fitted, which is an easy task. It is best to make

up a batch of fuel cans (nicknamed 'flimsies') and fit three on the hull (right rear).

Attention can now be turned to the turret. Working from the plan view, cut out the base plate, allowing for the thickness of the *kit* front plate and 20 thou. all round to allow for the sides; it is best to use 40 thou. (1mm) sheet for this part. Carefully cut out the side pieces from 20 thou. sheet and lightly chamfer the vertical sides where they join, which makes for a perfect joint. Where relevant, mark out the positions of vision slots and at each end of them drill a small hole. Using a rat's tail file, join these holes by filing, to make the slots. Cut from 40 thou. sheet a number of 1×1cm squares,

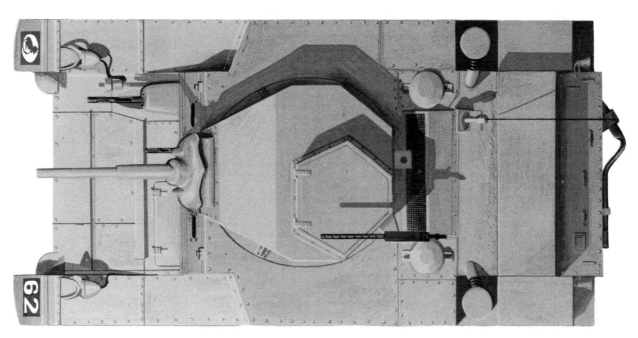

making sure that they are all *exactly* square. Fit the rear plate to the turret base first of all and ensure that it is at 90 degrees by gluing two of the 1cm squares to both surfaces as in the drawing. Attach the rest of the side plates, adjusting as necessary, then fit the kit front plate complete with gun, mantlet, etc.

Fit the turret roof from two pieces of 40 thou. sheet plastic, then attach the rest of the cupola sides, made from the same material, complete with vision slots. Fit a cupola roof and provide the hinges from slivers of plastic. The vision flaps at the sides are made up from small pieces of plastic card. Scribe a circle of 20 thou. sheet (see page 158) 2mm larger in diameter than the

kit turret ring, and fit it to the bottom of the turret. The machine-gun fittings are taken from the kit. Finally, assemble the kit turret and when dry carve off the turret fixing ring and glue it to the new turret. The completed model was allowed to stand for a week before being sprayed, as paint seems to have a definite solvent action upon fresh cement in conversions, more so than with basic kits.

A Bergepanzer from the Tamiya 1 : 35 Leopard

While the previous conversion cannot be classed as a 'soft option', the second one is as complex and complete an exercise as the modeller is likely to encounter. It is

Opposite *The M3 converted by Bill Evans to the earlier version with different cupola and other details, shown in the markings of the British 7th Armoured Division.* **Above** *The German Bergepanzer is currently in service and is based on a Leopard chassis. The dozer conversion from a Tamiya 1:35 kit of the Leopard represents one of several specialized versions. Model by Bill Evans.*

scratch-built from the chassis upwards, and is made only a little easier by using some kit parts such as the engine decking and cupolas. The main quality needed when tackling a conversion of this complexity is perseverance, as there is a lot of work involved.

Using the drawing as reference, a new hull rear plate was cut from 40 thou. sheet plastic and fitted. From the same material were cut the hull sides, top decking and the front glacis plate, complete with slots for the dozer blade arms. The engine hatch was cut out from the kit and then fitted into the top decking by cutting out the exact sized area. The sides were fitted to the model, next the decking and finally the glacis plate. The remaining crew compartment side plate was cut from 40 thou. sheet and fitted, as were the rear plates, from the same material. This basic structure was then allowed to dry completely. When it was dry the crew compartment was roofed with 20 thou. sheet. As can be seen from the drawings, part of the crew compartment roof is of cast construction and this part of the model is best carved from close grained balsa wood, firmly glued in

position using tube cement and then sanded as smooth as possible. The cupola base was made in a similar way from the same material. The wood was then coated with several layers of plastic solution, which fills the grain, and when dry sanded smooth with fine grade emery paper. A false rear roof was made from 10 thou. sheet and the cupola base fitted.

Hatches were scribed using the kit item as a pattern, and periscope covers cut from the kit were fitted. A lower nose plate complete with dozer arm cut-outs was cut from 20 thou. sheet and fitted and at this stage the model began to take shape. Crew access doors were cut from 10 thou. sheet, fitted and finished off with hinges made from thin gauge strip and plastic rod. Air intakes were modified by cutting off the raised portions, then using filler to build up the exposed shape as required, and the crane was a fairly easy, if precise, piece of 20 thou. sheet construction, using a nice new sharp blade to cut out the holes in the side pieces. The base and trunnions were fabricated from 40 thou. sheet.

The suspension was then fitted and final detailing could begin. Most of it can be taken from the kit or simply made from thin sheet or rod, or by delving into the spares box if one is available. Work of this nature is simple but tedious and exacting, and there is always the temptation to rush or skimp. This impulse must be checked and the detailing carried out as carefully and completely as possible, as it is responsible for the all-important finish of the model.

A dozer blade is easily made from 20 thou. sheet, while the frame carried on the engine decking is simply

Left and below *These drawings of the Bergepanzer, in association with the text, provide the information required to tackle a major conversion project, recommended only to modellers with some previous experience of conversion work. Study of illustrated armoured vehicle books will reveal considerable numbers of tank conversions such as mine flails, bridge carriers and many others which can add great interest to an armoured vehicle collection and provide a never-ending challenge to modelling skills.*
Opposite *Another picture of the completed Bergepanzer conversion.*

0			1			2		3 metres
0	1	2	3	4	5			10 feet

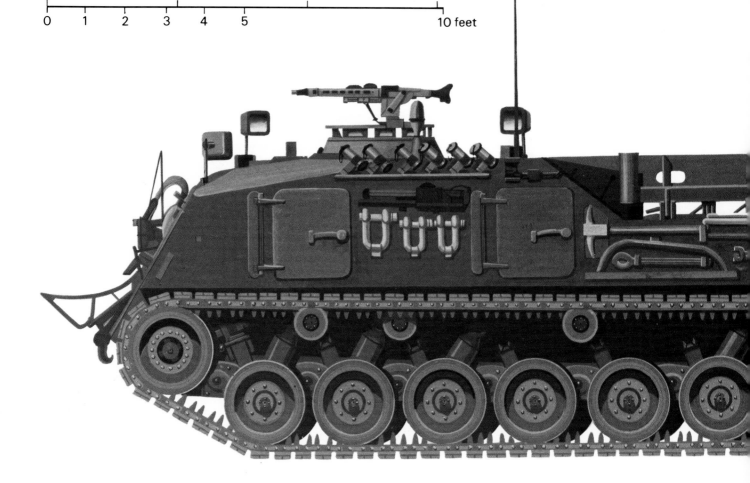

enough made up from 40 thou. sheet, strip and sprue from the kit. Much of the detail for the rear plate was carved off the kit plate. Once the model was completed, it was allowed to set.

An undercoat of grey shows, very distinctly, any flaws in the model, which can be filled or sanded off at this stage. Colour scheme is semi-gloss Olive Drab which has a distinct brown tone. Markings are as

photos. Weathering was restricted to a light coat of dust colour, just sufficient to bring out the detail, except for the dozer blade, which was made to look as if it worked for its living. Although the model was difficult to build it turned out to be very impressive indeed, well worth the effort involved. Once a project of this nature is successfully concluded, any other can be tackled with confidence!

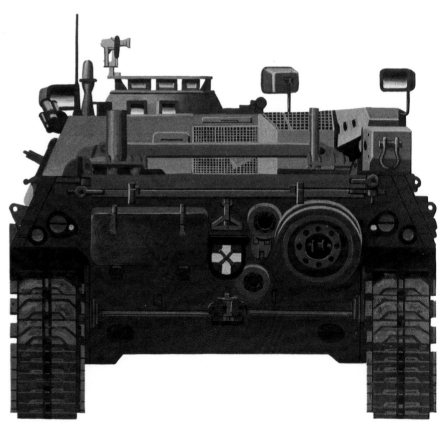

Scratch-building

If a model is not available and the subject is an attractive one to the modeller, it must be scratch-built. Before attempting scratch-building, it must be realized a great deal of effort is required, together with the modeller's highest standards of skill and attention to detail. If these demands are met, a unique model of top quality can result, but if interest flags the partially built model is usually abandoned which is a great waste of time, effort and material, and if work is rushed the result will be not nearly as good as it might have been. Confidence is important – it should always be remembered that a complex item is merely a number of simple pieces joined together, each of which is easy to make. More difficult skills such as heat-moulding plastic sheet or carving from the solid can be acquired easily with a little practice. Scratch-building therefore consists of building these basic units and joining them together, and this fact should always be borne in mind, no matter how daunting the initial task appears.

Below *The Renault FT17 'Char Mitrailleuse' is a good choice for a first attempt at scratch-building since, despite a fair amount of detail, it contains no compound curves apart from the cupola; even this is very simple and affords an easy introduction to heat moulding.*
Opposite above *Under construction, with the basic hull completed and work begun on the suspension. Materials for this model are available from most good model shops and represent a very small cash outlay. It is not, however, a one-evening project by any means!*
Opposite below *Bill Evans' completed tank is a handsome and worthy addition to any collection. It also has the attraction of being perhaps the most important armoured vehicle development not to have been made available in kit form.*

Before contemplating scratch-building a model, read all the latest magazines and catalogues carefully to find if any concern intends to release the model in the relevant scale; it has been known in the past for a scratch-built model to have just been completed when a kit of the same subject has appeared on the model shop shelves the next day! This sort of thing does nothing at all for morale.

In order to find a subject worthy of scratch-building, it is necessary to look beyond the most popular subjects. World War 1 is still a rich source of inspiration, and it is turned to for the Renault FT17, one of the most important AFV designs ever produced. From the point of view of a first scratch-built model this vehicle could hardly be bettered, as it is of flat plate construction. Neatness in working is essential, but once the basic units of hull, turret and suspension are made up and joined, the rest is an exercise in detailing and finishing. The edges of all plates are butt-joined to others in order to achieve neat, crisp joints.

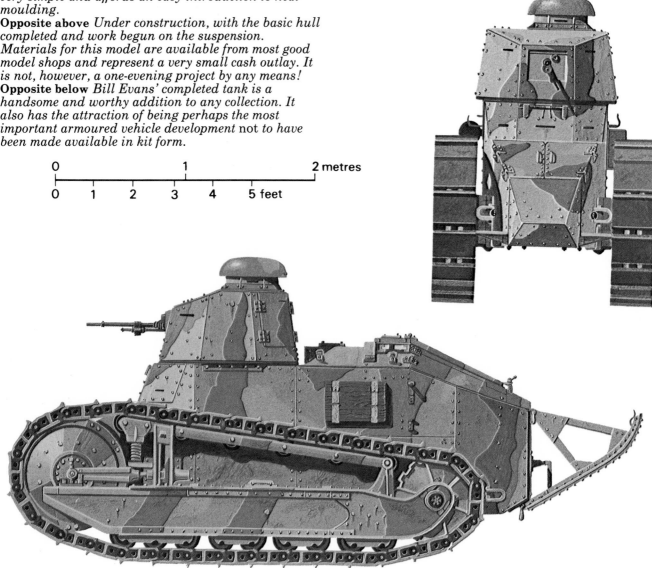

0		1			2 metres
0	1	2	3	4	5 feet

Construction began with the chassis, and a floor plate was cut from 40 thou. sheet plastic and the two main side portions from 30 thou. sheet. These two identical side portions were *very carefully* checked against each other to make sure that they were the same, as any difference would result in a distorted model; the same is true for all identical parts. Lines were scribed into the side pieces to represent the plate joins. The sides were then bonded to the floor with liquid cement and several oblong bulkheads with exactly square corners were installed to keep the sides true. This ensures a perfectly square basic structure, which is essential.

The forward part of the hull was then made in the same way and joined, as was the rear of the hull. All was again checked for squareness and lack of distortion and allowed to dry. The nose was made up from 20 thou. sheet and fitted, followed by the forward access hatch with the join line scored in. Next the hull roof was fitted from the driver's area right up to the sloping part, using 20 thou. sheet. The sloping rear plates were made from 20 thou. sheet and attached, left oversize at the sides and rear and when thoroughly dry trimmed to size. The forward part of the engine decking, which slopes from the middle to the sides, was made from two rectangular 20 thou. pieces and fitted, with the open end sealed with a shallow triangular-shaped piece of the same material. Then the three driver's plates were cut out, trial-fitted to ensure a snug fit and the vision slots cut in them as for the Honey. They were then attached to the hull and (again) the whole structure

Right *Methods of working styrene sheet.*
Below *Close up of a Panzer IV Ausf D turret with the hatches open. Model by John Wylie.*
Opposite *A 1943 Soviet T-34/76 with redesigned turret, yet another 1:35 scale Tamiya model, this time built by H. Grime.*

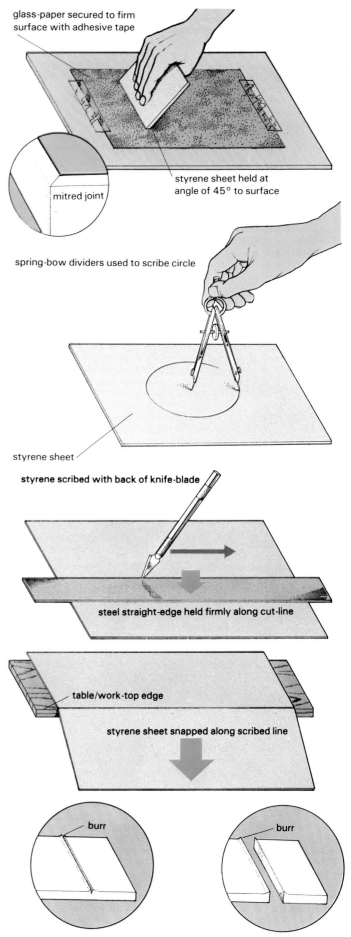

glass-paper secured to firm surface with adhesive tape

styrene sheet held at angle of 45° to surface

mitred joint

spring-bow dividers used to scribe circle

styrene sheet

styrene scribed with back of knife-blade

steel straight-edge held firmly along cut-line

table/work-top edge

styrene sheet snapped along scribed line

burr

burr

allowed to dry completely. This most important basic unit was now complete, and all the joints were given a wash of liquid cement to give extra strength.

The turret was a very simple item to construct, very similar in fact to that of the Honey described previously. It was different in that it was of the internal mantlet type, so the aperture was cut out and backed with a piece of 20 thou. sheet. Again only the basic unit was made up. Four suspension beams were cut from 40 thou. sheet, only the outer ones being detailed as the inner ones do not show. They were joined to make two separate units using 40 thou. sheet as spacers. The outer sides of the beams were detailed using 10 thou. sheet, with long strips of the same wrapped round the beams to form a shallow wall. Lengths of heavier gauge sheet, slices of sprue and short lengths of rod completed the detailing of these pieces. The front idler wheels were scribed with a pair of dividers from 40 thou. sheet and detailed with thin washers and discs, made in a similar fashion from 10 thou. sheet. The forward support brackets for the return roller bars were made up from sheet and fitted, then U-shaped mountings for the idler wheels were cut from 40 thou. sheet plastic. Support brackets for the idlers were made from scraps of sheet and short lengths of plastic tubing, fitted to the idlers, then attached to the suspension bearers. When this was done the U-shaped mountings were then fixed in

their correct positions and the whole areas detailed.

The forward springs consisted of fuse wire wrapped around lengths of thin sprue, and the rear support brackets were cut from 20 thou. sheet. Return roller bars were simple strips of 40 thou. sheet, detailed with tiny slices of plastic rod. Return rollers consisted of lengths of thickish sprue sandwiched between the bars. The completed bars were fitted to the support brackets. The forward springs were then attached as shown in the side view. Discs of 40 thou. sheet the size of the drive sprockets were scribed out and the teeth carefully cut into them. They were detailed with lengths of stretched sprue and mounted between the beams, using spacers also made from sprue. Road wheel units were cut from 20 thou. sheet in the form of shallow triangles with rounded ends. The road wheels themselves consisted of two slices of thick sprue with, in effect, a central axle of thin sprue, each road wheel resembling a miniature dumb-bell. The units were made up and fitted in position. Final detailing then took place, undemanding but essential work, and the units were allowed to dry.

Attention was then turned back to the hull. First the engine intake covers were made from 10 thou. sheet spaced out from the covers proper with small blocks of 40 thou. sheet. Spring clips made from scraps of rod and sheet were fitted to the driver's vision plate and hinges installed, where necessary, from squares of thin sheet

and short lengths of stretched sprue. The daunting task of providing rivet detail now arose. The positions of the rivets were marked in with pencil. Lengths of even section stretched sprue were chopped up into tiny 'rivets'. Each one was picked up with the point of the craft knife blade, held in position, then secured in place with a wash of liquid cement. This was a long, tedious task, the ideal occasion to tackle this being a wet Sunday afternoon. The turret was riveted during the same session. Handles on the front access plates and a deflection rail on the engine decking were made from thin plastic rod and put in position, while the last few fittings on the hull should be self-explanatory if the drawings are studied.

The suspension units were mated to the hull using two lengths of sprue both to hold them in position and space them from the hull. The hull was propped up from the ground so that the suspension units were just in contact with the work surface and the whole assembly allowed to set and dry. The cupola base on the turret was made from a length of dowel treated with plastic solution, while the cupola hatch was heat-moulded from thickish plastic sheet. However, it would have been equally simple to have carved one from wood or laminations of sheet plastic. The machine-gun was made from scraps of rod and card and put in position. The turret could have easily been made to work by fitting a peg to it and drilling a hole in the hull roof, but it was glued directly to the hull. Doors were fitted to the turret using thin sheet and hinges added. After all this work, the tail skid was child's play and easily constructed from various grades of sheet and fitted in place. The model was then nearly complete and, when 'set', was given a coat of matt Chestnut enamel with areas of dark green overpainting. Markings had to be hand-painted.

The most difficult and tedious bit had been left until

Opposite *Italaerei kits have a good reputation with AFV enthusiasts. This one is an M4 Sherman with the earlier 76mm gun. The use of sandbags for extra protection at the front gave crews confidence in the face of improved anti-tank weapons; there has been a race between armour specialists and anti-tank weapon designers ever since the first armoured vehicles appeared. Model by Mac Kennaugh.*
Above *Panzerjäger VI Tiger (P) Ferdinand (later called Elefant) with 8.8cm gun. Note anti-magnetic mine paste on outside and the score of seven tanks destroyed marked on the side. Model by John Sandars.*

last: the tracks. Each link consisted of ten pieces cut from sheet. The main part was made from two 40 thou. pieces of plastic sheet, and the inner one had to have a square hole cut in it to engage the driving sprocket. The best way to make these holes was to drill them, then square off with a craft knife. The links were edged with 10 thou. sheet capped with the same and detailed with strips of identical gauge material. Tiny triangular pieces of 10 thou. sheet must be added at the rate of four per link (a fiddly job) and note that the edging side pieces overlap. Then the plates must all be joined together and it was found best to make up lengths of track, cementing them in place as they became useful lengths. Once the tracks were in position, they were painted dull metallic grey and the whole model was lightly weathered, as there was no point in covering all that work up in mud!

If the model turns out successfully, there is a tremendous feeling of satisfaction in knowing that it owes its existence entirely to personal skills as opposed to those of the kit manufacturers. This vehicle is by no means the most complex one that it is possible to build, but it is an ideal introduction into this absorbing aspect of the hobby.

Artillery

Guns in action are among the first visions conjured up in most people's minds when they think of the word 'battle', but, surprisingly, comparatively few modellers concentrate on artillery subjects. This may partly be due to the impression that machine tools are needed to make successful model guns, though, as is shown in this chapter, this is not the case. Certainly the subject is fascinating and offers immense scope in construction and presentation; research is not difficult and a collection of a dozen or so models would embrace all the major steps in artillery development over the last 600 years.

A British gun crew in action with a 25-pdr during the North African campaign in World War 2. This simple but effective diorama was made by John Wylie.

History of artillery

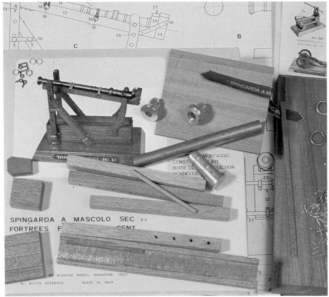

Left *A good example of a metal kit of an early cannon is this 15th century Fortress Falconet. Supplied by HGH Models and made by Mantua Models of Italy, it is shown here complete with box top, model parts and construction sheet.*
Right *A 12-pdr of 1800–1860 scratch-built by J. P. Coop.*

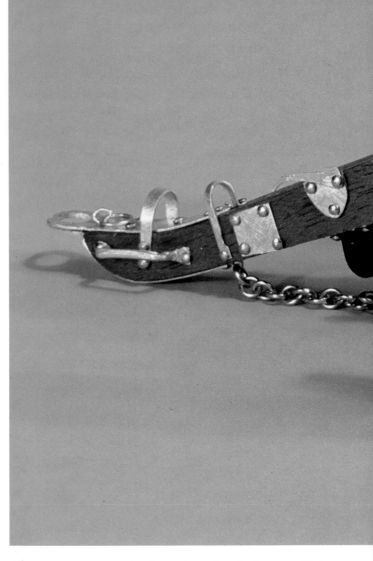

The single most momentous advance in weapon development was the application of gunpowder to cannon. Gunpowder, a mixture of sulphur, charcoal and saltpetre, is believed to have been known in Ancient China, but was introduced into Europe in about AD 1250. The most important of the ingredients was saltpetre, because it contained oxygen which enabled the other two substances to burn even when cut off from an air supply. It was soon realized that gunpowder, when ignited in a small space, created an explosion of sufficient power to propel missiles.

Early cannon, 1325–1550

Despite the immense significance of gunpowder, little subsequent research was undertaken to utilize it for military purposes by harnessing the created force to a missile. It was not until about 1325 that cannon were introduced. These were extremely simple, resembling large vessels or flower vases, tapering slightly from base to muzzle. Near the base was a touchhole through which the gunpowder charge, located within the bore, could be ignited by means of a hot iron or brand. It is not certain what method was employed to sustain the recoil. The guns were variously described as 'pot de feu' or 'vasa'; while the most popular missiles appear to have been large iron darts.

Guns became more sophisticated later in the 14th century. They consisted of hollow tubes constructed in a similar way to wooden barrels. Bronze, copper or brass rods were welded together around a wooden core and then strengthened with iron bands. These barrels were inefficient because the gases created by the explosion escaped through cracks, thus reducing the propellant power. Some cannon were breech-loaders on which breech and barrel were fashioned separately, the former being large enough to hold a cylinder containing both missile and charge. After firing, the empty cylinder was immediately replaced by a loaded one, which thus speeded up the rate of fire. The problem with these guns was the difficulty of achieving a secure joint between barrel and breech to prevent a major loss of gas compression, which naturally reduced missile velocity. Conversely, if the joints were too well sealed and the

charge too strong, the breech and cylinder would be blown apart – a fairly frequent occurrence.

The first missiles, apart from darts, were round stones and metal balls. Stones, an economical and easily obtainable form of ammunition, could be fired with a smaller charge than metal balls, an important factor in view of the crude construction of early guns which were liable to burst when over-large charges were employed, a serious hazard to anyone in the vicinity.

Related problems of barrel strengths and muzzle velocity were to a great extent overcome when iron casting was invented in Frankfurt-am-Main in about 1400. This enabled lighter but stronger guns to be made in one piece, capable of withstanding the high pressure required to propel iron missiles with effective velocity. Guns, therefore, became more efficient and cheaper because cast iron, being adequately resistant to corrosion, made the use of more expensive materials unnecessary.

Further gun improvements

Once guns proved useful, particularly in siege warfare, they steadily improved. Gun carriages (platforms to carry barrels), consisting of hollowed-out tree trunks, were developed, to which wheels were attached to increase mobility. Trunnions (pivots on each side of barrels) enabled barrels to be elevated without chocking them. To achieve rapid or concentrated fire, several guns would be combined upon one large carriage.

Eventually, it was realized that bronze was a more suitable although more expensive material for gun barrels because it cast more evenly than iron. This reduced the possibility of hidden barrel flaws and spectacular accidents. Soon, guns became larger because bigger ones could more rapidly achieve military objectives; enormous pieces were produced which were particularly successful against castles and fortified towns, but the problem was the heavier the gun, the

more cumbersome and less mobile it became.

Despite the invention of some multi-barrel small bore guns, cannon were of little value in field operations during the 15th century (the reduction of Constantinople was a notable exception) because they could not be moved quickly enough in sufficient numbers to required locations. By the early 16th century, the mobility problem had been overcome, to an extent, and larger numbers of small bore field guns were in use; by this time, guns had become standardized as smooth bore muzzle loaders variously described as bombards, petarara and culverins. Although these appeared similar, they actually varied considerably in bore size and weight. Two main patterns predominated, culverins firing balls between 6·8–8·2kg (15–18lb) and demi-culverins firing 4·1–5·4kg (9–12lb) missiles.

The first attempts to achieve gun/ammunition uniformity were made by the Emperor Charles V in 1544, be-

Above *A Calder Craft French Napoleonic 6in howitzer. This maker's kits are all metal.*
Opposite *Three stages of artillery development. At rear, a World War 1 Krupp 77mm field gun from a Pocher kit, left a Calder Craft English Civil War cannon and, right, a 12-pdr 'Napoleon' from the American Civil War, also by Calder Craft.*

cause he appreciated that standardization was a prerequisite to simplifying the logistic supply system. Meanwhile, gunnery soldiers were becoming more competent, knowledgeable and professional, and mathematical tables and instruments were introduced to ensure more accurate and devastating fire.

Military effectiveness

The first recorded field artillery employment was at Crécy in 1346. The French used it more successfully against the English during the Hundred Years War when it greatly contributed to their victories at Formigny (1450) and Chatillon (1453). However, cannon were still much more effective in their siege role, particularly against castles. The latter, previously a secure base for cavalry offensives and a means of dominating territory, thus lost these advantages, which decisively contributed to feudal decline; the expense of artillery caused it to become the virtual monopoly of kings and states. The Tudor monarchs of England (1485–1603) retained strong artillery trains to dominate and subjugate unruly nobles.

Artillery development, 1550–1820

During the early 17th century, artillery consisted of guns, howitzers and mortars, which were classified into use for siege and field purposes. Three types of gun were necessary because no one gun could undertake all necessary tasks: guns fired directly at static or moving targets, howitzers shot shells on high, curved trajectories to reach targets in dead ground (behind hills), and mortars fired at very high angles at extremely short range. The heavier versions of the guns mentioned were employed on siege operations, which became particularly important during the 17th century because defence by means of fortress networks dictated European strategy and tactics.

Although guns remained the same shape, many technical improvements were incorporated. It was fully appreciated, early in the 17th century, that field guns should give close fire support to infantry and cavalry. Consequently, carriages were changed to enable light guns to reach forward battlefield areas. The old, clumsy double bracket carriages which caused gun-laying and firing rate problems were modified. Gustavus Adolphus of Sweden (1594–1632) designed a very light gun which could be manoeuvred by two men or one horse. Later, this was replaced by a four-pound brass gun. Frederick the Great of Prussia also appreciated the value of artillery and formulated tactics for its use. He increased the number of guns allocated to infantry battalions and encouraged howitzer employment because they could provide cover over the heads of friendly formations. His most important innovation was the introduction of horse artillery (1759) which quickly provided fire support at specific locations.

Increased effectiveness of light guns caused the reorganization of artillery in European armies. Light

166

guns were permanently attached to infantry, and sometimes cavalry, and heavy guns were retained for specific tasks under army HQ control.

An important technical improvement was achieved in cannon barrel production. Hitherto, these had been cast with a core in the centre which formed the bore. It was then discovered that stronger and more accurate barrels could be produced by casting a solid metal cylinder into which a bore was drilled. Barrels were still smooth bore as gun rifling had not been introduced.

Aiming and sighting

Until about the mid-18th century, gun barrels were elevated or depressed (to achieve different ranges) by inserting hand spikes and wedges under the breech. The introduction of an elevating screw enabled rapid and more accurate sighting, and the later invention of a tangent sight improved aiming still further. However, despite these refinements it was still the training, skill and experience of gunlayers upon which shooting accuracy depended.

Ammunition

By about the middle of the 17th century, stone shot had been replaced by iron missiles. These were propelled by a gunpowder charge which was enclosed in a flannel or canvas bag. The charge was ignited by means of a priming charge inserted in the vent sited on top of the breech. By the end of the 18th century, ammunition had become standardized as:

Round shot/cannon balls

These were solid, cast iron balls of slightly smaller diameter than the bore of the field gun for which they were manufactured. This enabled more rapid loading, though suffered an appreciable loss of compression. Shot was either loaded loose or fitted to a wooden base to prevent turning in the barrel. Sometimes fixed ammunition was produced to increase firing rate, consisting of the shot and its base being included in the charge bag. Cannon balls were the most frequently employed form of ammunition.

Case/cannister

This was fired from field guns and howitzers at short range against closely packed formations. It consisted of a tin case, equivalent in size to the gun bore, filled with iron balls. On firing, the case split open, releasing a cloud of missiles over a wide frontage. Heavy case had about 40 heavy bullets, light case around 85.

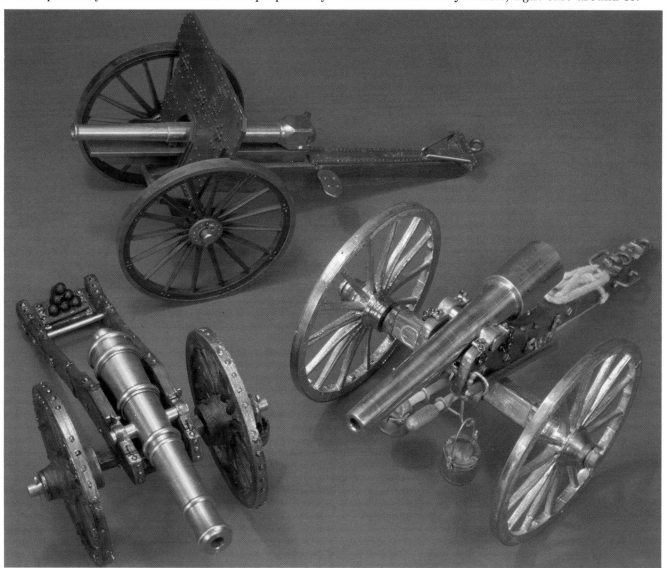

Opposite *A wrecked cannon forms part of a diorama by Belgian expert François Verlinden. All 54mm Historex parts.*
Right *Loading a 6-pdr anti-tank gun on a 7th Armoured Division Bedford QL 'portee', the sort of imaginative setpiece which adds interest to artillery modelling. Model by Mac Kennaugh.*

Shells

These were fired from howitzers only at medium/short range. The shell was a hollow iron ball containing a gunpowder charge connected to a fuse. When the latter burned down it ignited the charge, causing the ball to disintegrate into 'shrapnel' fragments which scattered up to about 32 metres (35 yards). The main purpose of shells was to strike at troops deployed out of sight, or at buildings and ammunition wagons which could thus be set on fire.

Shrapnel

This was an exploding shell invented by Henry Shrapnel. It was used by the British army, but never by the French, and was composed of a hollow cannon ball filled with musket balls and a gunpowder charge ignited by a fuse. The intention was to create an air burst over enemy infantry.

Gribeauval's reforms

The most far-reaching reforms were undertaken by the French General Gribeauval in the late 1760s. These gave France the best guns of the Napoleonic period and established a tradition of artillery competence and inventiveness which lasted until the 1920s. Gribeauval's purpose was to produce more mobile, reliable and accurate guns, while simultaneously simplifying the French artillery organization. He also attempted to standardize the armaments industry to ensure production of identical parts and patterns. This early attempt at economical mass production ensured that guns could be repaired on the battlefield by removing parts from those which had been partly damaged. The French therefore acquired splendid artillery which was later to be further developed by Napoleon. In 1770, French guns for field use were:

1) 4-pounders (later replaced by the 6-pounder) for light tasks with infantry battalions.
2) 8-pounders for medium tasks – at brigade.
3) 12-pounders for special heavy tasks – in reserve at army.

4) 6-inch howitzers – at brigade.
5) 8-inch howitzers – at army.

Towards the end of the 18th century, the British developed a new gun carriage with a single, instead of a double, trail. They possessed two excellent field guns, the 6-pounder and 9-pounder, which gave outstanding service during the Napoleonic wars.

It will be appreciated that the guns of the period lacked any form of recoil mechanism. Consequently, after firing the guns had to be pushed back into the firing position – a time-consuming and fatiguing operation. The heavier the gun, the longer it took to complete this task.

Some mention must be made of gun ranges. Round shot was much affected by the condition of the ground. A dry, hard surface would enable shot to skip much further than would a muddy surface. Effective shooting was also influenced by gunpowder smoke which frequently obscured targets. Round shot could reach about 1,370 metres (1,500 yards) but was most effective at about 900–1,000 metres (1,000–1,100 yards). Light case was employed at targets some 230 metres (250 yards) away, while heavy case was used at between 320–460 metres (350–500 yards). British armies tended to fire at shorter ranges than Continental armies. The latter fired shells up to about 900 metres (1,000 yards), while the British employed them at up to about 550 metres (600 yards). The general rule of ranges/effectiveness was that the closer the target the more devastating the firing result.

The growing importance of field artillery was notable in such battles as Brietenfeld (1631), Blenheim (1704), Dettingen (1743) and Minden (1759). However, it was during the Napoleonic wars that, for the French at least, it became a battle-winning arm. Napoleon latterly used it *en masse* to soften up areas selected for attack, and expanded his artillery corps to 100,000 men. The value and effectiveness of smooth bore artillery can be summarized by its use during the Waterloo campaign (14–18 June 1815). At Ligny, the Prussians positioned too many formations on dry, forward slopes, thus presenting frontal enfiladed targets. The French tore these apart with their 12-pounders; shots missing forward units skipped onwards and struck those behind.

At Waterloo, Napoleon deployed a grand battery of 84 guns which spent the day attempting to reduce the effectiveness of the Allied defence. Although many casualties were inflicted, the constant bombardments were unsuccessful because of the muddy ground and Allied deployment behind the ridge. The French used cannister to clear German troops from the Hougoumont Farm woods, but were then subjected to effective shrapnel fire from British guns. Despite the numerical superiority and greater use of French guns, it was the handling of British guns which contributed significantly to defeating French cavalry and infantry assaults.

Effects of industrialization, 1820–1914
The 19th century was a period of rapid scientific advance which caused major artillery changes. Guns remained categorized as siege and field, but the former increased in importance because of the network of fortresses, such as Strasbourg and Metz, which became established across the Continent. Such strongpoints contained huge long-range guns to keep besiegers at bay, while even larger ones were employed in attack. The difficulties of moving such vast pieces were resolved by complex transport organizations.

In 1847, Krupp of Essen perfected the production of cast steel gun barrels. This metal was more durable than iron or bronze, making it easier to achieve satisfactory rifling and breech mechanisms. The huge guns made by Krupp were successfully employed by the Prussians at Königgrätz (1866) and later in the Franco–Prussian war (1870–71) at Sedan and Froechswiller. In 1860, the British adopted the Armstrong rifled gun. This very accurate piece had a cast-steel rifled barrel surrounded with a wrought iron coil enclosed in wrought iron hoops. Shells became much more powerful and devastating due to the use of gelatinized nitrocellulose. The introduction of air and water pressure recoil systems, which cushioned the firing shock, obviated relaying guns after each shot. Consequently, firing rates improved considerably. Field guns also benefited from technological advances, and by 1914 had become standardized as rapid-firing breech-loaders which propelled high explosive shells up to about 4,600 metres (5,000 yards). Field gun effectiveness was clearly demonstrated during the Russo–Japanese war (1904–1905) where they contributed to Japanese victories.

By 1914, artillery had become the dominant field arm because guns could rapidly produce devastating fire from beyond the range of infantry rifles. Even troops out of sight could still be destroyed by artillery using indirect laying. Siege guns had become so powerful that fortresses lost their impregnability. Moreover, railways now greatly assisted in transporting huge guns and their supporting services.

The 20th century
At the start of World War 1, the principal contestants possessed similar categories of artillery, although the Germans had the most effective siege guns. Notable field guns were the French 75mm and the British 18-pounder. Artillery soon confirmed its battlefield supremacy and, in combination with machine-guns and magazine rifles, created a trench warfare stalemate. Artillery was initially successful in clearing enemy sectors, thus enabling their subsequent occupation by supporting infantry. However, ammunition stocks rapidly became exhausted soon after the war began, and it was then appreciated that long bombardments depended upon adequate industrial shell production and efficient re-supply systems. By the time the latter had been rectified, front line areas were much more elaborate, consisting of a network of several trench lines. Consequently, although mass bombardments frequently enabled infantry to capture sections of the first trench line, they rarely succeeded in completely neutralizing those behind.

Moreover, saturation shelling actually impeded sup-

Below *Scratch-built British 5.5in gun and Scammell tractor by M. C. Baskerville. This World War 2 gun remained in use at least until the late 1950s.*

Above *A German World War 2 75mm Pak 40 and crew. Figure animation is an important part of such setpieces. Diorama by Don Skinner.*

Left *One of the most numerous guns of World War 2 was the 40mm Bofors, which was very often used as a light anti-aircraft piece. This 1:32 scale scene of a British gun emplacement in the Middle East in 1942 was scratch-built by John Sandars.*

Below *The 8-ton Sd Kfz 7/1 Flakvierling half-track was a German anti-aircraft vehicle. This model by Don Skinner is made from a 1:35 scale Tamiya kit and shows the troops with typical winter clothing. Note the temporary winter white camouflage over the usual grey. The whole diorama in its display case is shown on page 191, and advice on how to create convincing snow scenes is given on page 189.*

porting infantry assaults because it churned up the ground over which troops were compelled to advance. Army commanders remained convinced, however, that artillery would break the tactical stalemate, providing that enough guns were employed for sufficiently long periods. At the battle of the Somme, British guns fired 1,738,000 shells during an eight-day bombardment. At Messines, 3,500,000 shells were fired during 17 days, while at the third battle of Ypres, 4,300,000 shells were expended in 19 days.

Despite the enormous casualties inflicted, none of these bombardments created situations ideal for decisive infantry breakthroughs. They failed to eliminate all enemy machine-guns which immediately went into action when the shelling ceased. Even the use of gas shells and gas mortar bombs was only momentarily successful in shaking the impregnability of entrenched infantry. The stalemate was eventually broken by a gun, but an armoured and mobile one – the tank.

Between the wars, guns were developed to combat the tank and the aeroplane. Very heavy guns declined in importance but were retained by the Germans, who deployed them efficiently by rail. In World War 2, artillery was categorized as heavy, medium and light, forming an integral part of combat formations. The most successful field gun was the British 25-pounder. Much effort was devoted to developing guns, particularly recoilless ones, to combat tanks which now dominated the battlefield. However, in the supremacy race between guns and armour, it was usually the former which lagged behind.

Early notable anti-tank guns were the French Hotchkiss 25mm and the British 2-pounder. The latter was soon replaced by a 6-pounder and later succeeded by the 17-pounder, a 3,050kg (3 ton) gun with noticeable firing flash. Sometimes the 17-pounder was mounted on a Valentine tank chassis. Much research was expended upon a 32-pounder gun which was found to be too heavy, either when towed or mounted upon a tank chassis. The most effective gun was the German 88mm, initially produced as the Flak 36 anti-aircraft weapon, but later employed most successfully for anti-tank tasks. Radar was used by artillery and, when adapted to anti-aircraft guns, much improved range finding.

The rocket was also a popular form of gun; the Germans introduced the Nebelwerfer 41, the 'Moaning Minnie', a towed six-barrel launcher which fired high-explosive rockets up to a range of about 6,400 metres (7,000 yards), later replaced by the Panzerwerfer 42, consisting of ten launching tubes carried on a half-track vehicle. The Germans sometimes employed even bigger rockets weighing 136kg (300lb) each. Much effort was also devoted by the Americans to rocket research and the 4·5-inch barrage rocket was extensively used in the Pacific campaign. The British used the Sea Mattress rocket which comprised massed 5-inch barrels firing a 13kg (29lb) high explosive shell. Germany's work on the V1 'flying bomb' and V2 rocket led to the post-war development of inter-continental and tactical ballistic missiles carrying nuclear warheads.

Since World War 2, artillery has become more sophisticated but is still generally categorized as heavy, medium and light, with an effective supporting range of anti-tank guns. Heavy guns/rockets are usually of long-

This Pak 35 37mm German gun is also a 1:35 scale kit from Tamiya. With figures crouched behind the gun and the ruined building alongside, Don Skinner has built a simple but very effective World War 2 diorama. Other artillery pieces from Tamiya include an 88mm gun, a 6-pdr anti-tank gun and a 20mm Flak 38.

range capability, firing nuclear missiles; the British 'Honest John' rocket and the American 155mm and 175mm guns are typical. The FH 70 155mm medium gun is an example of joint weapon production by NATO allies, with Britain, America, Italy and Germany all involved in its creation. Towed to the battle area, this gun can then move independently to the firing location, using its own motor. A typical light gun is the British 105mm, firing high explosive or anti-tank shells. The British 'Swingfire' is a long-range, optically guided anti-tank missile, with directions transmitted via a wire link contained in the missile housing. Mounted on an armoured personnel carrier, the missile can be fired either from behind cover, with the operator separated a short distance from the launcher vehicle, or fired from the launcher vehicle itself using an elevated periscope sight. With such weapons as these, the tank has become much more vulnerable to artillery than hitherto, as was conclusively proved in the Yom Kippur war.

Modern artillery now possesses lethal, long-range striking power on account of its nuclear capability. It also has considerable mobility, provided particularly by armoured, self-propelled guns such as the British Abbot. However, there is little doubt that due to the constant adaptation of modern technology it will become even more powerful and manoeuvrable within the next decade.

Artillery modelling

Model artillery can be split into three general areas, the small 15 and 25mm scales used mainly for wargaming, a reasonable range of which is available, 54mm scale, often used to complement a figure collection, and larger scale museum-type pieces which may be collected as individual models in their own right.

Paradoxically, modellers will find a wide selection but a narrow range of kits available. The Napoleonic Wars holding the strongest interest for modellers, it is no surprise to find the emphasis here, in plastic and in metal models. French Napoleonic gun teams are made by, among others, Rose Miniatures and Historex, the latter offering a choice of cannon or howitzer, as well as a caisson. Superior Models has a 90mm French Gribeauval 8-pounder and a crew to go with it, as well as, in 54mm, a German 88. Calder Craft, a division of Hinchliffe Models, produces several artillery sets in 1:32 scale, including a German World War 2 gun team and British Napoleonic and World War 1 teams, all with horses and crews, while Hinchliffe has a British 9-pounder in 1:32 scale for the 1798–1860 period. A World War 1 French artillery team is made by Monarch Miniatures, and American Civil War and Revolutionary War cannon kits are available from Imrie/Risley. The widest coverage of World War 2 artillery is by the Japanese firms, with emphasis on German weapons.

Hinchliffe and Historex, in particular, are prepared to supply spare barrels, wheels, and other parts for builders who do not wish to make up a standard kit; in the case of larger models the wheels in plastic or wood intended for model wagons can frequently offer a short cut.

The simplest way to scratch-build a gun model is to use plastic card, and the tools required are very few – a scalpel, steel rule, pin-vice and a pair of screw-adjusted dividers. These last are used to scribe circles, which may be quite tiny, on the card, and the screw adjustment prevents alteration of the setting, something which can happen all too easily with friction-set dividers. One other tool may be needed, a rivet simulator, which is made from a hypodermic syringe with the needle cut off square. In use the syringe is filled with white (PVA) glue and light pressure on the plunger produces a tiny droplet at the end of the needle. When touched on the card, the droplet will dry to form a perfect replica of a hemispherical rivet head. Practice is necessary to achieve consistent-sized droplets and absolute alignment and spacing of the 'rivets', but the method is simple and extremely effective.

To a modeller without access to a lathe, the prospect

Below *Methods of construction which do not require elaborate tools. The cannon barrel at the top illustrates the differences between reinforcement rings and astragals, and reasonable proportions, angles and barrel taper. The other illustrations show how to build steel and wooden gun carriages from styrene sheet. The wood grain can be simulated on plastic card by means of a large needle held in a pin vice, while rivets can be added with careful use of a syringe filled with PVA adhesive.*
Opposite *A scratch-built artillery piece and crew forms part of a World War 1 scene made largely in Plasticine by John Curran. Note the battle damage to the spokes of the wheel and the empty shell cases.*

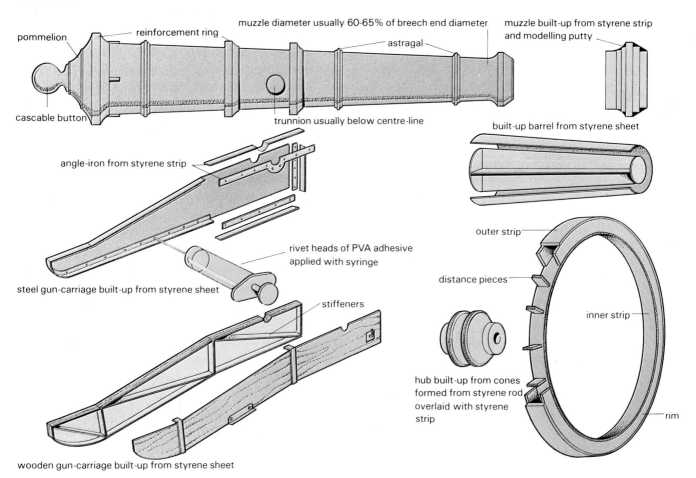

pommelion · reinforcement ring · muzzle diameter usually 60-65% of breech end diameter · astragal · muzzle built-up from styrene strip and modelling putty

cascable button · trunnion usually below centre-line · built-up barrel from styrene sheet

angle-iron from styrene strip

steel gun-carriage built-up from styrene sheet · rivet heads of PVA adhesive applied with syringe

stiffeners

outer strip · distance pieces · inner strip · rim

hub built-up from cones formed from styrene rod overlaid with styrene strip

wooden gun-carriage built-up from styrene sheet

of making wheels and barrels may seem daunting, but with a little practice at scribing, engraving, rolling, bending and sanding or filing plastic card, complete and convincing guns can be made entirely from this material or, if preferred, it can be used in conjunction with wood parts. For example, the illustration shows one side of a typical period carriage to be constructed in card, though it would be quite simple to make in solid wood. The riveted iron Victorian carriage in the same sketch, however, lends itself much more easily to plastic card; this, incidentally, is the basic form for more modern carriages.

A barrel can be made by cutting a section from a paint-brush handle of appropriate diameter and taper, or tapering a wooden dowel, and fitting a muzzle and breech. These can be made by cementing together circles of card and fairing them with modelling putty, as sketched, adding a bead or bearing ball and using narrow strips of thin card as necessary for reinforcement rings. This is probably the best method for small or modern barrels.

Larger barrels can be made entirely from card by joining a series of part-cones (conic frustums) together. Each section is made up by constructing a skeleton of card discs and splines, the more splines the better. This basic core is then wrapped in double-sided adhesive tape, and a pre-shaped thin card outer cover rolled on and trimmed to final length. One or two additional outer wrappers are then cemented on, staggering the joints. Casting details are then added, using plastic strip and rod, together with a muzzle etc. as described.

Wheels are made by scribing two rim faces and joining them with distance pieces, then adding a strip of card inside and out. The rims can be full circles or felloe segments joined together. Hubs are made in much the same way as barrels, from series of cones, except that the discs inside the cones are drilled and the whole assembly built up on a length of tube. The rim and hub for each wheel are then laid over a drawing of the wheel and the spokes cemented in place; these might be plastic tube or rod, or shaped spokes filed from rod or close-grained timber.

Wood grain can be 'engraved' on the plastic card by means of a large needle held in a pin-vice and the whole gun painted in its basic colours, then given a coat of matt varnish, preferably by spray. Colours vary — medium olive green for French Napoleonics, olive drab for American Civil War Union pieces or grey for the Confederacy, blue-grey or brown for the Americans of the Revolution, shades of khaki, grey or lightish brown for World War 1, and so on. Ironwork on early guns was often painted black, and black was a not uncommon colour overall for the defensive cannon in coastal forts and the like.

Experts apply similar weathering and dry brushing techniques to those for tanks and other AFVs when a gun is to be shown in natural surroundings, but a single gun as a display piece is usually shown in pristine condition. In a muddy diorama setting, a nice touch is to position scale boards under the wheels, a practice used in real life when there was a danger of the gun slipping or settling in soft ground.

Dioramas and display

A model on which many hours of patient skill have been spent deserves care and thought as to the best ways to display and protect it. Presentation may be formal, perhaps a single figure or horse and rider on a simple plinth with just a suggestion of ground around the feet, or the model may be incorporated with others or scenery to encapsulate an incident or tell a little story. Such a scene may be amusing or tragic, trivial or epic.

A diorama by Don Skinner showing a Tamiya 1:35 scale M3A2 half-track in a realistic wartime setting.

1/35 SCALE　TAMIYA　US Combat Group

DONALD SKINNER
MODELMAKER
TEL 0280703906

Presentation is the final stage in the construction of any model, and proper display is the crowning glory. Whether you have spent a great deal of your own time and effort to produce the model or whether you have purchased one professionally made and painted from a shop, it deserves consideration for the workmanship involved, and should be looked at, and looked after, in the best possible conditions.

To show off a model to its best advantage, many modellers build their work into a setpiece, or diorama. This consists of a display base to which the model is fixed, with a small scenic setting built around it. A certain amount of planning is necessary before starting construction. Having chosen your subject – infantry, armour, cavalry, or whatever – you must next decide on its location – town, country, woods or desert, and its situation, or reason for being there. Are the figures attacking the house on the corner, or sitting by the edge of a river making breakfast?

When all this has been decided, a wooden base must be made of the required size, this being largely dependent on the subject and scale of the model. A large-scale single figure loading his rifle could use the same size base as a 1:700 scale seaborne invasion. Conversely, one could be fitted in a matchbox, the other in an exhibition hall! A happy medium must obviously be reached. This chapter will deal primarily with 1:32 and 1:35 scale figures and vehicles, though the scenic methods used may be adapted to suit any scale.

A single figure should not be cramped on its base. On the other hand, neither should it be lost. There should be enough room for the figure, whatever it is doing, and a little bit left over. Try setting the figure on a flat piece of paper first, together with any scenic additions required – a piece of fence or wall, a tree stump, signpost etc. When you have decided on the correct size, transfer the measurements to a suitable piece of wood. Several commercial firms produce figure bases to a range of popular sizes, both in moulded plastic and in polished hardwood. Mahogany, teak, beech and oak are the most common. Some model soldier kits even have a display base provided.

A few small-scale plastic diorama kits have vacuum-formed display bases. These are fine for younger modellers or beginners, but they can be greatly improved if the hollow underside is filled with plaster of Paris. When it has set, glue the whole thing to a piece of board. If you are very careful, the plastic form may then be removed, leaving a plaster cast of the original. This, as well as being stronger, is far easier to paint and decorate. For larger groups or AFV dioramas one can use plywood, chipboard or blockboard, with hardwood veneers applied to the edge. Any wood less than 10mm ($\frac{3}{8}$in) thick should be avoided since the application of wet plaster may cause it to warp.

Square or rectangular bases generally are easier to work on, and of course are easier to fit with a showcase.

For the construction of a diorama base you will need to have various materials to hand. Polystyrene ceiling tiles are essential. They will rapidly become hillsides, walls, even whole buildings. Balsa wood of various thicknesses can be used for fences, beams, bridgeworks, etc, while cardboard, about 1mm ($\frac{1}{32}$in) thick, can make doors and signs. You will need commercial accessories like jerrycans, street lamps, oil drums and so on, plus various thicknesses of styrene sheet and strip. Plaster of Paris, builders' coarse grade plaster and a tub of readymix cement, like Tetrion or Porion, are used for groundwork. You will also need a bottle of PVA white glue (a water based glue), a tube of clear impact adhesive (UHU, Bostik, Testor's), and various paints and sprinkles. The term 'sprinkles' covers commercially dyed sawdust, small pebbles, railroad cork, bits of twig, etc., which are the final ground cover.

Opposite above *An M3 Stuart light tank being built into a diorama by Don Skinner.*
Opposite below *The whole of the Don Skinner diorama shown in part on page 32. Tamiya 1:35 figures are used and the ruined building is convincingly represented.*
Below *Diorama accessories are available in white plaster, resin, or sometimes vacuum-formed plastic, usually in 1:35 scale.*

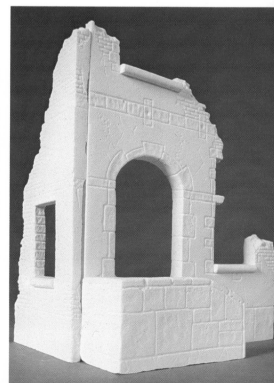

The tools required are relatively few – a modelling knife or scalpel, a pair of fine tweezers, a palette knife (for mixing and spreading plaster), a small drill, a pair of pliers and some paintbrushes. Other useful items include a small, fine mesh tea strainer, a draughtsman's ruling pen and, of course, a small bowl in which to mix the plaster.

In the following examples, the bases are of chipboard, 12mm (½in) thick.

Before doing anything, mix a small quantity of plaster of Paris in the bowl and let it harden! When it is hard, but not dry, break it up into small pieces. As it dries, keep breaking it down, with old scissors if necessary, into small 'rocks'. Put these aside and let them dry.

Next, PVA glue must be coated on both sides of the base. This is best done with a scraper. This glue coat will, in due course, bond the plaster to the top of the base, and the underfelt to the bottom. While this is drying, mix the builders' plaster in the bowl with the palette knife. Builders' plaster, like plaster of Paris, hardens chemically when mixed with water. However,

unlike plaster of Paris, it has a limited shelf life and, if kept too long, will not set chemically. The builder will then throw it away. This is when it is at its best for the modeller, since when used it will be mixed with PVA and will air-dry quite adequately. Mix equal parts of water and PVA, and sift in the plaster through the tea strainer. This takes a while, but the coarse grains left in the strainer make perfect scale pebbles. Put them in a small box for use later. Keep sifting in plaster until the mixture is thick enough to come away from the side of the bowl fairly cleanly. Unlike plaster of Paris you will have plenty of time to spread it to the shape you require, since being time-expired it will not harden until you want it to. These first stages are the same for all locations.

Below *Part of a diorama featuring a British Crusader Mk III tank from a 1:32 Airfix kit, built by H. Grime.* **Opposite** *'Balloon in Trouble', a 1:35 World War 1 diorama and exhibition prizewinner by R. Wright.*

No. 1 – Desert

You will need the following: plaster rocks of various grades; any extras such as sandbags, oil drums, barbed wire, etc., primed base, and builders' plaster mix.

Spread the plaster mix fairly flat over the base with a palette knife, then smooth it out with a large old brush (about No. 4) and water. Go over the whole surface like this to wet it, then sift dry builders' plaster over the entire base with the tea strainer. This will cover all the brush marks and give a texture like coarse sandpaper. Sprinkle small plaster rocks with the fingers, also some builders' plaster pebbles saved from earlier. Larger rocks, sandbags and any other extras may now be placed in the wet plaster, and the join smoothed over with the paintbrush and more rock and pebble sprinkles. If a sandbag wall is required, it is best to assemble it beforehand. Once in position on the base, all the holes between the bags should be filled in with plaster to make it solid. Wheel and trackmarks can be carefully pressed in the plaster, and the positions of the models marked.

Ideally figures for dioramas should not have bases. Instead drill a small hole up through a leg and fix in a length of wire. Plastic figures need only one leg drilled, metal figures both if possible. When all accessories have been fixed and the model positions marked, let the plaster dry. This can be hastened by placing it in the top of an airing cupboard. When it has thoroughly dried, mix water and PVA, this time about 60–40 and, with a medium-sized soft brush, carefully paint glue over the whole base. This must be done gently or the sandy texture will be lost. Make sure that everywhere is treated. This glue coat, when dry, will hold any loose rocks and pebbles in place, seal the surface of the plaster and make painting a great deal easier. When the glue has dried, clean up the edges of the base with a sharp knife and glasspaper.

The base can now be painted, using thinned down shades of light ochres, light browns, creams and dirty whites. It will be found that the use of several different colour washes will produce a more realistic effect than that of solid colours. Rocks and boulders should be

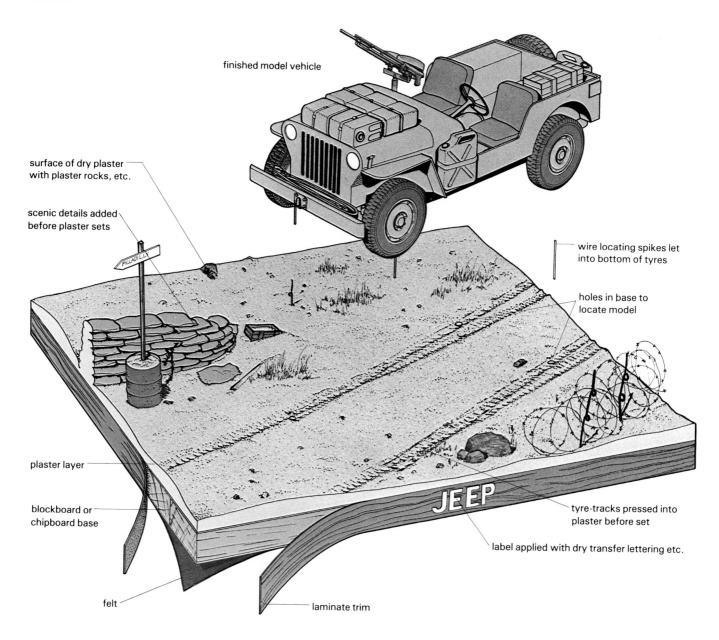

finished model vehicle

surface of dry plaster with plaster rocks, etc.

scenic details added before plaster sets

wire locating spikes let into bottom of tyres

holes in base to locate model

plaster layer

blockboard or chipboard base

tyre-tracks pressed into plaster before set

label applied with dry transfer lettering etc.

felt

laminate trim

picked out in lighter colours and the whole base finished off with a thin wash of brown. This will collect in small hollows and under rocks and produce an instant shadow effect.

A piece of felt or thick carpet underlay paper can now be glued to the bottom of the base with PVA. If you use self-adhesive felt there is, of course, no need to prime the undersurface of the base with PVA. The edges of the base can either be painted with a neutral colour or can be faced with wood veneer, according to your personal preference.

The models should be painted with colours which are compatible with those used on the base, with boots, tyres, etc., dusted with the same colour as the sand. They may now be fixed to the base by drilling their wires into their footprints, and gluing them with UHU. Wheeled vehicles are best fixed down with wire pins drilled into either two or four wheels, depending on the weight of the model. An easy way to match up the holes in wheels and base is by putting a small blob of white paint at the bottom centre of each tyre to be drilled. Carefully place the vehicle into its position on the base and remove again. The paint should have transferred to the right point to drill the hole. Drill a slightly larger hole in the base to allow for any inaccuracies. Glue the model to the base on all wheels.

Opposite The basics of a desert scene and details of mounting a model vehicle.
Above A diorama by Don Skinner showing a Tamiya 1:35 scale M3 Grant Mk 1 in desert-type surroundings. Desert landscape can be made effectively out of plaster.

Tracked vehicles must be wired down before the underfelt and edging are applied. They need only be fixed at two points, at front and rear opposite corners. Place the model in position and mark on the ground under the tank the centre point of the second wheel on each side. Remove the model and drill two holes about 3mm ($\frac{1}{8}$in) either side of this point, so that a wire can be passed up through the base and the track, round the axle of the wheel, and back down through the base again. This is a tricky job, but will be easier if a piece of wire 150mm (6in) long is bent in half and put round the axle and through the track first. On the underside of the base, where the two pairs of holes come out, two grooves must be cut. Pass the wires down through the holes and twist together tightly. The AFV should now be firmly fixed. Cut the twisted wires off about 10mm ($\frac{3}{8}$in) from the base and fold up flat into the groove. The under-paper or felt can now be applied to the bottom. Finally, titles may be added to the front edge of the base.

No. 2 – Town

You will need ceiling tiles, lamp post, medium thickness card, and a strip of 3mm ($\frac{1}{8}$in) balsa.

It is difficult to depict a town in a limited space. The small portion you model must suggest that there is more; therefore rather than model one building, it is better to show two halves of different buildings next to each other, or a street corner. Other details, like direction signs, house numbers and street lights, all help to increase the illusion. Since the location is probably a battle zone, or has recently been, there must be signs of war. Bullet holes, damaged shutters, broken glass and rubble can all be modelled to produce this effect. Remember also that houseproud civilians will do what they can to protect their property. Windows will have their shutters closed and shop windows will be boarded up, awaiting the time when hostilities have passed and business can continue with a hopefully intact shop-front. This generally makes modelling that much easier. Unless your StuG III is actually driving through the building, you can get away with a few strips of balsa nailed across an imaginary window.

Study photographs and when you have found a suitable building, sketch on a piece of paper how much you need to model. Using the following rough guides, plan out the building frontage on to the ceiling tile. Doors, on average, are about 2m (6ft 6in) high. This should be slightly higher than the figure. Windows can start about 1m (3ft) from the ground, and finish level with the top of the door. Floor heights are about 3m (10ft). Naturally, the design and construction of doors and windows

is infinite, and the above measurements can only be approximate.

Cut out window and door apertures with a sharp knife. Window sills, string courses, copings and plinths should be modelled in card or thin styrofoam strip, and fixed in place with PVA. Doors should be modelled in card and glued to the back of the tile. Windows can be made from clear styrene or celluloid, with window bars of thin card or balsa. Put a piece of black or dark grey card behind the windows, unless you want to model the interior. Shutters are made from card and should be applied later. An additional detail, often forgotten, is a drainpipe. This can be made from round section plastic sprue, with the bottom end curved and drilled out.

When the modelling is complete, glue the building to the base. Take a strip of balsa about 3mm by 10mm ($\frac{1}{8}$in by $\frac{3}{8}$in) and glue it to the base parallel to the building. This will be the kerb. Spread some thick mix builders' plaster with the palette knife between the kerb and the building to form the pavement (sidewalk). Smooth it out with a wet palette knife; then, with the large old brush, paint the plaster over the balsa and on to the road to hide any sign of the join. Paint the building with a very thin plaster and PVA mix, and sift

Below *A 1:35 scale Panzerkampfwagen V Panther built into a street scene by Don Skinner.*
Opposite *Street scenes can form backgrounds for many different dioramas. Note the effective though simple method of representing louvred shutters. Study of photographs will provide correct details.*

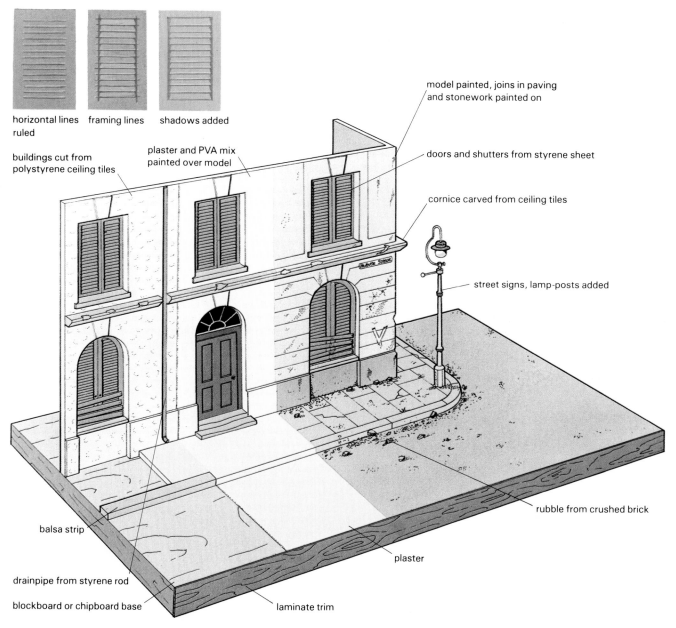

horizontal lines ruled

framing lines

shadows added

buildings cut from polystyrene ceiling tiles

plaster and PVA mix painted over model

model painted, joins in paving and stonework painted on

doors and shutters from styrene sheet

cornice carved from ceiling tiles

street signs, lamp-posts added

rubble from crushed brick

plaster

balsa strip

drainpipe from styrene rod

blockboard or chipboard base

laminate trim

plaster through the tea strainer on to the face of the building. This will disguise the tell-tale texture of the ceiling tile. Repeat the procedure on the road and pavement, then sprinkle pebbles on the ground, with a slightly heavier build-up in the gutter and against the building. Mark the position of the street light by pushing it into the wet plaster. Allow the plaster to dry and carefully coat the entire base with thinned PVA as before.

While this is drying, make the shutters from card, painting them in sombre colours. The louvred effect can be achieved by painting with a ruling pen. First, paint the card a darker tone of the final colour of the shutters. When dry, rule horizontal lines of the final colour 1mm ($\frac{1}{32}$in) apart, across the shutters. Now, using the dark tone again, rule a framing line 3mm ($\frac{1}{8}$in) from the edges of the shutter. Against this, paint a shadow on to the louvres in the dark tone, using a fine paintbrush. Finally, rule and paint the frame in the main colour. This system, although perhaps not quite as good, is a great deal quicker and easier than building it up properly.

The building should now be given a white undercoat, the road and pavement a pale grey. When dry, give the building several thin washes of greys and browns. Rule the paving stones with black or dark grey. The slabs can be given varying colour washes, together with the gutter and kerbstones. Give the road and building a wash of runny black shadow coat and, when dry, shutters, road signs and the lamp post may be fitted.

To add a few more signs of war, try sprinkling some brick dust and rubble about. This is easily manufactured by pounding a piece of brick with a hammer until only tiny bits remain! Save them all carefully, together with the dust. Try several colours of brick and mix them together. The same system can be used on stone and concrete. It is a good idea to add a few pieces of stone to the brick mix, and some brick to the stone mix. Paint areas of the road, gutter, pavement and window sills with thinned PVA, and sprinkle on the rubble with the fingers. Only a small amount will be needed. The figures and vehicles may now be added, using the same techniques as before. Add underfelt, finish the edges and apply titles.

No. 3 – Ruined buildings

You will require a ceiling tile, lamp post, strip of 3mm ($\frac{1}{8}$in) balsa, 1mm ($\frac{1}{32}$in) balsa sheet, and plaster of Paris rocks.

Mark off the building frontage as before on to the tile, modelling window sills and other details in thin styrofoam or card, but break the tile off at random across the top, suggesting that the top half has been destroyed. You can also break off pieces around the door and window frames. Glue the wall to the base and spread a good quantity of thick mix builders' plaster on the ground inside the building. Make the pavement the same as before with the balsa strip and thick mix, piling the mix up against the wall and in low heaps on the pavement, gutter and road. Paint the building and road with thin plaster, and sift builders' plaster over all. Press plaster of Paris rocks into the plaster inside the building and into the heaps in the road, and sprinkle about a few pinches of pebbles. Mark the position of the lamp post in the wet plaster of the pavement.

Below *A dilapidated barn offers a home for this German field kitchen with a 'goulasche kanone' in the foreground. Built by Mac Kennaugh.*
Opposite *A country setting for an American War of Independence diorama by K. M. Yuill.*

When the plaster has dried, paint on the thinned PVA sealer coat and set aside to dry again. Give the building a white undercoat and the road grey, also giving the heaps of rubble and any broken sections of wall a coat of red brown colour. Rule the paving stones and apply various colour washes to the slabs and the building. Model the door frame and window bars in 1mm ($\frac{1}{32}$in) balsa strip and paint them a dirty brown colour. They can then be glued into the openings in the wall with PVA. Finish with a fairly heavy runny black shadow coat, adding dark brown to the rubble heaps. It does not matter if this colour runs on to the road, since it will add to the impression of dust and rubble. The door is made from 1mm balsa, with horizontal and diagonal bracing on the back. Hinges can be made from card, the door handle from a pin or bent wire. Paint the door the same dirty brown and, when fully dry, it can be 'shot up' with a pair of tweezers and fixed at an angle in the door frame. Paint all rubble heaps and broken areas of wall with thinned PVA and sprinkle real brick rubble on to them. It is best if brick dust only is applied to broken parts of walls. The lamp post can be glued in place with UHU and dust and rubble put around its base. Patriotic slogans may be daubed on the walls if you wish. Drill in the figures and wire down the vehicle; apply underfelt, edges and titles.

The same method can be used for stone buildings, substituting ochres and browns for red areas, and stone rubble for the brick.

No. 4 – Country

You will need plaster rocks, 1mm balsa, ivy root, sphagnum moss, and a piece of ceiling tile.

A scene may depict a short length of road on which to display the model. It can be flanked by stone wall, fence or hedge depending on personal preference. A field gate and a telegraph pole may be added for interest.

If the wall is required it should be made from a strip of tile, with the top edges roughened. Glue it to the base with PVA. Only one verge need be modelled, unless a farm track is called for, so apply thick mix along the side of the road, levelling off for the gateway; paint thin plaster over the road and sift on the texture. Impress wheelmarks through the gateway using an old, heavy tread model tyre. If the scene is to be muddy, allow some plaster from the gate to spread on to the road. Press one or two rocks into the verge and sprinkle a few pebbles along the side of the road. Allow the plaster to dry, paint on the PVA sealer and dry again.

It is important that the plaster should be absolutely dry before the application of the sealer coat. If the PVA is put on too soon, the plaster will not harden sufficiently, and may go mouldy or fall off.

Paint the road pale grey and the earth brown; rocks and pebbles can be picked out in pale greys, creams and browns. Wash runny black over everything, and while it dries, construct the gate and fenceposts from balsa strip painted dirty brown. The posts should be about 10mm ($\frac{3}{8}$in) longer than necessary as they will be drilled into the plaster. Drill and glue the posts with PVA, add the gate, open or closed, and either glue wooden fence bars from post to post or fix black- or brown-painted 10 amp fuse wire. Paint grass areas with thinned PVA, sprinkle a mixture of dyed sawdust, finely ground dyed foam rubber and tea leaves. Drill the telegraph pole and glue with UHU, drill and glue the figures, wire down the vehicle, and apply underfelt, edges and titles.

After any greenery sprinkling, shake off the excess on to a sheet of newspaper and save in a plastic bag. Small bits of twig and wisps of sphagnum moss can also be added, together with a few tea leaves, and the whole mixture becomes a general field mix. Used tea leaves, well washed and dried on a paper kitchen towel or in gentle heat, are very useful to the diorama modeller. They can be sprinkled along road edges and under hedges to represent fallen dry leaves, or added to the general ground mix to vary the colour.

If long grass is required it should be made from clusters of sisal string pushed into the wet plaster. Planting it so early in the construction of the base presents problems later with painting and fixing ground cover, but although tedious and tricky to do is very effective when completed.

Realistic hedges and bushes can be modelled using ivy roots and moss. Stay clear of lichen, as it always appears toy-like. Drill and glue a few sprigs of root along the hedgerow and glue fluffy pieces of washed and dried sphagnum moss between and round them with PVA. Do this carefully, since the glue will turn the moss a brilliant green. It is wise to sprinkle some dark green sawdust and tea leaves on to the wet glue to prevent the colour coming through. Trees can be made from suitably chosen pieces of root drilled and glued with PVA. Several commercial firms are now producing excellent tree kits, e.g. John Piper Accessories. Trunk and branches are cast in white metal which must be assembled and bent to the desired shape. The foliage is added using rubberized horsehair and green sprinkle usually supplied with such tree kits.

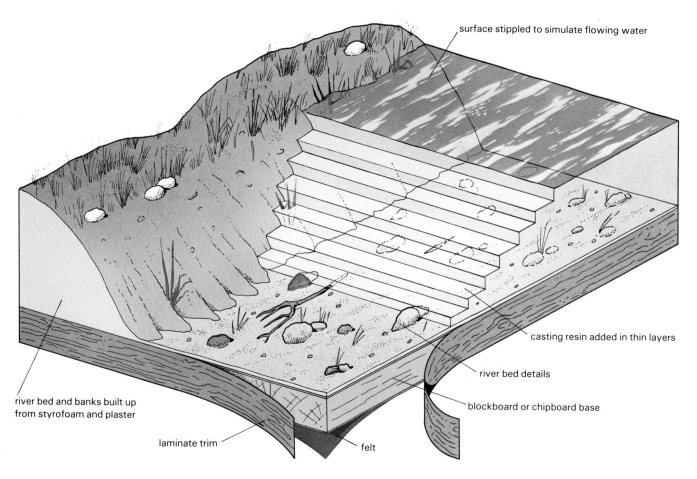

surface stippled to simulate flowing water

casting resin added in thin layers

river bed details

blockboard or chipboard base

river bed and banks built up from styrofoam and plaster

laminate trim

felt

No. 5 – Water

You will need plaster of Paris, nerve and luck!

This is just one way of modelling water. Many people use clear casting resin to very good effect for rivers and streams but it is very slow, can be poured in only limited depths at any one time and may attack some paint finishes. We'll come back to this. The following method, using plaster of Paris, is reasonably fast to model and represents the average river or stream, relying mostly on paintwork to simulate the correct effect.

If the model is to be partly submerged in the water, or if a river bank is required, they must be completed before construction of the water is begun. Using the techniques described in the preceding examples, make, paint and finish all items, river bank, soldiers, vehicles etc., and fix them in the position required. Using pieces of styrofoam, build up to a level just below the final water surface, leaving about 3mm (⅛in) gap around the model, along the river bank, and around the edge of the base. Mixing only small quantities of plaster of Paris, as it hardens so quickly, apply it carefully around the edge and across the top of the styrofoam. When this has set make a very runny mixture of plaster and pour it into the gaps around the model, at the same time spreading it with an old paint brush across the already set surface. Repeat the procedure along the river bank, again with the brush, smoothing the joins and modelling the surface. Be careful not to get plaster on the model above the waterline as it will be hard to remove. When you are satisfied with the sculpting of the base, clean up the edges of the base with a knife and glasspaper, making sure that the sides of the water are smooth.

When dry, sealer coat it with PVA as before, and paint browns and greens across the whole water surface and down the sides, keeping the paint wet, but not too runny, so that the colours blend together. While the paint is still wet, stipple small amounts of white paint over the surface and down the sides, using a piece of sponge. Let the white blend with the green/brown base colour, then add some more, again with the sponge. If the colour is becoming too pale, stipple on some more green and brown. This must all be done fairly rapidly so that the application of white produces a range of shades from pale green through to white. The white should by now appear to be foam and bubbles on the bow wave and in the wake of the model. Finally paint the water with clear polyurethane varnish. With a water diorama, it is more effective to paint the edges of any ground with a neutral colour, following the line of the ground under water, but leaving the water as a painted block. Apply veneer only to the wooden part of the base. Apply underfelt and titles.

The alternative scheme to the plaster method of modelling water is the use of one of the numerous clear casting resins available for home jewellery making and decorative encapsulating – we've all seen those sea-horse paper weights and the wristwatches reduced to their component parts suspended in blocks of clear resin! The system has the drawback that, while the liquid resin cures, it (a) may generate heat and (b) can attack some paint finishes. For this reason it is advisable to employ the method only for modelling flowing water like rivers and streams and for pools and boggy ground which do not actually have models in direct contact. However, the resin does not seem to attack models finished in water-based paints and artist's oils, and if you experiment first on an unimportant model it is easy to avoid any complications. The finished result is certainly worth the extra care.

The water surface should be built up in layers, each a few millimetres thick. The first of these is poured over the already painted river bed surface which can have pieces of twig, pebbles, grasses and sisal string (to represent bullrushes) located on it. When the first layer has set a second can be poured on and if additional pieces of flotsam are added between each pouring of resin it is possible to create a most effective impression of depth to the water which is not possible to achieve by any other modelling means. On the final or top surface layer one can even introduce ripple or wavelet effect by adding extra hardener to the two-part mix but, again, experimentation is strongly advised beforehand.

Snow and ice

Arctic and wintry settings can be used to set off models, vehicles especially, to good advantage, and there are several ways of achieving this. The effect of thick, newly fallen snow is best achieved with fairly thinly mixed white plaster (plaster of Paris is ideal, though any commercial plaster-type filler is also suitable) and this should be applied to the base with a spoon. Try to achieve build-ups and the effect of drifts by tilting the base board while the plaster sets and add grasses and twigs sticking up through snow by drilling small holes in the dry plaster. The finished snow surface should be painted matt white and an aerosol can or an airbrush is best for this.

To achieve the effect of a light dusting of snow, a choice of methods can be employed. One of these is quite simply to spray the finished, painted base very lightly with an aerosol can of matt white enamel, taking care to apply the spray from only one direction. A slightly heavier coating of snow in local areas of the diorama can be modelled by first painting the areas in which the snow is to appear with white PVA adhesive, using a large soft brush. Before the glue dries, sprinkle on commercial medicinal salts in exactly the same way as flock powder is sprinkled on conventional dioramas. For heavy snow clinging to the tops of fences, signposts and hanging from the corner of gutters etc. one well-known British modeller uses generous applications of a commercial white leather shoe cleaner (Meltonian Sports White Buckskin and Canvas Cleaner) applied with a small sponge or brush to add a little 'body' to the snow.

For frozen water a very effective result can be achieved simply by painting, using alternative washes of light grey and white but, for a really quality effect, some top modellers use candle wax heated by holding an electric iron very close to it so that it melts and forms its own, perfectly flat, surface in the required areas of the diorama base. The result is a realistic representation of frozen water, ideal for model ponds, puddles, open water butts and the like.

The methods used in these examples are all based on long experience where ease and speed of construction have been essential. Sometimes as many as eight dioramas a week have been produced! A scenic base should give an impression of a location without showing any more than is absolutely necessary. A piece of railing and some brick rubble suggest that somewhere nearby is a ruined building, without actually having to show it. A sloping section of road with low walls either side suggests a bridge, though no bridge need be modelled. Remember, a diorama base should enhance the model to the maximum, with the minimum of visual effort. It is up to the individual to test his skill and imagination, to experiment and adapt the systems in his own way.

Opposite *A river diorama made from layers of resin.*
Below *A Tamiya 1:35 Sd Kfz 7/1 half-track in a typical snowy setting. Model by John Wylie.*

Display

Having mastered the techniques of displaying the model on a base, one then has to display the base.

Probably the most common place for home display is the open bookshelf, though the danger of accidental damage, and the inescapable problem of dust, necessitate more protection. A bookcase with glass doors is the logical solution. Many modern furniture systems, with wall-mounted racks and brackets, have modular units to fit to them. Almost all have an ideal glass-fronted cupboard unit which may already have a small strip light. However, even cabinets with glass doors are not entirely dust free, so models should have an occasional careful dusting with a soft brush. Remember that a model should never be touched or handled by anything other than its display base. The oils from the skin of the fingers will transfer to the paint surface of the model, and will leave fingerprints which are impossible to remove.

Should your display cabinet have internal lighting, it is not advisable to leave the lights on for too long, since some metals and paints may be adversely affected by the build-up of heat and change of atmospheric conditions. If you make your own display cabinets, on no account must you use turpentine or oil-based paint on its interior. The fumes from these paints will react with some models. Use only water-based paints and allow them to dry thoroughly before placing the models inside.

There are, of course, any number of display possibilities. Glass bell jars, much favoured by the Victorians for housing stuffed birds, although expensive and hard to find these days, make most attractive display cases. A well-known American collector has used an old brass coach lamp, emptied of its working parts, to show off a large-scale figure of Napoleon to great effect.

At the less exclusive end of the scale, clear plastic seed propagators or picnic and lunch boxes can become useful dust covers. However, the clarity of the plastic, while allowing you to see what you have in your sandwiches, may not be of adequate quality for a true display case.

Perhaps the most versatile method of display is a rectangular showcase, which can be constructed relatively simply from glass or acrylic sheet. The more readily obtainable of the two is glass, but the weight, and the difficulty of assembly, are disadvantages. Your local glazier will cut sheets to your specifications, and if the size required is not too expensive, may even assemble the case for you. Acrylic is lighter and easier to work with, but still has problems. There are several brand names – Perspex, Oroglas, Plexiglas, etc. – and ready-made cases can be obtained from commercial firms. Acrylic in sheet form, cut to the size required, is readily available from trade suppliers. A brief search in your local trade directory or Yellow Pages telephone directory will soon bring them to light.

Acrylic will scratch. It must be cleaned with a soft cloth or kitchen roll, soaked in a light soapy solution. If a dry cloth is used, static electricity will be generated, attracting more dust than you wipe off! An anti-static liquid is available, together with an anti-static cloth, which should solve this problem. Your supplier will also sell Perspex adhesive. Alternatively, you can use dichloromethane, a liquid chemical similar to chloroform, which bonds the Perspex together. Assemble the case together with clear adhesive tape, and apply the liquid with a No. 4 brush, flooding it along the inside edges. Do not allow the glue to touch the tape or the Perspex will be marked. Small surface marks may be removed by polishing with toothpaste.

Carefully sand all corners and edges with fine glasspaper since Perspex has edges like glass, and will easily cut fingers!

The case may be attached to the base with countersunk screws, or left free standing.

Final display is as much a personal choice as the model itself, and each person must decide for himself how to gain the most pleasure and satisfaction from his prized model.

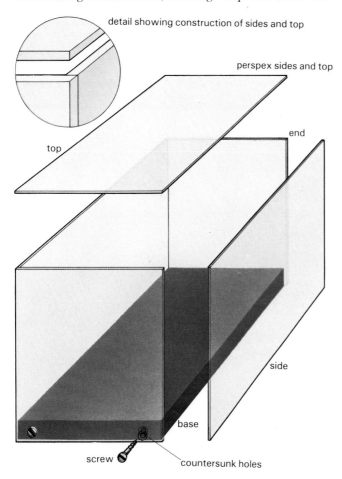

detail showing construction of sides and top

perspex sides and top

top

end

side

base

screw

countersunk holes

Left *Construction of a Perspex or Plexiglas case. Any acrylic plastic is subject to static electricity build up, so a periodic wipe with an anti-static cloth is necessary.*
Opposite above *A Panzer IV D of the 11th Panzer Division rumbling through a street diorama by Don Skinner. The crew all wear the typical German black tank uniforms with pink piping around the collars indicating their branch of service. The Panzer IV is probably the most popular tank model.*
Opposite below *An Sd Kfz 7/1 half-track with multiple flak gun, from a 1:35 Tamiya kit, by Don Skinner. Detailed models are almost impossible to dust adequately and a case is therefore a very desirable addition to protect many hours of patient work.*

Index

For simplicity, only the most important references have been indexed.

Acknowledgements

Illustrations and artwork by Terry Allen Designs Ltd: Lyn D. Brooks, Roger Courthold, Bob Stoneman and Nigel Waller
Uniform illustrations by Bob Marrion

Insignia on pages 96 and 97 provided by Rusty Jenkins and co.

Additional assistance: Ken Jones

Books illustrated on pages 39 and 141 courtesy of Phoebus Publishing Company (History of the Second World War)

The publisher would like to thank all the individuals and companies who allowed their models to be photographed. Whilst every effort has been made to credit the modellers in the captions, in some instances this information was not available to us.

The publisher would like to thank the following for their kind permission to reproduce the photographs in this book. Mike Dyers 11 top left; Bill Evans 157 above; Alec Gee 22, 26 right, 28 above, 64 below, 89, 92, 95 top left, bottom left and right, 102 top, 106, 112 above, 130–131, 164–165, 167; Marc Riboud/John Hillelson Agency 10; Under Two Flags 11 top right.

All other photographs by John Wylie